A DISTINCT
TWENTY-FIRST CENTURY
PENTECOSTAL HERMENEUTIC

A DISTINCT TWENTY-FIRST CENTURY PENTECOSTAL HERMENEUTIC

Harlyn Graydon Purdy

WIPF & STOCK · Eugene, Oregon

A DISTINCT TWENTY-FIRST CENTURY PENTECOSTAL HERMENEUTIC

Copyright © 2015 Harlyn Graydon Purdy. All rights reserved. Except for brief quotations in critical publications or reviews, no part of this book may be reproduced in any manner without prior written permission from the publisher. Write: Permissions, Wipf and Stock Publishers, 199 W. 8th Ave., Suite 3, Eugene, OR 97401.

Wipf & Stock
An Imprint of Wipf and Stock Publishers
199 W. 8th Ave., Suite 3
Eugene, OR 97401

www.wipfandstock.com

ISBN 13: 978-1-4982-1780-4

Manufactured in the U.S.A.   06/11/2015

The following monograph is first dedicated to my Lord and Savior Jesus Christ who made it possible for this project to be completed. Second, it is dedicated to my patient, loving wife, Helene, who endured long hours of silence while this project was in progress. I cannot neglect Dr. Glenn Wooden who read the pre-publication draft, asked probing questions that promoted clarity of thought and expression, and made several helpful suggestions along the way. Finally, I dedicate this monograph to the many teachers, students, and colleagues who have contributed in various ways to the thinking and experimentation that has led to this project's completion.

CONTENTS

Foreword | ix

Chapter 1
Why A Distinct Pentecostal Hermeneutic | 1

Chapter 2
Defining Pentecostalism and Its Early Hermeneutic | 30

Chapter 3
Biblical Foundations For A Twenty-first Century Pentecostal Hermeneutic | 61

Chapter 4
A Distinct Twenty-first Century Pentecostal Hermeneutic:
The Starting Point | 77

Chapter 5
Twenty-first Century Pentecostal Hermeneutic Method | 88

Chapter 6
Twenty-first Century Pentecostal Hermeneutic Strategy | 103

Conclusion | 153

Appendix A | 157
Pentecostal Bible College of Malawi—A Twenty-first Century Pentecostal Hermeneutic—PR3211—Syllabus | 159

Course Description | 164

Appendix B
Definitions | 179

Bibliography | 183

FOREWORD

This text argues for a distinct Pentecostal hermeneutic that utilizes several interpretive methodologies and a quadradic strategy. Chapter 1 argues for the legitimacy, and necessity, of a distinct Pentecostal hermeneutic on the basis of academic activity and challenge, a changed world environment, and the need for Pentecostals to make a theological contribution to the Christian church. To lay a foundation and identify Pentecostalism's ethos for the proposed hermeneutic, chapter 2 traces Pentecostalism's roots. Chapter 3 lays a biblical foundation by examining the interpretive strategies employed in Acts 2 and 15, Matthew 1:23, John 10:34–36, and Jude. The early Pentecostal hermeneutics, especially that of D. Wesley Myland, are examined in chapter 4 to establish a starting point for the hermeneutic argued in this monograph. Chapter 5 argues that a distinct twenty-first-century Pentecostal hermeneutic must engage interpretive methodologies that enable meaning and meaningfulness to emerge through a dynamic interaction between text and interpreter, and that a legitimate role for the traditionally dominant historical-grammatical method must be limited. Chapter 6 presents the quadradic strategy that embraces a dynamic interaction between Scripture, Spirit, Community, and Trained Leader. This strategy allows for meaning and significance to emerge as text, Spirit, and interpreter engage in creative interaction so that original/authorial intent no longer has absolute control over meaning. Scripture's primacy is maintained and Scripture and community establish appropriate limitations on the interpreter's creative imagination. A bachelor-level course to teach the proposed hermeneutic forms an appendix.

CHAPTER 1

WHY A DISTINCT PENTECOSTAL HERMENEUTIC

Introduction

IT MUST BE ACKNOWLEDGED from the outset that I am a Pentecostal[1] by affiliation and experience and my approach is as an insider. As a youth and young adult businessman I was an active participant in congregational life, serving as an elder, Sunday school teacher, and in other roles until sensing a call to full-time ministry. I attended Eastern Pentecostal Bible College (now called Master's College and Seminary) in preparation for pastoral ministry. After entering ministry I recognized the need for further training so I enrolled at Acadia University and earned a BA in Psychology and then

---

1. The term "Pentecostal" is used in a variety of ways and with numerous nuances of meaning. For the purpose of this monograph "Pentecostal" is used inclusively to refer to Classical Pentecostals, Charismatic Pentecostals, and Independent Pentecostals as a group. The term "Classical Pentecostal" refers to denominations such as Pentecostal Assemblies of Canada, Assemblies of God (U.S.A.), Church of God, and other Trinitarian Pentecostal groups that trace their roots to the Azusa Street revival and hold the view that tongues are the initial evidence of baptism in the Spirit. "Charismatic Pentecostal" refers to those Pentecostals who do not necessarily have roots in the Azusa Street Revival and would not accept tongues as the exclusive evidence of baptism in the Spirit. Independent Pentecostals refers to congregations without denominational alliance, hold a view similar to Charismatic Pentecostals but operate as independent congregations. The terms "Pentecostalism" and "Pentecostalization" are used in an inclusive manner and refer to Classical, Charismatic, and Independent Pentecostals. The term "Pentecostal hermeneutic" is used in an inclusive manner to apply to Classical, Charismatic, and Independent groups.

A Distinct Twenty-first Century Pentecostal Hermeneutic

completed graduate work in theology. This book is written to add to the discussion of Pentecostal interpretation and provide a resource for pastors, teachers, and students.

Through each stage of training I maintained a full-time pastoral ministry serving in both small rural and larger urban congregations. I was also privileged to serve for nearly five years as lead pastor at West Pembroke Pentecostal Assembly in Bermuda. This was an indigenous, black congregation. (It is interesting to see some of the cultural similarities between this congregation and the African people I now serve among.) It has been my privilege to serve in national and district level leadership roles. Serving as adjunct faculty I taught several courses for Master's College and Seminary, Faith School of Theology, and Global University all of which are "Classical Pentecostal" institutions. Currently I serve as President of Pentecostal Bible College (PBC) in Malawi, Africa where I function in both teaching and administrative roles. I also currently teach at All Nations Theological Seminary (The Assemblies of God training institution in Malawi).

Throughout my career I have become increasingly concerned about some of the trends occurring within Pentecostalism. My greatest concern is in the area of biblical interpretation as evidenced in the preaching practiced by many pastors. There has been a trend toward unrestrained imagination being passed off as revelation by the Holy Spirit. This practice is especially problematic within the African context, perhaps the Majority World as a whole.[2] In Africa, the more innovative the interpretation and "charismatic" the delivery the larger the audience a preacher can expect. This reality drives a trend toward unrestrained imaginative interpretation presented in the guise of revelation knowledge and Holy Spirit anointing. Although the presentation tends to be more sophisticated in North America the trend is no less real or dangerous.

Allegorization or spiritualization is a popular, perhaps preferred, interpretive method in Africa and lends itself neatly to imaginative interpretation and can easily escape scrutiny by claiming revelation knowledge as its source. For example, the five stones in David's battle with Goliath (1 Sam 17:40) have been claimed to represent the five wounds of Jesus, the five

---

2. My current context is Africa. I cannot speak from a direct personal experience of other Majority World contexts. However, I can speak from personal experience and exposure of the African context. My reading, cross-cultural experiences and conversations with those from other majority world contexts suggests there are both remarkable similarities and clear differences between Africa and other majority world contexts. I do not want to overgeneralize.

Why A Distinct Pentecostal Hermeneutic

letters in the name JESUS, the fivefold gifts to the church (Eph 4:11) and the Pentateuch among other things.[3] The effectiveness of this method to attract crowds and establish a reputation for the preacher lend to its popularity. The potential for heretical interpretation is obvious; therefore, an appropriate corrective for the abuse of allegorization among Pentecostals must be found. As the influence of African Pentecostals increases this need will increase but a distinct twenty-first century Pentecostal hermeneutic will meet this critical need.

Beside allegorization, I have heard interpretations of Scripture that have produced a chuckle and others that aroused serious concern and anxiety. One imaginative interpretation offered by an African Pentecostal pastor was based on Genesis 6:1–8. Tying this text to the scripture that tells us we may entertain angels unawares (Heb 13:2) the pastor claimed that angels (the sons of God) continue to marry the daughters of men. These marriages in the contemporary setting, according to this pastor, "celestial marriages," are to be highly desired. The children of these marriages in Genesis produced offspring that were men of renown and this was interpreted to mean children of these "celestial marriages" were specially gifted spiritual individuals who would serve as powerful prophetic and apostolic voices in the church. This pastor then encouraged the women in the congregation to pray that they might be so honoured and be chosen for a celestial marriage. This is one of the innovative interpretations I have heard or had reported to me by students in my classes.

The great danger I see is that unrestrained, imaginative interpretations will carry Pentecostalism over the cliff into heresy. A number of pastors in North America and in the Majority World have already plunged over this cliff at least partly due to unrestrained imaginative interpretation. I believe there is a great need for a hermeneutic[4] that embraces Pentecostalism's dis-

---

3. Reported by students in the Bible college during discussion on proper hermeneutical practice.

4. The art and science of hermeneutics is the search to discover meaning in a written text. The interest of this book is hermeneutics applied to Scripture. There are two separate, yet closely connected, elements to this process. First, is the engagement of clearly defined tools to discover the content of the text to answer the question, "What does the text say?" Exegesis is the technical term associated with this side of the hermeneutical process. Second, is the exercise of sometimes less precise tools to answer the question, "What does the text mean?" Hermeneutics is the term generally associated with this activity although hermeneutics is at times used so as to include exegesis. The two elements are so closely connected that it is likely impossible to truly separate them. The focus of this book is on the second element of the hermeneutical process. The tools and

tinctiveness, escapes the restriction of authorial intent, static meaning and the autonomy of the historical-grammatical method while also establishing appropriate boundaries around creative interpretation.

My interest in a Pentecostal hermeneutic began in Bible college during my second-year course in "Pentecostal Distinctives." In this class I became acutely aware that the historical-grammatical method could not support the doctrine of tongues as initial evidence of baptism in the Spirit. This initiated a personal search to determine "how" or "if" the doctrine could be scripturally supported. Using a literary approach I was able to settle the question for myself.[5] My search led me to an emerging discussion concerning hermeneutical theory taking place within the church in general and among Pentecostals specifically.[6] My reading and thinking have led to this book.

When considering a distinctive Pentecostal hermeneutic one is immediately confronted with numerous questions. Is it appropriate to discuss and define a distinctive "Pentecostal" hermeneutic? Where do Pentecostals fit into the theological spectrum? What criteria should drive the discussion? What aspect/s of Pentecostalism require/s specific address as they relate to hermeneutics? Does the term "distinctive" suggest the normative hermeneutics of evangelicals in general do not apply? These and many other questions will guide the way through the issues that must be explored.

---

process of exegesis will be part of the discussion as is necessary. However, it is the second element that is open to greater subjectivity and therefore more in need of address from the Pentecostal perspective.

5. I am not suggesting that Pentecostalism's *a priori* faith statement (i.e., initial evidence) govern hermeneutical discussions or decisions. Scripture is the starting point and hermeneutics serves to promote the understanding of Scripture, not the protection of distinctive doctrines. As a Pentecostal I would rather reject our distinctive doctrines than twist Scripture to support them.

6. Anderson is typical of the majority of Pentecostal academics. He argues that the historical-grammatical method is the proper exegetical method. Anderson, "Pentecostal Hermeneutics," 20. Anderson expresses concern that some contemporary Pentecostal pastors have embraced heretical belief and practices because they did not use the proper historical-grammatical method of interpretation. I agree with Anderson that some Pentecostals (pastors and laity alike) have embraced heretical beliefs and practices. I am not convinced that using the historical-grammatical method properly would have prevented these leaps into error. Currently there is a growing minority voice calling Pentecostals to develop a distinctive Pentecostal hermeneutic that moves away from the exclusive use of historical-grammatical methods. It is among this minority group that the present author stands.

Why A Distinct Pentecostal Hermeneutic

It is the premise of this book that a distinctive Pentecostal hermeneutic for the twenty-first century must take into account Pentecostalism's roots, its contemporary context and contemporary hermeneutic theory.[7] However there is a legitimate question, "is there a need for such a hermeneutic?" Chapter 1 argues the case on several grounds and answers with a resounding "yes." Such things as Pentecostal and non-Pentecostal academic perspectives, contextual changes, the place of community in contemporary theory, and Pentecostalism's development over time are offered as evidence that a "distinct" hermeneutic is legitimate and necessary.

The concept of an independent objective observer is almost universally rejected today. It is widely accepted that both writer/speaker and reader/hearer bring context to the communicative event. Pentecostals as a distinctive group within Christianity bring specific predispositions, biases, and presuppositions to the interpretive task, hence chapter 2 seeks to describe and define Pentecostalism, traces early Pentecostalism's[8] roots, and identifies the early Pentecostal ethos. The hermeneutical practices of early Pentecostals are considered since they aid in understanding the Pentecostal ethos and community metanarrative. These background issues help bring to light the contextual issues Pentecostals bring to the interpretive process and point toward a methodology and strategy for a distinct interpretive approach for the twenty-first century.

---

7. Archer proposes to "move beyond the impasse created by Modernity and push Pentecostals into the contemporary context by critically re-appropriating early Pentecostal ethos and interpretive practices for a contemporary Pentecostal community" (Archer, *A Pentecostal Hermeneutic*, preface). The proposal in this book does not follow Archer's stated intention of re-appropriating early Pentecostal interpretive practice. The early Pentecostal interpretive practices and ethos do help identify the essential nature of Pentecostalism and are considered from that perspective in this book. However re-appropriating early Pentecostal interpretive methods may worsen rather than correct some of the current problems. Bradley Noel also argues that contemporary Pentecostals follow the interpretive methods of the early Pentecostal leaders. See Noel, *Pentecostal and Postmodern Hermeneutics*.

8. In this book "early Pentecostals" refers to the Pentecostals of the late nineteenth and early twentieth centuries (1890–1920). I am aware that a number of Pentecostals have attempted (without success in my view) to trace Pentecostals and Pentecostalism in a continuous, unbroken, line, back to the Pentecostal outpouring of Acts chapter 2. However, even the most ardent supporter of a continuous, unbroken line from the Acts 2 Pentecost to the modern day must admit that for most of that time period Pentecostal experience was extremely limited until the great revivals of the last decade of the nineteenth century and the first decade of the twentieth century. For this reason the term "early Pentecostals" will refer to that group of restoration revivalists of the late nineteenth and early twentieth centuries rather than to the Acts 2 context.

A Distinct Twenty-first Century Pentecostal Hermeneutic

Chapter 3 offers a biblical foundation for a distinct twenty-first century Pentecostal hermeneutic. Acts chapters 2 and 15 are presented as hermeneutical models, while Timothy and Titus are considered as foundational for the role of a trained leader as critical to a Pentecostal method and strategy in their hermeneutic. The New Testament's use of Old Testament texts is considered as it strengthens the position that a trained leader is a foundational element.

Chapter 4 considers the role of hermeneutics along with early Pentecostal interpretive practice, including the influential Myland approach, in order to identify some important aspects of Pentecostal identity. The Myland interpretive method with its Latter Rain motif is shown to be a powerful informer of Pentecostal self-understanding and identity. This self-understanding and identity are vital elements in the Pentecostal metanarrative and ethos that function as presuppositions in a Pentecostal hermeneutic.

Chapters 5 and 6 argue through the complex issues and difficult task of identifying appropriate methods and strategy. It is shown that from a Pentecostal perspective methodology must allow a creative dance to exist between text and reader in the interpretive process. A place for the interpretive tools of historical-grammatical method is recognized but it must operate in conjunction with various literary methods and a limited use of semiotic theory. A quadradic interaction among Scripture, Spirit, community, and trained leader is presented as a fitting interpretive strategy. The distinct twenty-first century Pentecostal hermeneutic proposed here engages an eclectic use of interpretive methods from a clearly Pentecostal perspective embracing the quadratic strategy previously noted.

One of the questions asked earlier was whether a distinctive Pentecostal hermeneutic is legitimate or necessary. The answer is a resounding yes as will be shown in the next several pages. Academics, both Pentecostal and non-Pentecostal, a changed world, theoretical developments in communication theory, Pentecostalism's distinctiveness as a community, its unique story and worldview, development, and theological contribution all combine to support the claim that this hermeneutic is both legitimate and necessary.

Why A Distinct Pentecostal Hermeneutic

Literature Review

Pentecostal hermeneutics has been a subject of discussion among Pentecostals for the past three decades. Pentecostal scholars argue for one of two positions: the majority hold that Pentecostals practice hermeneutics as evangelicals; however, a minority voice calls for a distinct Pentecostal hermeneutic. The hermeneutic proposed in this book aligns with the minority voice and puts forward a distinct hermeneutic for Pentecostals in the twenty-first century. To lay an appropriate foundation for our discussion we present a brief literature review. The following review is not exhaustive but presents the primary voices and identifies the major approaches being proposed and establishes the background against which the hermeneutic proposed in this book arises.

Appropriately this literature review begins with the renowned Pentecostal scholar Gordon Fee. Fee has written several monographs, chapters in monographs, and articles dealing with exegesis and hermeneutics, and these monographs are frequently used as texts for hermeneutic classes taught in Pentecostal Bible colleges around the world. Fee is representative, perhaps the icon, of the majority camp that rejects the idea of a Pentecostal hermeneutic proposing that Pentecostals do hermeneutics as evangelicals. After reading only the first two chapters of *Gospel and Spirit: Issues In New Testament Hermeneutics* it is clear that Fee believes Pentecostals ought to do exegesis and hermeneutics like all other evangelicals.[9] He presents the historical-grammatical method as the appropriate exegetical method, argues for authorial intent, and original intent as the proper means of accessing meaning in a text, and rejects the view that historical precedent[10] has a place in doctrinal development. The volume *How to Read the Bible For All Its Worth* (a "how-to" in the use of the historical-grammatical method) coauthored with Douglas Stuart is frequently used in Pentecostal Bible colleges as a hermeneutics textbook.[11] Fee's chapter in Russell Spittler's volume

---

9. Fee and Stuart, *Gospel and Spirit*, 51. A clear indication that this is Fee's approach is found in his conclusion for chapter 3: he says, "I would thus urge that evangelical hermeneutics in the years ahead must increasingly think of Scripture less as law to be obeyed and more as gospel to be proclaimed . . ." See also: Fee, "Hermeneutics and the Historical Precedent"; Fee, *New Testament Exegesis*. Gordon Donald Fee is an American-Canadian Christian theologian and an ordained minister of the Assemblies of God. He currently serves as Professor Emeritus of New Testament Studies at Regent College in Vancouver, Canada.

10. Historical precedent refers to the events related as occurring in the book of Acts.

11. Fee and Stuart, *How To Read The Bible*.

A Distinct Twenty-first Century Pentecostal Hermeneutic

Perspectives on the New Pentecostalism critiques Pentecostals for using "historical precedent" and narrative material for doctrinal development. Fee consistently argues for historical-grammatical method and evangelical hermeneutics for Pentecostals, rejecting the concept of a particular Pentecostal hermeneutic. Fee is locked into a modernist position that rejects the value and importance of a role for the reading community, among other things, that are well recognized in postmodern hermeneutical theories. Fee argues for a "gospel lens" to interpret the Epistles while disallowing a Lukan lens (with emphasis on Acts) as proposed by many who call for a distinct Pentecostal hermeneutic. Fee contributes much to the field of hermeneutics but, in the opinion of this writer, his approach eliminates the Pentecostal voice and disables Pentecostals bringing their distinctive interpretations and understandings of Scripture to the attention of the broader church.

Howard M. Ervin stands at the opposite end of the spectrum from Fee.[12] Ervin argues for a distinct Pentecostal hermeneutic on the basis of his understanding of the role of the Spirit in the interpretive process. Ervin argues that a "pneumatic epistemology firmly rooted in the Biblical faith with a phenomenology that meets the criteria of empirically verifiable sensory experience"[13] is required for proper interpretation of Scripture. Ervin distinguishes between exegesis (what the text says) and hermeneutics (what the text means), contending that hermeneutics begins where exegesis ends. Ervin argues that traditional hermeneutics is weak in that it is insensitive to the numinous, asserting that the distance between text and contemporary reader is traversed by the Spirit. He says, "This distance renders the word ambiguous until the Holy Spirit, who 'searches even the depth of God' (1 Corinthians 2:10), interprets it to the reader."[14] Although Ervin makes a positive contribution by highlighting the role of the Spirit in the interpretive process, he is elitist in claiming Pentecostal experience advantages the Pentecostal hermeneut. Ervin's article promotes the development of a distinct Pentecostal hermeneutic and highlights the need for careful and clear thinking about the appropriate role of the Spirit and Pentecostal experience of the Spirit in this hermeneutic, but his concept of the "pneumatic factor" results in a strong elitist position that this writer rejects. As will be seen, the

---

12. Ervin, "Hermeneutics," 11–25. Howard M. Ervin (September 21, 1915—August 12, 2009) was an American scholar, pastor, and professor at Oral Roberts University.

13. Ibid., 12.

14. Ibid., 17.

Why A Distinct Pentecostal Hermeneutic

hermeneutic proposed here includes a place for the Spirit and Pentecostal experience while rejecting the elitist position held by Ervin and others.

In 1992 Roger Stronstad wrote an influential article entitled, "Pentecostal Experience and Hermeneutics."[15] Here Stronstad argues that a Pentecostal hermeneutic properly consists of four elements: 1) charismatic experiential presuppositions, 2) the pneumatic, 3) genre, 4) exegesis and experiential verification. Unlike Menzies, who places personal experience at the end of the interpretive process as a verifier, Stronstad places personal experience at the beginning of the interpretive process. Stronstad wants to retain the historical-grammatical method and holds firmly to the view that the role of the Spirit is not different for Pentecostals than for non-Pentecostal hermeneuts (an important correction to Ervin) in the interpretive process. He breaks from Fee and embraces narrative material as having didactic value. In 1993 Stronstad made another important contribution to Pentecostal hermeneutics. Although agreeing with Fee that Pentecostals ought to engage the historical-grammatical method and follow evangelical hermeneutical practices, in an article published in *Pneuma* he argues that historical precedent as found in the book of Acts is appropriately employed in developing Pentecostal theology and doctrine.[16] Stronstad's work suggests that Pentecostals bring something distinctive to the interpretive task that impacts the formation of meaning thereby implying the appropriateness of a *distinct* Pentecostal hermeneutic.

Timothy B. Cargal takes a bold step in 1993 and argues that Pentecostals should move away from the historical-grammatical method and adopt newer, postmodern, forms of hermeneutical method.[17] Cargal's article identifies the dissonance between scholars such as Fee and Pentecostal pastors, saying "Pentecostal preachers . . . generally continued traditional modes of Pentecostal interpretation with their emphasis on the immediacy of the text and multiple dimensions of meaning."[18] Cargal briefly reviews and compares the modernist and postmodernist philosophical paradigms and hermeneutics in order to ground his hermeneutical proposal. He argues that

---

15. Stronstad, "Pentecostal Experience and Heermentuics," 16–28. Roger Stronstad is professor of New Testament at Summit Pacific College, Abbotsford, British Columbia.

16. Ibid., 222. He states, "I conclude that there needs to be a paradigm shift in the hermeneutical debate."

17. Cargal, "Beyond the Fundamentalist-Modernist Controversy," 163–87. Timothy B. Cargal is the Associate for Preparation for Ministry in the Office of the General Assembly of the Presbyterian Church (U.S.A.).

18. Ibid.,164.

A Distinct Twenty-first Century Pentecostal Hermeneutic

Pentecostalism is more in line with postmodern views of meaning than the modern concept that only what is historically and objectively true is meaningful. Cargal argues that Pentecostalism has an affinity with postmodernity; therefore, Pentecostal interpretation should follow postmodern interpretive concepts in order to effectively address this worldview. He discusses the role of "pneumatic illumination," "Pentecostal experience," and an "emphasis on narrative texts" and their connection to meaning, postmodern thinking, and a distinct Pentecostal hermeneutic that embraces these phenomena. His discussion of "Pentecostal experience" and its influence on interpretation is insightful; however, he seems to border on an elitism with which this writer is uncomfortable in his discussion of "pneumatic illumination." Scripture is God's word expressed in human words; therefore, Scripture is comprehensible apart from pneumatic illumination. Although Cargal may go too far in his understanding of pneumatic illumination and its place in a Pentecostal hermeneutic his arguments do support the need for Pentecostals to develop a distinct hermeneutic.[19] Cargal provides a profitable discussion proposing Pentecostals move away from historical-grammatical methods and embrace postmodern approaches to interpretation and this is perhaps his greatest contribution to the ongoing debate.

Arden C. Autry takes up the issue of Pentecostal hermeneutics in his article for the *Journal of Pentecostal Theology*.[20] Autry identifies the tension within hermeneutics as one between *correct* and *creative* reading. He contends that the Pentecostal experience heightens the Pentecostal's concern for both correct and creative reading, and proposes a theoretical framework, consisting of five dimensions, for a Pentecostal hermeneutic: 1) history, 2) language, 3) existence in time, 4) transcendence, 5) and community. Autry briefly develops each of the five dimensions presenting a hermeneutic that attempts to bridge between correct and creative meaning. Under his discussion of "history" and "language" Autry recognizes a need for historical-grammatical investigation but argues that by itself it is inadequate for the interpretive task, especially in the Pentecostal context. "Existence in time" refers to the impact the interpreter's own historical context

---

19. It is important to note that, in a brief article, Robert P. Menzies critiques Cargal's position suggesting that Cargal goes too far and ends up at a position that shifts meaning from author/text to the reader. I agree that some of Cargal's presentation is elitist and extreme, but I agree that there is a need for a shift toward the reader's involvement in meaning and interpretation. Menzies, "Jumping Off," 115–20.

20. Autry, "Dimensions Of Hermeneutics," 29–50. Arden C. Autry is associate professor at Oral Roberts University.

Why A Distinct Pentecostal Hermeneutic

has on the interpretive process. "Transcendence," his term for one's present experience of the God of the Bible, is Autry's bridge between "then and now." The difficulty here is twofold: first, how might variation among interpreters' experience of transcendence impact interpretation; and second, if transcendence is encountered how does one determine which encounters are *with God* and which are not? For Autry, community functions as a critique of private interpretation. Autry's contribution adds to the discussion and understanding of how a Pentecostal hermeneutic might appropriately embrace a *correct* and *creative* reading of Scripture, but lacks solid protection against sinking into unrestrained subjectivity.

Gordon L. Anderson discusses the subject of a distinctive Pentecostal hermeneutic in his article titled, "Pentecostal Hermeneutics."[21] Anderson offers a description of six elements that he believes are "necessary elements" in every hermeneutic: 1) historical/grammatical exegesis, 2) Holy Spirit, 3) genre, 4) personal experience, 5) historical experience, 6) and theological presuppositions. Anderson begins by identifying what he believes a Pentecostal hermeneutic is not. Two of his observations were especially influential for this writer's thinking: first, he argues a Pentecostal hermeneutic is not a new exegetical method; and, second, he argues that Spirit baptism does not result in special insight. Anderson argues for a unique, identifiable, Pentecostal hermeneutic that engages historical-grammatical methods while deliberately and purposefully including one's personal experience of salvation and Spirit baptism in the hermeneutical process. He further calls for the Pentecostal theological positions to exercise a "formative effect on the interpretation of Scripture,"[22] while also being open to revision should the text call for such. Anderson argues for the primacy of the author-intended meaning, while allowing the hermeneut to bring some things to the text that impact on interpretation.

French L. Arrington proposes an elitist position, arguing that the experience of Spirit Baptism enables the Pentecostal hermeneut to gain insight unavailable to the non-Pentecostal.[23] He inaccurately claims that a

---

21. Anderson, "Pentecostal Hermeneutics: Part 1," 1–11. Anderson, "Pentecostal Hermeneutics: Part 2," 13–21. Gordon L. Anderson is president, North Central University, Minneapolis, Minnesota. North Central University is an Assemblies of God, USA college.

22. Anderson, "Pentecostal Hermeneutics: Part 2," 21.

23. Arrington, "The Use of the Bible by Pentecostals," 101–7. French L. Arrington is Professor Emeritus of New Testament Greek and Exegesis at the Pentecostal Theological Seminary.

A Distinct Twenty-first Century Pentecostal Hermeneutic

Pentecostal, "interpreter relies on illumination by the Holy Spirit in order to come to the fullest comprehension of the significance of the text."[24] Arrington identifies the real issue facing Pentecostalism is the function of Scripture, role of the Spirit, the Christian community, grammatical-historical research, and personal experience in the interpretive process. He minimizes the place for historical-grammatical research and greatly elevates the role of the Spirit. For Arrington the Spirit is the continuum between the text (then) and the current context (now) and is able to enlighten the interpreter. The Pentecostal experience of Spirit Baptism, in Arrington's view, results in greater illumination for the Pentecostal interpreter. The value of Arrington's presentation is his description of how the interpreter might rely on the Spirit's illumination. In summary, he argues that submission of the mind to the Spirit, genuine openness to the witness of the Spirit, personal experience of faith, and response to the transforming call of God's word is how the interpreter relies on the Spirit for illumination. This is helpful when considering what the interpreter brings to the text, but is seriously detrimental if viewed as elevating the insight of the interpreter. Although we would reject his position as elitist, these four suggestions offer dialogical points for discussing the place and role of the Spirit in the hermeneutical process.

In an article John Christopher Thomas also argues for a distinct Pentecostal hermeneutic.[25] He argues that a Pentecostal hermeneutic must move away from rationalism toward a greater embrace of the Spirit. Drawing upon his interpretation of Acts 15:1–29 Thomas develops his brand of Pentecostal hermeneutical strategy. His conclusion is that community, Spirit, and Scripture (his order) engage each other in a dynamic way that produces interpretive meaning. In his discussion Thomas makes a revealing observation; he says, "Acts 15 reveals that the text's authority is not unrelated to its relevance to the community."[26] For Thomas the interpretive event begins with community experience and then comes round to Scripture's comment or critique of that experience. In his conclusion Thomas states that Scripture remains authoritative and the community's experience must submit to its scrutiny.

24. Ibid., 105.

25. Thomas, "Women, Pentecostals and The Bible," 41–56. John Christopher Thomas earned his PhD at the University of Sheffield and is professor of New Testament at the Pentecostal Theological Seminary. He also serves as editor of the *Journal of Pentecostal Theology*.

26. Ibid., 50.

Why A Distinct Pentecostal Hermeneutic

Thomas proceeds to apply his model to the issue of women's role in the ministry of the church with an interesting outcome. (He claims this is a particularly hot topic among the Pentecostals with whom he is acquainted.) He argues that the ultimate conclusion of Acts 15 is one of practicality and function (a decision enabling table fellowship between Jew and Gentile) and is not necessarily binding for all time. He concludes that a study of Acts 15 suggests there "may indeed be a distinctive hermeneutical approach to Scripture contained in the New Testament itself."[27] Thomas' understanding of the community, Spirit, and Scripture in the interpretive process underlies Kenneth Archer's proposed hermeneutic, which is also the primary conversation partner for the hermeneutic proposed in this book.

Mark D. McLean argues on the basis of a distinct "Pentecostal theology" that a distinct Pentecostal hermeneutic is essential.[28] He argues for a distinct Pentecostal hermeneutic that carefully navigates between the historical-grammatical method and the extreme existential form of interpretation represented by the "rhema word" camp within Pentecostalism.[29] McLean argues that much of contemporary theology either challenges the actual existence of God (consequently Scripture is nothing more than spiritually sensitive writers imposing a God figure upon natural phenomenon) or limits God's activity to biblical times. Pentecostals, on the other hand, hold a worldview in which God acted and continues to act within history and human experience; therefore, the activities of God recorded in Scripture are also present possibilities. According to McLean, Pentecostalism's understanding of God's presence among his people is distinctive and requires a distinctive hermeneutic. McLean's is perhaps the strongest of the earlier voices arguing in favor of a distinct Pentecostal hermeneutic for the twenty-first century. His argument is philosophically rooted and revolves around the essential distinctiveness of the Pentecostal community.

---

27. Ibid., 54.

28. McLean, "Toward a Pentecostal Hermeneutic," 35–56. Mark D. McLean received his PhD from Harvard University and is affiliated with the Assemblies of God, USA. He taught Biblical Studies and Philosophy at Evangel University, Springfield, Missouri.

29. Some charismatic Pentecostal groups argue that the Holy Spirit will give a "rhema" word to the believer. A rhema word is authoritative because it is the result of the Holy Spirit making a particular scripture, or concept, real to the individual through revelation. The danger is that the rhema word could replace the canonical word. McLean says, "If we lose our hold on the Bible, that infallible rule of our faith, and conduct, we are lost" (McLean, "Toward a Pentecostal Hermeneutic," 36).

A Distinct Twenty-first Century Pentecostal Hermeneutic

Kenneth Archer's monograph is the primary conversation partner for this book.[30] This work is a comprehensive presentation for a distinct Pentecostal hermeneutic. Tracing the early roots and background of modern Pentecostalism, surveying the early ethos, and describing the early hermeneutics of this group Archer lays his foundation for, and argument supporting the need of, his proposed hermeneutic. An important contribution of this monograph is Archer's explanation of early Pentecostalism's use of the Lukan lens (focusing on Acts) and Latter Rain motif resulting in a distinctive application of the Bible Reading interpretive method. Archer presents a hermeneutic that moves away from the historical-grammatical method (though allowing for its limited use) to employ newer methodologies and semantic theories that allow an important place for the interpreter in the creation of meaning. He presents a "hermeneutical strategy" consisting of three elements, Spirit, Scripture, and community engaging each other in dynamic dialogue. An important contribution of Archer's argument is its generous discussion of the Pentecostal community, its Central Narrative Convictions, and the significant role this plays in the interpretive process.

More recently, Bradley T. Noel has written on this subject.[31] Noel's work is focused on postmodern youth and a hermeneutic that responds to that group's worldview and emphasis of experience, emotion, and intuition over the supremacy of reason. He develops a distinct hermeneutic for Generation Xers and Millennials. This work is also specific to "classical" Pentecostals and is not inclusive of Charismatic Pentecostals. Noel critiques Fee's view of hermeneutics and rejects Fee's emphasis on authorial intent and original meaning. A weakness of this work is that it seems clearly to be written to the Pentecostal community that would uncritically accept some of Noel's assertions. Noel argues that the interpretive approach of early Pentecostals (that which predates the Pentecostal turn to adopting the historical-grammatical method) fits well with the postmodern Generation Xers and Millennials. Noel's presentation adds to the evidence that a distinct Pentecostal hermeneutic is both relevant and necessary.

Douglas P. Lowenburg writes on the subject and adds a Majority World perspective to the discussion.[32] Perhaps the greatest contribution of

---

30. Archer, *A Pentecostal Hermeneutic*, 1–196. Kenneth J. Archer is the associate professor of Theology at the Pentecostal Theological Seminary.

31. Noel, *Pentecostal and Postmodern Hermeneutics*. Bradley T. Noel is the Director of Pentecostal Studies and Assistant Professor of Christian Ministry at Tyndale University College, Toronto, Ontario.

32. Lowenburg, "A Twenty-first Century Pentecostal Hermeneutic," 1–41. Douglas P.

Why A Distinct Pentecostal Hermeneutic

this work is its insistence that any Pentecostal hermeneutic must adequately engage the African context. An important contribution made by this article is its review of interpretive methodologies, especially those employed within the African Pentecostal church. Lowenburg takes the position that the historical-grammatical method is helpful in determining what the text says but getting to the broader hermeneutical concern of a text's meaning requires methodology that engages both author-text and text-reader interactions in the process. To arrive at his Pentadactic (his term) model of interpretation, Lowenburg investigates Acts 2 and Acts 15. The interpretive model presented consists of five elements: Spirit, Theophany, Individuals, Community, and Scripture engaging each other. The discussion of theophany as an interpretive element is unconvincing and some aspects of his position on the Spirit's activity are elitist. The separation of individual leaders and community in the interpretive process leavened the thinking of this writer and helped lead to the hermeneutic proposed in this book.

This review identifies some of the primary thinkers and literary works dealing with Pentecostal hermeneutics. Although far from exhaustive, the review presents examples of the major positions and issues involved in this discussion. Clearly there are two camps within Pentecostalism: the one rejecting the idea of a *Pentecostal* hermeneutic, the other calling for a distinct Pentecostal hermeneutic. Among the second group there is wide variance in terms of method and strategy to be employed within a distinct Pentecostal hermeneutic. While it is a minority position this review indicates that it is legitimate to consider and argue for a distinct Pentecostal hermeneutic; therefore, this author contends that it is reasonable to argue for and present the hermeneutic proposed in this book. As a follow up to this literature review we now turn our attention to discuss the call from academics for such work to be done.

A Call From Academics

As we answer the question, "Why a distinct Pentecostal hermeneutic?" we begin by considering the call from academics. Hermeneutics is essential to all Christians since scholars and laity alike depend on it to obtain meaning in the biblical text. Answering the questions, "What does the text say?" and "What does the text mean?" hermeneutics moves biblical truth to the

---

Lowenburg is the J. Philip Hogan Professor of World Missions at the Assemblies of God Theological Seminary, Springfield, Missouri.

A Distinct Twenty-first Century Pentecostal Hermeneutic

arenas of belief and practice. Ferguson says, "In the last several decades, hermeneutics has moved to the forefront of the theological discussion. Today it continues to be a prime concern for all who endeavour to understand the Christian faith."[33] More recently Peter Enns notes that the subject of hermeneutics continues to hold a critical place.[34] The recent Scripture and Hermeneutics Series edited by Craig Bartholomew and Anthony Thiselton (with volume 7 released November 2006) is indicative of the ongoing academic interest in hermeneutics and recognition that there is a continued discussion related to interpretive approaches.

For Pentecostals, hermeneutics is doubly important. It is important to Pentecostals for all the reasons it is important to believers as a whole. It is also important to Pentecostals for it is the only means by which Pentecostalism, in the contemporary setting, can be biblically validated. The words of Gordon Fee are appropriate here:

> But as a New Testament scholar, even though convinced of the basic rightness of Pentecostalism's historic concerns, I realize our articulation of those concerns left much to be desired hermeneutically. We tended to argue on the basis of historical precedent what was disallowed to others on the same basis. Indeed, I think it is fair to say that this tradition has lacked both hermeneutical sophistication and consistency. On the one hand, we adopted a hermeneutical stance that seemed perfectly evident to us—and therefore should be to others; hence, one can find very little in the early literature of this movement that either articulates or defends its particular kind of "restorationist" hermeneutics. But the basic problem with all such restorationist hermeneutics, of course, is consistency. Based on all kinds of cultural and experiential factors, various "restorationists" pick and choose on the basis of their own set of concerns.[35]

---

33. Ferguson, *Biblical Hermeneutics*, 3. Although nearly three decades have passed since Ferguson made this statement it continues to be accurate.

34. Enns, "Preliminary Observations," 220. Enns asks the question, "How can practitioners, theologians, and biblicists contribute together to an overall approach to Scripture that is constructive while also being open to critique by the various disciplines?" Enns' question and his presentation of an interpretive model indicate that hermeneutics continues to hold a significant place within the academic community.

35. Fee, *Gospel and Spirit*, x. I agree with his recognition that there have been problems with Pentecostal interpretation but I am not as critical as Fee. Fee assesses early Pentecostal hermeneutics through modernist eyes; therefore, he concludes their pre-critical Bible Reading method is unsophisticated. This does not mean their method or interpretations are not valuable. Pentecostals, using their "unsophisticated" hermeneutics

Why A Distinct Pentecostal Hermeneutic

This statement by Fee points out that the time has come for Pentecostals to effectively struggle with the development of a distinctive hermeneutic and offer a legitimate, if at times challenging, Pentecostal interpretation of Scripture.

The conviction that the whole Bible is the word of God lies at the heart of Pentecostalism, hence, for Pentecostals, the Bible is a reliable revelation of God and conveys the truth the Holy Spirit intended. This truth, inspired by the Holy Spirit, is expressed through the words of men and women. This text is the governing principle for Pentecostal faith and praxis so they come to Scripture with openness to its re-formational activity. Scripture has what Anthony Thiselton calls "formative power;"[36] therefore, a proper interpretation and application of the Bible is essential to Pentecostalism.

French Arrington, a Pentecostal scholar, claims that the real issue facing Pentecostalism is hermeneutics.[37] Robeck also acknowledges that Pentecostals must engage in a serious exercise of developing a distinctive hermeneutic for the twenty-first century. He says, "Critical to our survival and our ability to speak to and be heard by the larger church is our willingness to engage in hermeneutical self-understanding."[38] In reference to Pentecostal hermeneutics Roger Stronstad states, "there needs to be a paradigm shift in the hermeneutical debate."[39] Hyun-Sook Kim argues for what he calls "the hermeneutical-praxis paradigm,"[40] and Sam Oleka writes "the Bible demands interpretation in contemporary Africa" for adequate understanding and effective obedience.[41] Lowenburg continues the discussion for a Pentecostal hermeneutic into the second decade of the twenty-first century[42] as does Bradley Noel.[43] Both Pentecostal and non-Pentecostal scholars continue to energetically discuss hermeneutics as one of the church's primary issues and all indicators suggest it will be an urgent topic for some

produced engaging, challenging and insightful interpretations. It is the view of this author that Pentecostals should continue to resist the pressure to be totally absorbed into the evangelical world. Pentecostals ought to continue to be a distinctive voice in the world of biblical interpretation.

36. Thiselton, "The Hermenetical Dynamics," 5.
37. Arrington, "The Use of the Bible by Pentecostals," 101–7.
38. Robeck, "Taking Stock of Pentecostalism," 60.
39. Stronstad, "Pentecostal Hermeneutics," 222.
40. Kim, "The Hermeneutical-Praxis," 419–36.
41. Oleka, "Interpreting and Applying," 104.
42. Lowenburg, "A Twenty-first Century Pentecostal Hermeneutic," 1–41.
43. Noel, *Pentecostal and Postmodern Hermeneutics*, 1 ff.

A Distinct Twenty-first Century Pentecostal Hermeneutic

time to come. Archer observes that Pentecostals must develop a distinctive hermeneutic or risk the undermining of their identity and practice.[44]

Conversations, articles, and monographs of the last two decades support the view that there is a great need for a distinct Pentecostal hermeneutic. A very brief and superficial review of the literature reveals a wide range of opinions among Pentecostals concerning hermeneutics and how Pentecostals should go about interpreting Scripture. Some positions seem contradictory and mutually exclusive demonstrating that there is a clear and present need for a careful, academic response to this burning issue.

Timothy Cargal makes a very interesting observation by arguing that the Fee–Stronstad–Menzies debate about the theological intent of Luke–Acts[45] demonstrates the evangelicalization of Pentecostal biblical scholarship in North America.[46] This points to the deep divide among Pentecostal academics and a separation between scholars and those engaged in Pentecostal ministry. Pentecostal preachers continue to engage in traditional Pentecostal interpretation that emphasizes the immediacy of the text, recognizes multiple dimensions of meaning and is open to the Spirit's aid in interpretation while many scholars such as Fee, Stronsdad, and Menzies, with their commitment to the historical-grammatical method, would reject the idea of multiple meanings in a text. The emphasis on the immediacy of the text and the possibility of multiple meanings among Pentecostal preachers and laity points to the growing gap between Pentecostal academics and Pentecostals in general. This suggests there is a genuine need to engage in the work of developing a distinctive Pentecostal hermeneutic for the twenty-first century.

A critical question is the nature and function of Scripture and the roles of the Holy Spirit, community, methodologies, the individual, experience, etc. in the interpretive process. Now that we are in the twenty-first century and a postmodern age, Pentecostalism must wrestle with these hermeneutical issues and establish a clear path forward for the task of biblical interpretation. Failing to do so will allow the current chaotic state to worsen and even possibly silence the *Pentecostal* voice completely.

---

44. Archer, *A Pentecostal Hermeneutic*, 3.

45. Luke–Acts is the biblical center for Pentecostals. Pentecostals interpreted all Scripture through the Lukan lens. For example, Pentecostals understood Jesus' miracles as due to his being "filled by the Spirit" (Luke 4:14) rather than due to his deity.

46. Cargal, "Beyond the Fundamentalist-Modernist Controversy," 163–87.

Why A Distinct Pentecostal Hermeneutic

The Twenty-first Century: A Changed World

The call of academics is joined by the fact that the first decade of the twenty first century saw radical change in the world. Globalization, 9/11, the recession of 2008, a series of major disasters, and ongoing international economic, political, and social crises combine to create a world that must be addressed in new categories. The development of postmodernism during the last half of the twentieth century also calls for new paradigms in the communication of the old gospel message of Scripture. Pentecostals as the largest Christian community worldwide next to the Roman Catholic Church must speak to this new world. To do so, as Robeck stated, Pentecostals must establish a distinct Pentecostal hermeneutic for the twenty-first century.

To suggest it is time to develop a distinctive Pentecostal hermeneutic is not to suggest that Pentecostals have not been practicing hermeneutics. Indeed they have! Part of the current problem is that after 1920 they abandoned their distinctive hermeneutic and adopted the hermeneutic of the evangelical community.[47] This resulted in the loss of a distinct Pentecostal interpretation and adoption of the historical-grammatical method. The Pentecostal voice needs to be heard again and a fresh hermeneutic is necessary for this to occur.

The Christian church looks vastly different at the beginning of the twenty-first century than it did at the turn of the twentieth century. Anderson states, "The Pentecostal and Charismatic movements in all their multifaceted variety constitute the fastest growing group of Churches within Christianity today."[48] The five largest churches in the world are Pentecostal and are located in the Majority World not the West. Christianity's "next wave" may come in the form of Pentecostalism as an outcome of its sheer size.[49] We may also speak of the Pentecostalization of all denominations, even the Roman Catholic Church, in the Majority World if not in the

---

47. Archer, *A Pentecostal Hermeneutic*, 131. He states, "As Pentecostals entered the universities and academic seminaries, they abandoned the early Pentecostal 'Bible Reading Method' and adopted the Historical Critical approaches of Modernity" (Bray, *Biblical Interpretation*, 223). Bray claims that by 1945 virtually all professional biblical scholars had accepted Historical Critical principles.

48. Anderson, *An Introduction To Pentecostalism*, 1.

49. The BBC web site notes that Pentecostals are the fastest growing denomination in the UK. It cites Pentecostal numbers as between 250,000,000 to 500,000,000 worldwide as of 2006 (http://www.bbc.co.uk/religion/religions/christianity/subdivisions/pentecostal_1.shtml).

A Distinct Twenty-first Century Pentecostal Hermeneutic

West. This Pentecostalization is such a phenomenon that Pope Francis I recently identified Pentecostals as Roman Catholicism's primary competition in Africa. With its continued growth and its unique understanding of Christian experience, Pentecostalism promises to reshape Christianity in the twenty-first century by default if not intentionally.[50] "The Pentecostal movement is not simply a new denomination," says Margaret M. Poloma of the department of sociology of the University of Akron. She continues, "The rise of Pentecostalism is more analogous to the rise of Protestantism in Christianity than the birth of a new denomination. It's an example of the restructuring of Christianity." This alone is sufficient reason for serious work in developing a distinct Pentecostal hermeneutic for the twenty-first century.

Theoretical Developments

Added to the call from academics and a transformed context is contemporary hermeneutical theory's recognition that one's communal metanarrative significantly influences the process of exegesis and the understanding of meaning.[51] Walter Brueggemann says, "The status of the interpreter (or interpreting community) is now an important one. What one finds in scripture is to some (large?) extent determined by what one brings to the text."[52] Since Pentecostals are a distinct group with a particular metanarrative, a distinct hermeneutical strategy is legitimate and necessary. It is important to understand how narrative tradition works as a pre-understanding and influences interpretation since one's community narrative acts as an interpretive lens. The potential for interpretive excesses resulting from the community influence must be filtered out. It is also essential to knowingly allow this pre-understanding to enable the Pentecostal hermeneut to arrive at new and fresh interpretations.

50. Poloma, "Spirit Bade Me," n.p.

51. Stout, "Theological Commitment," 44–59. Stout demonstrates that an inescapable relationship exists between the community to which one belongs and how one explains past religious experience. Alasdair MacIntyre argues convincingly that a community's "narrative tradition" (metanarrative) determine one's interpretive practices. See MacIntyre, *After Virtue*. See also Murphy, Kallenberg and Nation, *Virtues and Practices*. Archer writes, "the narrative tradition of a community becomes an essential part of any hermeneutical strategy, for the making and explaining of meaning is inherently communal" (Archer, *A Pentecostal Hermeneutic*, 96).

52. Brueggemann, *The Book That Breathes New Life*, 3.

Why A Distinct Pentecostal Hermeneutic

Hermeneutical theory is also revising its view of the grammatical-historical method. Though this method held a dominant role in biblical study and exegesis for a long time it is losing its place if it has not already done so. There is a growing consensus that grammatical-historical method is inadequate for the hermeneutical task. The great disillusionment with the grammatical-historical method is, according to Autry, due to its inability to edify.[53] Edification is why Pentecostals read Scripture; therefore, their interpretive methodology must be more than the continued adoption of the grammatical-historical method. Disillusionment and rejection of this modern method, the postmodern adoption of literary critical method, contemporary interpretive theory that includes reader/hearer in the creation of meaning, all indicate that the twenty-first century Pentecostal hermeneutics must move beyond the current methodological approaches.

A Distinctive Community

Hermeneutic theorists' recognition of community as a significant influence in the interpretive process requires we consider the real status of the Pentecostal community. Obviously the early Pentecostals were a distinctive community and even in the contemporary church, Pentecostals remain distinctive. Within Pentecostalism itself there has been a great deal of differentiation take place over the past half century. However, Pentecostals of all stripes continue to stand apart as a distinct expression of Christianity. Denominations and individuals alike would easily identify themselves as Pentecostal or as not belonging to that group.[54] Even the most cursory study of early Pentecostal writings and sermons will show that Pentecostals understood themselves to be a distinct community within Christianity. The response of the larger Christian body to early and, to some extent, contemporary Pentecostals indicates others see them as distinct also.[55] This recog-

---

53. Autry, "Dimensions Of Hermeneutics," 32.

54. Miller, *Canadian Pentecostals*, 45. Miller describes how the Mennonite Brethren in Christ moved to renounce and oppose Pentecostalism.

55. Ibid., 45. Miller writes, "Many of the new Pentecostal groups in Ontario were the by-product of local opposition. At Vineland, in the Niagara Peninsula, Mrs. Henry Snyder and Mrs. George Stewart heard of the Toronto outpouring and came to join in the blessing. When they tried to share their experiences with their pastor and congregation at home, they were expelled. . . . This pattern—reception of the Baptism in the Holy Spirit with tongues and subsequent testimony to others, followed by persecution and expulsion—was followed many times in the decade following the Toronto outpouring

A Distinct Twenty-first Century Pentecostal Hermeneutic

nition of Pentecostals as a distinct expression of Christianity promises to continue worldwide within Christendom.

Douglas Jacobsen effectively argues that every community has "Foundational Narrative Convictions."[56] These Foundational Narrative Convictions form the primary story giving reason for the community's existence and serve to differentiate the group (community) from all other groups. An important role of these Foundational Narrative Convictions is to inform the group of the duties they are to perform, their *raison d'etre*. Clearly one's Foundational Narrative Convictions would color their interpretation of Scripture. Being a distinctive community with distinctive Foundational Narrative Convictions means that Pentecostals will engage in a distinctive hermeneutical strategy. They will either do so intentionally or unintentionally and the danger is that they will accidentally do hermeneutics in a distinctive manner; therefore, intentionality is important for it is the only way one can purposefully correct for excesses and attempt to avoid extremes and serious error. Since Pentecostals are a clearly defined group within orthodox Christianity, a distinct twenty-first century Pentecostal hermeneutic is legitimate and necessary.

A Unique Story

Along with Foundational Narrative Convictions the Pentecostal community grew and continues to grow out of shared experience. The more intense the experience the stronger the bond it creates within a group. The formative years of Pentecostalism beginning with Azusa Street were intense and spiritually dynamic. Miller's description of early Canadian Pentecostalism's development portrays an intense, dynamic movement spreading outward from the Hebdon Mission, Toronto (sometimes referred to as "the Canadian Azusa").[57] Pentecostals shared a spiritual experience called baptism in the Spirit with the supernatural evidence of speaking in tongues and a story of mission with all its reported success. They also shared the experience of persecution from within and without the Christian church. Shared testimonies increased awareness and the intensity of this shared story and ultimately produced a deep sense of identity among Pentecostals. They saw themselves as the apostolic church of Acts restored.

---

of 1906."

56. Jacobsen, "Pentecostal Hermeneutics," 13–15.

57. Miller, *Canadian Pentecostals*, 39–69.

Why A Distinct Pentecostal Hermeneutic

Obviously, Pentecostals are part of the larger Christian body but they are also a distinct group within that body. Whether one is a Classical Pentecostal, Charismatic Pentecostal, neo-classical, or Independent Pentecostal they are recognizably distinct within Christendom because of their distinctive pneumatology and historical journey. Their form of worship also sets them apart. The Pentecostal openness, even expectation of, the immediacy of God's presence evidenced by the Charismata distinguishes them from other faith communities. Any reading of recent church history will clearly show that Pentecostals from the very beginning are a distinct expression of Christianity.[58]

Liberal and Fundamentalist[59] alike rejected the early Pentecostals. Even the Holiness movement from which they sprang rejected them and many considered them heretical, even demon possessed.[60] The rest of Christendom responded to the early Pentecostals in such a way as to set them apart as a distinct group. Their journey through the last century has been in some important ways distinct from the journey of the rest of Christendom. Pentecostalism has (and in some cases continues to) produced joyful reception and bitter contention. The Pentecostal story through the twentieth century and into the twenty-first century is distinctive and distinguishes them as a clearly identifiable community within the broader Christian community.

---

58. Pentecostal distinctiveness in the twenty-first century is perhaps less remarkable. The Charismatic movement has brought Pentecostal experience within the walls of most, if not all, denominational structures. Roman Catholic and Baptist alike would have among them individuals who claim a Pentecostal experience. Hostility toward Pentecostals has radically diminished, in some cases all but disappeared, in the past four decades. However, I believe it is still possible to say that Pentecostalism is a distinct form of Christianity. Pentecostals continue to share a metanarrative that is distinct and continues to influence their reading of Scripture.

59. Russell Spittler states that Pentecostals and Fundamentalists are "arch enemies" when it comes to tongues and healing as proper expectations in today's church. As to their approaches to the Bible, "precritical and uncomplicated," Spittler argues they are identical. He goes on to say that Fundamentalists and Pentecostals must be kept distinctive for a number of reasons. Spittler, "Are Pentecostals and Charismatics Fundamentalists?," 106.

60. Miller, *Canadian Pentecostals*, 42.

A Distinct Twenty-first Century Pentecostal Hermeneutic

A Unique Worldview

As will be shown in chapter 2, Pentecostals also have a particular worldview. They differ from Fundamentalists, Liberals, non-Christians, mainline denominations, and Roman Catholicism in their fundamental understanding of reality. According to Middleton and Walsh "worldviews give faith answers to a set of ultimate grounding questions."[61] A worldview answers identity questions for the community and individuals within it while also explaining what is wrong with the outside world and how it should be repaired. An important part—perhaps the central, controlling aspect—of the early Pentecostal worldview was their self-perception as a "marginalized people of the 'Latter Rain.'"[62] Both Scripture and the present reality were interpreted through this lens.[63] For Pentecostals the Latter Rain motif understood Acts 2 as a defining, historical moment when God poured out his Spirit on a saved and sanctified church with the biblical sign of speaking in tongues. They further saw the church becoming apostate after the death of the apostles. This apostasy was worsened when the church embraced the Roman Empire with the conversion of Constantine and was complete after the split between East and West. From this point onward Pentecostals see only fragmented sparks of life remaining in the church but a faithful, persecuted remnant always existed.[64] For Pentecostals, the Reformation prepared the church for the Latter Rain outpouring. This outpouring meant that Jesus was coming soon and the task of world evangelization must be completed as soon as possible.

---

61. Middleton and Walsh, *The Transforming Vision*, ch. 2. See also Middleton and Walsh, *Truth Is Stranger*.

62. Archer, *A Pentecostal Hermeneutic*, 116. Faupel effectively argues that the Latter Rain motif was/is the centerpiece of the Pentecostal self-narrative. Faupel, *The Everlasting Gospel*, 19–43. See also, Miller, *Canadian Pentecostals*, 39 "Latter Rain People."

63. Miller, *Canadian Pentecostals*, 30–31. Further, on page 75 he states, "All that Argue needed to complete his doctrinal system, and fulfill the model of a first-generation Canadian Pentecostal preacher, was a conviction that the Second Coming of Christ was imminent. This theological certainty was quick in coming, as the Rapture of the Church was almost immediately highlighted among the Latter Rain believers. In fact, the very term 'Latter Rain' signified their conviction that they were the forerunners of the last great move of God on earth prior to the Second Coming."

64. Some Pentecostal church historians went to great lengths to trace this remnant through history. They seized on any mention of behavior, etc. that might be interpreted as a Spirit Baptism experience. Eisegesis was common in their reading of some history and biographies of prominent church leaders.

Why A Distinct Pentecostal Hermeneutic

The supernatural, divine healing and the charismatic gifts were important elements in the early Pentecostal worldview as a consequence of their Latter Rain motif. They saw themselves as a unique people—the endtime church that would complete the command to take the gospel to the whole earth and then experience the return of Christ. This motif with its belief that Christ's second coming was imminent provided a strong impetus for missions among Pentecostals.[65]

Some of Pentecostalism's self-understanding has modified during the past several decades. The Charismatic movement, over time, reshaped some aspects of Pentecostalism as many Charismatics left their mainline denominations and joined Classical Pentecostal congregations. The effectiveness of Pentecostal missions has brought millions from the Majority World into the Pentecostal community. Each of these factors, and others not mentioned here, have reshaped the Pentecostal community from its early days yet twenty-first century Pentecostalism retains the core of the early self-understanding. Most Western twenty-first century Pentecostals would not see themselves as marginalized and most would not recognize or be able to accurately define the term "Latter Rain." However, the essential beliefs of the Latter Rain theology continue to be essential Pentecostal belief and teaching. The soon return of Christ, expectancy of the supernatural, an association of the baptism in the Spirit with Joel and the belief that they represent the church as Christ intended it to be remain pillars of Pentecostalism. The need to fulfill Christ's mandate to preach the gospel to the whole world remains a high priority among Pentecostals. Pentecostalism was and is an identifiable group within Christendom and, as such, must purposefully develop a distinctive hermeneutical strategy.

Unlike Liberals and Fundamentalists, Pentecostals neither completely rejected nor fully embraced modernism. They employed elements of modernism in their evangelism and missions programs. In contrast to Liberals, Pentecostals held a high view of Scripture, accepting it as authoritative and inspired. They differ from Fundamentalists in that they are not cessationist, do not adopt all the "fundamentals" nor do they accept all the tenets of Dispensationalism. Pentecostals differ from the mainline denominations in that they did not initially adopt higher criticism and the grammatical-historical method of biblical interpretation. They did not embrace liturgical worship forms and so are distinct from Roman Catholicism and Episcopalian groups. Obviously, Pentecostalism is a distinct expression

---

65. Miller, *Canadian Pentecostals*, 42.

of Christianity and cannot be easily grouped within any other tradition including Evangelicalism. Considering current hermeneutic theory it is reasonable to conclude that Pentecostals require a community specific hermeneutic.

Pentecostalism's Development

Contemporary Pentecostalism is also different from the early Pentecostal community. Archer fails to adequately recognize the difference between the early twentieth century Pentecostal community and that of the twenty-first century. Over one hundred years after Azusa Street Pentecostals, especially in the West, are far more educated, wealthy, and influential. They continue to believe in the return of Jesus but are less likely to believe it will happen in their lifetime and views of the rapture vary among contemporary Pentecostals. Charismatic and independent Pentecostal congregations make up a large and growing percentage of the Pentecostal community. The vast majority of Pentecostals now live and worship in a Majority World context. Views on tongues as initial evidence and end times are varied and sometimes differ from that of the early Classical Pentecostals but Pentecostals remain highly missional and committed to evangelizing the world before Jesus returns. They continue to expect the manifest presence of the Spirit in worship with accompanying signs and wonders. The Lukan lens continues as the Pentecostal interpretive lens and they continue to hold to charismatic signs as evidence of baptism in the Spirit. A distinctive Pentecostal hermeneutic is required so that traditional doctrines and newer challenges can be addressed effectively.

Pentecostal Theological Contribution

Arguably Pentecostalism engaged in a significant theological development in the field of pneumatology a century ago. Adopting the Old Testament as their Scripture, the first-century church adopted the Jewish belief that the Father was God. There does not seem to be any theological debate over this truth in the early church. The first council of Nicea, in 325 CE, resulted in the creedal declaration of the deity of Christ and a recognition of the deity of the Holy Spirit. The terminology of Constantinople (381 CE) confirms the deity of the Holy Spirit and uses language that became normative for orthodox Christianity so it is clear that the doctrine of Trinity develops

Why A Distinct Pentecostal Hermeneutic

over a long history. In 110 CE Ignatius of Antioch speaks of God in terms of Trinity and several of the church fathers, including Tertullian, discuss the nature of God and use trinitarian language. However, not until the end of the fourth century CE does the doctrine of Trinity basically reach its current form with the Cappadocian fathers bringing the discussion of Trinity into language that resonates with contemporary understanding.

Interestingly the discussion and outcome of the Council of Nicea says little of the Holy Spirit beyond declaring his deity. Throughout the discussions of the church fathers, church councils, and creeds, the focus is on Christology rather than pneumatology. Little attention is given to the Holy Spirit. The second Council of Constantinople, in 381 CE, affirms the deity of the Holy Spirit and uses the controversial phrase "proceeding from the Father and the Son." Systematic theologies have treated the Holy Spirit as the third person in the Trinity and describe his person and work. What Pentecostals brought to the table was a theology of the Spirit that described how the Spirit was experienced in worship and life. They further brought a clear means by which one might know they have been baptized in the Spirit—they spoke with tongues. With the appearance of Pentecostalism at the turn of the twentieth century, pneumatology comes to the foreground and arguable it is Pentecostal theology that develops an understanding of the activity of the Holy Spirit within the life of the church.

The Pentecostal movement of the early twentieth century moved pneumatology to the foreground of Christian debate. Understanding of the Charismata develops within the context of Pentecostal theologizing and Pentecostalism motivates the discussion concerning the nature, work and role of the Holy Spirit over the past century. Prior to the Pentecostal revival the Western church seems content to simply acknowledge the deity of the Holy Spirit and allow his presence and activity to exist in the mystical realm. With the Pentecostal revival, theology is pushed to begin seriously reconsidering pneumatology and so Pentecostals have made a significant contribution to Christian theology because of their focus on the Holy Spirit. As Pentecostals effectively employ a distinctive hermeneutic they will continue to contribute positively to theological discussions and biblical interpretation for decades to come.

A Distinct Twenty-first Century Pentecostal Hermeneutic

Conclusion

Pentecostalism from its beginnings has been a distinct expression of Christianity. Its interracial worship, belief that the baptism in the Spirit is evidenced by tongues, restorationist zeal, and Latter Rain perspective set it apart. Fundamentalists rejected Pentecostals because of their pneumatology; and their high view of Scripture, among other things, distinguished them from Liberals. Although they used Dispensational language to express their eschatology, they rejected Dispensationalism's cessationist view of the charismata and thus were unacceptable in the Fundamentalist camp. Their Armenian soteriological position set them apart from mainline denominations and the "come-outism" that developed, clearly marked Pentecostals as distinct. The church's negative response to Pentecostalism's theology and worship practices identify the latter as a distinct expression of the Christian faith.

The world of the twenty-first century Pentecostal is vastly different from that of the early decades of the twentieth-century Pentecostal revival. The development of the Charismatic movement impacted Pentecostalism in significant ways. First, it introduced an expression of Pentecostalism that did not hold to tongues as the sole evidence for baptism in the Spirit. Second, many charismatics remained within their denominational structures even though they were frequently relegated to the church basement; therefore, their influence was slowly felt throughout the congregation. This resulted in what might be called a mild form of Pentecostalization within other Christian denominations. One might argue that Pentecostalism's distinctiveness is altered and less intense as a result of the Charismatic movement but it remains true that Pentecostalism is a distinct expression of the Christian faith even if that distinction is no longer connected to denominational affiliation or a "come-outism" mindset.

Twenty-first century Pentecostals must address a very different audience and context than their forefathers. In the twenty-first century they face the challenge of revisiting their doctrinal positions. New social issues have arisen and require a biblical response from the Pentecostal community. The problems of life are the same at their core but they find expression in vastly different forms today than a century ago and temptations, though the same in essence, are very different in appearance. The twenty-first century world differs technologically, geographically, economically, politically, etc. from that of the first half of the twentieth century and challenges Pentecostals to

Why A Distinct Pentecostal Hermeneutic

develop a distinct hermeneutic in order to effectively speak to a twenty-first century world.

Contemporary theory clearly recognizes the significant role community plays in the task of interpretation. Pentecostals, though a distinct and obvious community within the broader church, share much in common with all Christians but it is also clear that they own a worldview, story and theology that distinguishes them. The extent of this distinction may have been more acute in the early years of Pentecostalism than the contemporary context but the distinguishing marks still remain and call Pentecostals in the twenty-first century to develop a distinct hermeneutic.

There remains a place for Pentecostals to contribute to the theological and practical development of the church, but to contribute effectively they must speak with a clearly Pentecostal voice. If they speak only with an evangelical[66] voice or, even worse, with an unclear voice, they cannot contribute to the church's continued growth and ongoing need of biblical direction for belief and practice. They cannot engage in the current conversation the Holy Spirit is using to move the church toward the final eschaton if their voice is not clear. They can only be part of the conversation God is using to reveal his will to his people in the twenty-first century if they speak with a distinctive voice and to do so they must interpret Scripture as Pentecostals; therefore, a distinct hermeneutic is legitimate and necessary.

---

66. This is not to suggest Pentecostals are not evangelicals or that they should in any way disassociate with the evangelical camp. However, Pentecostals are a distinct group within the larger evangelical body. Evangelicalism is enhanced as Pentecostals learn to speak with their distinct voice.

CHAPTER 2

DEFINING PENTECOSTALISM AND ITS EARLY HERMENEUTIC

Introduction

WE HAVE ARGUED THAT a distinctive Pentecostal hermeneutic is legitimate and necessary, partly because Pentecostalism is a distinct community, and community is currently recognized as an essential aspect of interpretive theory. Pentecostalism's roots are deeply imbedded in the holiness, revivalist movements of the late nineteenth and early twentieth century. Pentecostal revivalist fervor, charismatic experientialism, and welcoming spirit attracted large numbers of the lower class resulting in Pentecostalism appearing to some to be the religion of the poor and socially marginalized. Pentecostals, as we shall discover, developed a specific worldview that was informed by restorationism and a Latter Rain motif that was reinforced by a distinct use of the Bible Reading method of interpretation. As a result, Pentecostalism quickly developed a distinct ethos and self-understanding that continues into the twenty-first century. Since a distinctive hermeneutic is not the use of unique methods, but is the way a particular community uses interpretive methods, we now turn our attention to both describing Pentecostalism's community identity and their interpretive strategy.

Defining Pentecostalism and Its Early Hermeneutic

Pentecostalism's Roots

It is our position that modern Pentecostalism has roots in the Bethel Bible College, Topeka, Kansas, under the direction of Charles Fox Parham, and the Azusa Street revival under the direction of William Seymour.[1] Parham began his investigation of the Holy Spirit baptism as early as 1899/1900. He apparently taught his students in 1900 that there must be a further experience from salvation called the baptism in the Holy Spirit.[2] This was not a new or unique theology, but it was part of the Wesleyan Holiness movement's teaching also. In December of 1900 he left his students to search the scriptures specifically for the biblical evidence that a person had been

---

1. Miller, *Canadian Pentecostals*, 28. There is general agreement that modern Pentecostalism began with the Topeka, Kansas Bible College. However, there is debate over whether Parham or Seymour should be considered the founder of North American Pentecostalism. Some contend the movement began in Topeka Kansas and should be associated with Charles Fox Parham. Others argue the movement began at Azusa Street and is associated with William Seymour. This author agrees with Miller that both places hold a critical, foundational place for the North American Pentecostal movement. The small Bible college led by Parham, in my view, is the foundation for the Pentecostal distinctive doctrine of glossolalia as initial evidence for Spirit Baptism. Azusa Street, under the leadership of Seymour, serves as the fountainhead from which the Pentecostal movement sprang and spread and may be said to be the birthplace of full-blown Pentecostal revival experience.

The Azusa Street revival under William Seymour is certainly a major contributor to modern Pentecostalism. Miller correctly concludes, "It was at the Azusa Street Mission that all these strands of 'Pentecostal' theology coalesced to form a basis for 20th century Pentecostalism" (Miller, *Canadian Pentecostals*, 28). Many of the early leaders travelled to Azusa Street and received the baptism in the Spirit while there. From there they brought the message of Pentecost to their various localities. The racially integrated, African American style of worship at Azusa Street was also influential. It is important to note that William Seymour was a student at Parham's Bible College and received his theological training there. It is also important to note that several Pentecostal leaders were baptized in the Spirit under the ministry of Parham in Zion City in 1906.

Stone Church, Chicago under the leadership of William Piper also played a significant role for the Canadian Pentecostal movement. Some of the prominent early leaders of the Canadian Pentecostal movement received their initial Spirit Baptism experience at Stone Church. Stone Church became Pentecostal in 1907 and the Pentecostal movement there seems to be independent of Azusa Street. A. H. Argue, a prominent leader in PAOC, travelled to the North Avenue Mission, Chicago and received the Baptism in the Holy Spirit with evidence of speaking in tongues. William Durham, pastor of North Avenue Mission, was filled with the Spirit after travelling to Azusa Street. Rudd, *When The Spirit Came Upon Them*, 36; cf. Stronstad, "Trends in Pentecostal Hermeneutics," 1–11.

2. Miller, *Canadian Pentecostals*, 28.

A Distinct Twenty-first Century Pentecostal Hermeneutic

baptized in the Holy Spirit. The evidence, contrary to Fee,[3] seems to suggest that Parham's students came to the conclusion that tongues was the biblical evidence an individual had been baptized in the Spirit.[4] On January 1, 1901, Agnes Ozman (one of Parham's students) received the baptism in the Spirit and spoke in tongues. Some suggest this occurred before the student body clearly came to a conclusion concerning the biblical evidence of baptism in the Spirit, but Sarah Parham claims the scripture search precedes Ozman's experience.[5] Edward Irving, leader of a failed attempt at charismatic renewal in the 1830s, identified glossolalia as the "standing sign" of the baptism in the Holy Spirit.[6] Since the movement initiated by Irving is part of Pentecos-

---

3. Fee and Stuart, *Gospel and Spirit*, 86. Fee says, "in general the Pentecostal's experience has preceded their hermeneutics." Fee contends that the Pentecostal doctrine of subsequence concerning Spirit-baptism arose from experience not hermeneutics. He holds the same position with regard to the doctrine of tongues as initial evidence of Spirit Baptism. The evidence does not seem to support Fee's position. The issue of subsequence is related to the Holiness background of Pentecostalism (see discussion later in this chapter). The issue of initial evidence is a bit more murky but the evidence challenges Fee's definitive position. I agree with Fee that the Pentecostal approach to hermeneutics is experientially biased, perhaps even driven, and inadequate but I disagree with Fee as to how Pentecostal's initially came to these positions. The evidence seems to point more toward a hermeneutical origin than an experiential one; therefore, the role and place of experience in Pentecostal hermeneutics, past, present and future, is of critical importance and will be addressed latter in this book.

4. Stronstad, "Trends in Pentecostal Hermeneutics," 1. Stronstad says, "the locus of Pentecostalism . . . is not the uniqueness of this experience, but the new hermeneutical/biblical understanding of this experience. Charles F. Parham bequeathed to the Pentecostal movement its definitive hermeneutics, and consequently, its definitive theology and apologetics. His contribution arose out of the problem of the interpretation of the second chapter of Acts and his conviction that Christian experience in the 20th century 'should tally exactly with the Bible. . .'" Stronstad argues that hermeneutics preceded experience. See also Miller, *Canadian Pentecostals*, 28 and Parham, *The Life of Charles F. Parham*. Sarah Parham's account supports the view that the scripture search preceded the experiential component. Sarah Parham was the wife of Charles Fox Parham and her much later report of these events are not conclusive. It must be admitted that the evidence is somewhat murky. Which source one uses and what weight is given to each source will determine how one interprets the evidence. Fee acknowledges that his position lacks a certain historical certitude but contends there is an experiential component driving the scripture search. Fee's point is important and must be given due consideration.

5. Parham, *The Life of Charles F. Parham*, 51–56.

6. Synan, "The Origins of the Pentecostal Movement," 1. It cannot be proven that Irving's understanding of glossolalia as the sign of Spirit Baptism was hermeneutically produced or merely deduced from experience. It is also impossible to determine to what extent Irving's view may have influenced Pentecostal hermeneutics in relation to initial evidence. Synan points to Edward Irving's nineteenth century ministry as an important

Defining Pentecostalism and Its Early Hermeneutic

talism's historical roots it is reasonable to assume Irving's view was known by Parham and early Pentecostal leaders with a holiness background. The evidence suggests that Pentecostals have, at least partially, a hermeneutical root and starting point for their distinctive doctrine of baptism in the Spirit. William Seymour, a black African-American and the leader of the Azusa Street Pentecostal outpouring, was influenced by Parham's teaching in Houston, Texas before travelling to Los Angeles to pastor.[7] Seymour assimilated Parham's theology, and through the Azusa Street revival spread it, and the experience of baptism in the Spirit with evidence of speaking in tongues around the world. Parham, likely more than any other person, was responsible for the theological shift to understanding tongues as the evidence of Spirit baptism,[8] but Seymour, through the Azusa Street ministry, was largely responsible for exporting Pentecostalism globally.

Although controversy exists over Pentecostal origins and who should be considered founder of Pentecostalism there is agreement that early Pentecostals all shared a commitment to the "Full Gospel" message and an ecstatic religious experience associated with Spirit Baptism.[9] They shared the belief that the miracles of the Gospels and Acts should be normative for the contemporary church, and their experience of healings and Spirit Baptism evidenced by speaking in tongues confirmed to them that their belief was correct.

---

precursor to Pentecostalism. He says, "Edward Irving and his friends in London suggested the possibility of a restoration of the charisms in the modern Church . . . Irving led the first attempt at 'charismatic renewal' in his Regents Square Presbyterian Church in 1831. Although tongues and prophecies were experienced in his church, Irving was not successful in his quest for a restoration of New Testament Christianity . . . While his movement failed in England, Irving did succeed in pointing to glossolalia as the 'standing sign' of the baptism in the Holy Spirit, a major facet in the future theology of Pentecostals." Synan was the director of the Holy Spirit Research Center and is now Dean of the College of Divinity, Regent University.

7. Although segregation was in full force in the Southern U.S., William Seymour was allowed to sit in the hallway and listen, through an open door, to Parham's Bible College lectures.

8. Anderson, *An Introduction To Pentecostalism*, 35.

9. Miller, *Canadian Pentecostals*, 17. Miller identifies Salvation, Baptism in the Spirit, Divine Healing and the Second Coming as the four cardinal doctrines commonly referred to as "the full gospel." There was a shared belief and proclamation of the four (or five) fold understanding of the work of Jesus as Savior, (Sanctifier), Spirit Baptizer, Healer and Soon Coming King. There was also the shared belief in tongues as the initial evidence of Spirit Baptism.

A Distinct Twenty-first Century Pentecostal Hermeneutic

Parham's influence on early Pentecostalism in North America cannot be ignored; however, Seymour and Azusa Street far surpass him in significance. Seymour and Azusa Street are at the root of how Pentecostals define themselves. The Azusa Street emphasis on evangelism and mission resulted in over twenty-five missionaries being sent to more than twenty-five nations in two years.[10] Missions and evangelism are at the centre of Pentecostalism's self-understanding. Pentecostalism is a significant revival movement motivated by the belief that every person must, and can, be saved. They are further driven by their belief that Jesus' return is imminent.

The Azusa Street revival, lasting some three years, was a spiritual and social revolution where the marginalized and dispossessed found equality, acceptance, and place.[11] African American spirituality helped form the ethos of Azusa Street and became embedded in the fabric of Pentecostalism.[12] We agree with Robeck and Faupel who argue that the Azusa Street prototype of Pentecostalism must remain a source of inspiration for theological and spiritual renewal if Pentecostalism is to remain strong and continue its phenomenal growth in the twenty-first century.[13]

Western and African Pentecostalism are in need of an infusion of Azusa Street spirituality. Pentecostalism in Africa is often far too segregated while a critical element of Azusa Street spirituality was its interracial worship. This author has noted that Pentecostal congregations in Africa frequently fail the interracial test. We have noted that congregations in urban areas led by white pastors are likely to be more racially mixed than those led by black pastors. This book is not the place to debate or attempt an explanation of these observed phenomena, but it is noted to highlight the point that Azusa Street spirituality with its racially mixed worshipping community continues to hold a noteworthy place as a model for Pentecostal congregations.

Initially many of the early Pentecostals were believers from various traditions but came primarily from a Holiness background.[14] Some, dissatisfied with their current religious experience, heard of the revival in Los Angeles and went to see what was happening and many who travelled to

---

10. Faupel, *The Everlasting Gospel*, 182–86, 208–9, 212–16.

11. Anderson, *Introduction to Pentecostalism*, 45.

12. Nelson, *For Such A Time As This*, 157–58.

13. Robeck, "Pentecostal Origins From A Global Perspective," 179; Faupel, *Everlasting Gospel*, 309.

14. Miller, *Canadian Pentecostals*, 21–22.

Defining Pentecostalism and Its Early Hermeneutic

witness these revivals were baptized in the Spirit and spoke in tongues. On their return home they became vociferous proponents of this new experience, and their message reached many who were dissatisfied with the church and their current religious experience. This dissatisfaction created an openness to the message of Spirit baptism proclaimed by those newly baptized in the Spirit, and many who heard were baptized in the Spirit and a great movement was born.

Most Pentecostals did not initially intend leaving their former affiliations, but wanted to see their present faith tradition embrace this new experience. The response was mixed, but most faith traditions resisted and or rejected these new phenomena. Consequently, large numbers left their former traditions to gather together with like-minded believers and eventually fellowships and denominations were born. As these groups and fellowships developed and grew it became clear that pastoral leadership would be necessary. Some of the newly baptized were clergy from other traditions, and many of them naturally filled the role of pastoring these new congregations.[15] Men like James Eustace Purdie[16] (an Anglican priest) became important voices in early Pentecostalism aiding in the establishment of doctrinal positions, etc. More normative was the case where individuals untrained in theology and Scripture became pastors of these fledgling congregations.

Amid the fervor of revival many heard the call to preach and went out to bring the full gospel message to crags, crannies, hollows, villages, and towns. They preached a simple gospel and called people to repent and be baptized in the Spirit. The success of their ventures is well documented, and many came to faith and were baptized in the Spirit speaking in tongues. Miracles, healings, etc. accompanied these early preachers, and

---

15. For a number of examples see Miller, *Canadian Pentecostals*, 39–98. Miller, referring to early Canadian Pentecostals, states, "A considerable number of the early leaders had some formal training in their former denominations; men such as A. G. Ward, D. N. Buntain and J. E. Purdie" (201). See also, Rudd, *When the Spirit Came Upon Them*. Rudd provides excellent biographical information for a number of early Pentecostal leaders in Canada. It is interesting to note how many of these individuals had pastoral training and were engaged in ministry prior to their experience of baptism in the Spirit.

16. See, Craig, "'Out and Out For The Lord.'" This thesis by James Craig provides an excellent description of the role of Dr. James E. Purdie (originally from Charlottetown, PEI) in the development of PAOC. Thomas Miller writes, "One of J. E. Purdie's chief aims, in establishing the Bible school in Winnipeg, was to combat this tendency among Canadian believers" (Miller, *Canadian Pentecostals*, 107). The tendency to which Miller refers is the tendency to "undue subjectivism in doctrine and in practice."

congregations were established almost faster than count could be kept. Leadership became an issue since pastoral leadership fell to persons not trained or prepared for the role. This reality likely led to some of the hermeneutical inconsistency, even disregard, noted by Fee.

Many of those in early Pentecostalism "came out"[17] of denominational churches, often not by choice but because they were expelled. Early Pentecostal history contains numerous examples of individuals that returned to their home assemblies, having been baptized in the Spirit with the evidence of tongues and filled with a new fervor. Their exuberant testimony and attempts to lead others to share this experience frequently brought them into conflict with their congregation's leadership. In not a few instances this led to individuals being given an ultimatum to discontinue their activity or be expelled. Many left rather than capitulate, but some remained and were eventually expelled. Those who left or were expelled brought with them a denominational heritage and theology that impacted their interpretation of Scripture.[18] This historical reality impacted the early Pentecostal's understanding of Scripture, and their practice of hermeneutics. Consequently the background of these early Pentecostals is important since it helped shape their identity and ethos.

So who are these Pentecostals and what is their background? Harvey Cox writes, "The Pentecostal movement is diverse, volatile and mercurial

---

17. The "come-outism" movement began in the 1880s. It was a pejorative term applied to radical Wesleyan preachers who were calling people out of the established Methodist churches to join independent holiness churches. John P. Brooks is a prominent leader of the movement. See Synan, *The Holiness-Pentecostal Movement*, 42–54. Pentecostals used this terminology for several decades but it does not seem to be in common use today. It was the terminology used by many Pentecostals in their testimony. As a boy, teen, and young adult I noted that testimony services were common elements in the Pentecostal liturgy of the Sunday evening service. Frequently those giving testimony would refer to the time when they "came out" of a certain denominational church. This was often related to their conversion experience and subsequent Baptism in the Spirit.

18. I acknowledge that many early Pentecostals held a negative attitude toward their former denominations. Many times, especially in reference to main line denominations, this negative attitude resulted in the rejection of academics as theology and education were often demonized as the culprits that led these denominations to be sterile, lifeless, anti-Pentecostal and void of the Spirit. The emphasis on the Spirit, invigorated worship and evangelism led these early Pentecostals to focus more on practice than theology and doctrine. However, the power of the underlying doctrine, theology, and understanding of scripture that these persons brought with them from their various denominational backgrounds should not be underestimated.

Defining Pentecostalism and Its Early Hermeneutic

. . . it is highly paradoxical."[19] Pentecostalism has its roots deep in the soil of late nineteenth- and early twentieth-century social and religious context, and a time of revivalist fervor, social chaos,[20] and theological transitions in Europe and North America. Modernism had powerfully impacted theology, and the Tubingen school dominated biblical scholarship. Liberalism and scholasticism held sway in the mainline churches. Amid these varied conditions the Pentecostal revival erupts in North America.[21]

Revivalist fervor in North America, with its emphasis on personal salvation and its emotional appeals, meant that crusades and campaigns were frequent occurrences. The experiential focus of the revival movement coupled with the "second work" theology of the Holiness groups provided the fermenting soil of early Pentecostalism. The theological and social environment of the late nineteenth and early twentieth centuries produced theological, social and philosophical predispositions that were brought into the milieu of the Pentecostal revival of the early twentieth century. These predispositions combine with the Pentecostal experience to impact the hermeneutics they practiced; therefore, they must be taken into account in our discussion. We now turn to identifying the theological, social, and philosophical roots of early Pentecostalism, and their hermeneutics to gain insight into Pentecostalism's ethos, doctrine and self-understanding. This foundation provides an essential starting point for our discussion of a distinct Pentecostal hermeneutic for the twenty-first century.

---

19. Cox, *Fire From Heaven*, 184.

20. Noll, *A History of Christianity*, 295. He argues that from the American Civil War until the Great Depression immigration, urbanization, and industrialization reshape North America. As a result social problems became increasingly troublesome. The revivalists believed that personal moral reform was the key to social reform. This belief fueled the revivalist fervor and was inherited by many early Pentecostals.

21. It should be noted that there were Pentecostal revivals occurring in other parts of the world around the same period. To what extent, if any, these influenced the North American revival of 1906 could be debated. Let it suffice here to say that there was likely some cross pollination between these events; however, the 1906 revival of Azusa Street, Los Angeles is universally accepted as the primary ignition point for the Pentecostal revival of the twentieth century following.

A Distinct Twenty-first Century Pentecostal Hermeneutic

The Holiness Influence

As noted Pentecostalism's immediate background is primarily in the nineteenth-century Holiness movement;[22] therefore, it is rooted in the biblical interpretation and teaching of John Wesley.[23] Central to Wesley's Methodism was the doctrine of a crisis experience subsequent to conversion variously called "entire sanctification," "perfect love," "Christian perfection," or "heart purity." The "second blessing" doctrine, as interpreted through the U.S. Holiness movement, greatly influenced Pentecostalism.[24] John Fletcher's speaking of sanctification as the baptism with the Holy Ghost linked the "second blessing" with an experience of receiving the Spirit.[25]

North American Pentecostalism[26] is deeply rooted in the Holiness movement, and is multicultural, multiracial, diverse, and complex. The Holiness movement, from which most of the early Pentecostals come, was not

---

22. Synan, "Origins of the Pentecostal Movement," lines 26–28. He says, "Perhaps the most important immediate precursor to Pentecostalism was the Holiness movement which issued from the heart of Methodism at the end of the nineteenth century. . . . Indeed, for the first decade practically all Pentecostals, both in America and around the world, had been active in holiness churches or camp meetings. Most of them were either Methodists, former Methodists, or people from kindred movements that had adopted the Methodist view of the second blessing. They were overwhelmingly Arminian in their basic theology and were strongly perfectionistic in their spirituality and lifestyle." See also, Miller, *Canadian Pentecostals*, 21–28.

23. Research for this book did not identify any scholarly discussion of the Wesleyan Quadrilateral in relation to Pentecostal hermeneutic practice. This is a strange oversight since some of the early leaders of Pentecostalism were trained as Methodist pastors and likely would have employed the Wesleyan Quadrilateral in their hermeneutics.

24. Anderson, *Introduction To Pentecostalism*, 27 Anderson says, "The outstanding characteristic of the Holiness movement—literal-minded Biblicism, emotional fervor, puritanical mores, enmity toward ecclesiasticism, and above all belief in a 'Second Blessing' in Christian experience—were inherited and perpetuated by the Pentecostals. . . . Except for speaking in tongues, in the early days there was little to distinguish the Pentecostal believer from his holiness brethren" (Anderson, *Introduction to Pentecostalism*, 28).

25. Turner, "The Baptism in the Holy Spirit," lines 32–34.

26. Historical research clearly reveals a number of independent Pentecostal revivals occurring around the globe during the last decade of the nineteenth century and first decade of the twentieth century. To date no one has effectively shown a clear linkage between them all. Therefore it is essential that we not over generalize the background influences but North American Pentecostalism clearly rests on a Holiness background. However, when it comes to presenting a Pentecostal hermeneutic for the twenty-first century, the Pentecostal movement worldwide shares enough commonality to make such a hermeneutic universally valid.

Defining Pentecostalism and Its Early Hermeneutic

theologically homogeneous with both Wesleyan and Keswickian adherents joining the Pentecostal movement, and they significantly impact the theological foundation on which early Pentecostals stood.[27] This background provides the platform from which the search for evidence of baptism in the Spirit sprang, but it is the Keswickian understanding of Spirit baptism as a baptism of power that provides the basis for the Pentecostal understanding of the purpose for baptism in the Spirit.

The African American influence upon the Azusa Street mission, and its connection to most, if not all, North American Pentecostals cannot be ignored since Seymour was African American. The largest North American Pentecostal denominations (Assemblies of God, The Church of God In Christ, and The Pentecostal Assemblies of Canada) along with more than twenty others trace their roots to Azusa Street.[28] In reference to Azusa Street, Anderson says, "Although events have moved a long way from these heady days, this formative period of North American Pentecostalism should be seen as its fundamental essence."[29] Any discussion of Pentecostal hermeneutics must take these early years into account. Seymour was initially invited to come to Los Angeles to pastor a Holiness congregation. Seymour held a holiness theology, and Parham's conviction that baptism in the Spirit is evidenced by speaking in tongues. His theology, as the leading figure of the Azusa Street revival, ministry style, and African American spirituality helped shape early Pentecostal theology and identity.

The Church of God, Cleveland, links its roots to the 1896 revival in North Carolina among the group called Christian Union.[30] Some 130 persons were reported to have spoken in tongues at this camp meeting revival, and between 1895 and 1905 over twenty Holiness denominations were established. Among these groups the concept of "second blessing" was associated with power for service and witness more so than with sanctification. Phoebe Palmer, one of the most prominent Holiness leaders, referred to holiness as "the full baptism of the Holy Ghost," and Asa Mahan wrote

---

27. Synan, "Origins of the Pentecostal Movement," lines 18–24. He states, "Although the Pentecostal movement had its beginnings in the United States, it owed much of its basic theology to earlier British perfectionistic and charismatic movements. At least three of these, the Methodist/Holiness movement, the Catholic Apostolic movement of Edward Irving, and the British Keswick 'Higher Life' movement prepared the way for what appeared to be a spontaneous outpouring of the Holy Spirit in America."

28. Miller, *Canadian Pentecostals*, 28.

29. Anderson, *Introduction To Pentecostalism*, 45.

30. Ibid., 27.

A Distinct Twenty-first Century Pentecostal Hermeneutic

of the baptism in the Spirit with the consequence being power.[31] Several prominent Holiness preachers near the end of the nineteenth century connected spiritual gifts to the power of the Spirit and rejected the notion of cessation. Some even used the term "third blessing" in an attempt to separate sanctification and the baptism in the Holy Spirit.[32] Early Pentecostals continued this eschatological and pneumatological emphasis.

Pentecostalism's Holiness background provides a structured understanding of *subsequence* and *purpose* for the baptism in the Spirit. The Keswick Convention recognized the "new birth" and "fullness of the Spirit" as two distinct experiences. The influence of leaders such as South African Andrew Murray resulted in the Holiness movement understanding baptism in the Spirit more in terms of *empowering for service*[33] than in terms of holiness. Andrew Murray's ministry may have provided the foundation for understanding glossolalia (speaking in tongues) as the evidence of baptism in the Spirit. According to Faupel the idea of a "baptism with the Spirit" as distinct from salvation, and for the purpose of giving power for service was a major theme in North American revivalism by the end of the nineteenth century.[34] At the turn of the twentieth century there were three distinct holiness groups: the Wesleyan position (second blessing is entire sanctification); the Keswick position (second blessing or baptism in the Spirit was an endowment with power for service); and the "third blessing" position (second blessing of sanctification and "third blessing" of baptism with fire). Pentecostalism is most closely aligned initially with the "third blessing" position and understood the third blessing to be baptism in the Spirit evidenced by speaking in tongues.[35] It is the belief that tongues serve as evidence of the baptism in the Spirit that ultimately separates Pentecostals from their holiness family.

---

31. Dayton, *Theological Roots of Pentecostalism*, 88–89.

32. Synan, "Origins of the Pentecostal Movement," line 116.

33. The idea that Spirit Baptism (or second work) was for empowerment rather than holiness is a vital shift which enabled early Pentecostals to connect their view of Spirit Baptism evidenced by tongues with the Holiness concept of a second (or third) work of grace. This was a forerunner to the Pentecostal doctrine of Spirit Baptism.

34. Faupel, *The Everlasting Gospel*, 84–87.

35. Anderson, *Vision of the Disinherited*, 28–46.

Defining Pentecostalism and Its Early Hermeneutic

Revivalist Roots

As already noted, the turn of the twentieth century was a time of social chaos, and revival was seen by the revivalists as the only means to transform, since society could only be altered through *individual* transformation. For several decades revivalists like D. L. Moody proclaimed their message of personal salvation in the belief that revival was the only way to heal society. Revivalism emphasized a personal salvation *experience*, and the altar call is iconic of the revival movement. The call to repent and receive Christ as savior generally involved an *emotional* appeal with individual experience taking center stage. Revival services were lively, emotional, and encouraging; therefore, they were very attractive to many, especially those caught in deprived economic and social conditions.

Amid the revivalist fervor a phenomenon known as "come-outism" emerged as some radical Methodist preachers were calling people to "come out" of the established Methodist churches and join independent Holiness groups.[36] This movement began in the 1880s, and continued into the twentieth century with Pentecostalism emerging at the high point of "come-outism."[37] Pentecostalism continues to call individuals to come out of the world, and churches that do not experience the rich, emotive, immediacy, and expectancy of God's presence evidenced in the operation of spiritual gifts. The early Pentecostals also embraced the message and methods of the great revivalists with altar calls for salvation and healing occurring in every service. Although this practice may be less normative for some Western Pentecostal congregations today, it continues as the norm in the Majority World context.

The immediacy of God's presence mediated through the Holy Spirit was, and continues to be, one of the core elements in Pentecostal identity. Pentecostal belief and practice is *experiential* in nature, and Pentecostals expect the experiences found in the Gospels and Acts to occur within the church and everyday life. Scripture is understood and interpreted among the early Pentecostals through this lens.

---

36. Norwood, *The Story of American Methodism*, 300.

37. Come-outism has all but disappeared in twenty-first century Pentecostalism. However, during my early years in Pentecost (1960–1980) testimonies often contained the phrase "I thank God for the day I came out of . . . ." It is impossible to measure but I suspect that the impact of "come-outism" continues in the DNA of Pentecostalism even today. It is closely associated with Pentecostal belief that Pentecostalism is the authentic apostolic Christianity as seen in Acts.

A Distinct Twenty-first Century Pentecostal Hermeneutic

Essential to understanding the hermeneutics of early Pentecostals is recognizing this fundamental ethos, and Pentecostalism is best understood through its emphasis on experiencing life with God as described in Acts. Cox refers to Pentecostals as having a narrative theology whose central expression is the testimony and points to "mystical encounter" and an emphasis on experience "so total it shatters the cognitive packaging" as the core ethos of Pentecostalism.[38] Mystical encounter may not be the "core," but it is certainly an important contributor to Pentecostal ethos and identity. Pentecostals see the outpouring of the Spirit at the turn of the twentieth century as the latter rain of Joel, and understand the baptism in the Spirit as a divine encounter with eschatological implications.[39] Early Pentecostals read and hear Scripture through this eschatological lens. The hermeneutics of early Pentecostals was informed by their belief that they were the generation that would see the return of Christ. This self-understanding was, and continues to be,[40] an important element in Pentecostal hermeneutics, and is a factor in the interpretive method and strategy proposed in this book.

Pentecostalism's Holiness background provided a theological foundation, and revivalism gave Pentecostals a method to promote the belief that apostolic Christianity had been restored to the church. The revival meeting gave a recognized format for the proclamation of the "Full Gospel" with signs following, and the altar call served as an ideal means of encouraging individuals to seek salvation, healing, baptism in the Spirit, and an encounter with God. Significant aspects of Pentecostalism's ethos are associated with this Holiness, revivalist heritage.

---

38. Cox, *Fire From Heaven*, 58, 68–71.

39. Miller, *Canadian Pentecostals*, 30, 31, 39–45, 72–79. Miller notes the Latter Rain motif was so influential that Pentecostals were sometimes called "the Latter Rain people." For most, if not all, Pentecostals the outpouring of the Holy Spirit at the turn of the twentieth century was evidence of the soon return of Jesus. This eschatological expectation influenced everything the early Pentecostals and, to a large extent, contemporary Pentecostals believed and practiced. It motivated an intense sense of mission. Most Pentecostal denominations organized around the belief that world evangelization must occur quickly before the imminent return of Jesus. It would be impossible to overestimate the influence this eschatological perspective had on Pentecostalism.

40. The imminent return of Christ is a theological position of all Pentecostals and charismatics. However, there is wide variance as to the stress given this doctrine in recent years. There would also be a wide variance of beliefs around 'end times' theology among twenty-first century Pentecostals.

Defining Pentecostalism and Its Early Hermeneutic

Modernity's Influence

As well as the Holiness background we must also consider modernity's influence on Pentecostalism. Timothy Weber claims that modernity pushed many evangelicals into various forms of theological liberalism.[41] Biological and sociological evolution theory challenged the existence of God undermining the foundations of Christian belief while higher criticism seemed to undermine the inspiration and veracity of Scripture. The economic uplift of modernity and its emerging middle class resulted in many denominations mainstreaming to appeal to this steadily growing, and influential group. Pentecostalism protested what it considered *spiritual sterility*, and the accommodation of modernity's worldview within the mainline denominations.[42] They embraced the biblical injunctions of separation and simplicity as per their Holiness background. Non-Pentecostals often ridiculed them for their stance while academicians dismissed them, and this persecution resulted in a strong bond among Pentecostals who viewed the more traditional churches as lukewarm and compromising. They moved away from, even protested, the cold formalism that grew from the mainline denominational embrace of modernity in both their worldview and theology. Pentecostals saw persecution[43] as evidence they were correct in their doctrine and practice.

Pentecostal worship was spirited and animated, and it focused on the experiential manifest presence of the Holy Spirit; therefore, many were attracted to this enthusiastic, experience oriented form of worship. Pentecostalism was in many ways a counter-culture movement, and a protest against modernity. Cheryl Johns writes, "In an era of the 'war to end all wars,' Pentecostals were pacifists. In an era when women were excluded from public voice, Pentecostals were ordaining women as ministers. In an era of the KKK [Ku Klux Klan], Pentecostal blacks and whites were worshipping together."[44]

The early Pentecostals were totally committed to proclaiming the "full gospel message" to everyone, since everyone needed, and could receive,

---

41. Weber, *Living in the Shadow*, 86.

42. Blumhofer, *Restoring the Faith*, 98.

43. Fundamentalists, with whom Pentecostals would have much in common, rejected Pentecostals. Vinson Synan, in his forward to Bartleman's *Azusa Street: The Roots of Modern Day Pentecost* states that fundamentalists had disfellowshipped Pentecostals by 1928 (Bartleman, *Azusa Street*, xxi).

44. Johns, *Pentecostal Formation*, 110.

salvation. The Latter Rain motif, with its focus on end-times harvest, added urgency to the mission of evangelizing the world, consequently Pentecostals were interested in spiritual reformation rather than social reform without conversion. They were convinced of Christ's soon return, and rejected evolutionary theory's belief that humanity was evolving toward utopia.

Pentecostal fervor was stimulated by the belief that theirs was the generation that must complete the task of world evangelization. A. J. Thomlinson,[45] addressing the 1912 General Conference of the Church of God (Cleveland, TN), called his generation to complete the task. He said, "Foreign countries should be occupied, and the gospel given to them as rapidly as possible."[46] Some believed and taught that the gift of tongues was for the purpose of missionary evangelization.[47] Early Pentecostals read and heard Scripture through this eschatological, pneumatological, and soteriological lens, and understood the great commission of Matthew 28:19 as Jesus' word to them.

Modernity was promoting science as mankind's savior, but early Pentecostalism's roots led them to see personal salvation as man's only hope for social reform. Modernity looked to social and theological evolution as the hope for the future, but early Pentecostals presented personal salvation, and a personal baptism in the Spirit as *the* hope for the future. Modernity tended to remove God from history, as immediately available, and challenged the existence of miracles and God's intervention in human affairs. It also questioned the veracity and validity of Scripture. Retaining the Holiness high view of Scripture, and their experience of signs and wonders, baptism in the Spirit, and the supernatural, led Pentecostals to reject and contradict modernity's claims. Modernity may be said to influence early Pentecostals in that it forced them to think through, and respond to the widely accepted modernistic worldview. Their response was to reject modernity's interpretation of reality and embrace a scripturally informed pneumatic understanding of reality.

---

45. A. J. Thomlinson was the first overseer of the Church of God (Cleveland, TN). He was elected to this office in 1907.

46. Willis, *Assembly Addresses*, 1986.

47. Some taught that the gift of glossolalia enabled an individual to speak an unlearned language immediately. Discovering what your language was would indicate your country of ministry. Others taught that upon arriving in a place to which you felt called the Holy Spirit would supernaturally enable you to speak the language. These extremes resulted in many spiritual casualties. I am aware of no confirmed cases where such supernatural phenomena occurred.

Defining Pentecostalism and Its Early Hermeneutic

Within the context of modernity Liberalism and Fundamentalism move in two different theological directions,[48] and the ministry of John Alexander Dowie, a healing ministry evangelist, forged a third position providing an alternative to both Liberalism and Fundamentalism.[49] Early Pentecostalism, following this third option employed a biblical theological hermeneutic strategy that differed from both Fundamentalism and Liberalism.[50] Archer claims that the early Pentecostal hermeneutic identifies them as a "paramodern group"[51] because they used the Bible Reading method of their Holiness predecessors, but employed a Latter Rain lens. Thus, early Pentecostals did not use a unique method, but engaged a common method in a distinctive manner. Understanding this aspect of early Pentecostal hermeneutical strategy helps lay a foundation for a distinct Pentecostal hermeneutic for the twenty-first century.

Social Marginalization

Added to modernity's influence on Pentecostalism is the impact of social and economic marginalization since many of the early Pentecostals came from among the socially marginalized.[52] Their revivalistic, experience-oriented worship was appealing to those who were often shunned by mainline congregations and sidelined by society. Early Pentecostals, energized by the belief in a near rapture, were driven by a sense of call and often travelled from place to place with no support to proclaim the full gospel message. There was no price too high to pay for the purpose of preaching the full gospel, and the frequent opposition they received from society and the organized church served to unify and build community. In this

---

48. Murphy, *Beyond Liberalism and Fundamentalism*, 11–85. Murphy identifies both Liberalism and Fundamentalism as modernistic yet they come to differing views concerning the authority and inspiration of Scripture.

49. Faupel, *Everlasting Gospel*, 121–35. Fundamentalists employed Common Sense realism building upon the philosophy of Reid. Liberals drew on Schleiermacher and Kant.

50. Archer, *A Pentecostal Hermeneutic*, 2.

51. Ibid., 33.

52. Blumhofer, *Pentecost in my Soul*, 15. Anderson would identify early Pentecostalism as composed of a socially heterogeneous and eclectic group. Anderson, *Vision of the Disinherited*, 165. Most historians would accept the view that a large number of the early Pentecostals came from the edges of society and or from among the socially marginalized.

A Distinct Twenty-first Century Pentecostal Hermeneutic

context the socially marginalized found acceptance, meaning, and opportunity to function in positions of importance because they could exercise the charisms, testify, participate in the worship services, and hold offices within Pentecostalism.

Pentecostal preachers, energized by their eschatological fervor, preached wherever they could find space and, due to financial restraints, their locations were often storefronts, warehouses, etc., making them both accessible and appealing to marginalized persons. They often worked along the fringes of the established churches since their message appealed to those who had already been turned off (or turned away) by the cold, cerebral religion of mainline denominations. Pentecostal preaching offered hope, the promise of God's immediate presence in the person of the Holy Spirit, and assurance of salvation. They emphasized the availability of the charismata described in Acts and the New Testament for the contemporary church, and demonstrated them in their services. Their worship was highly emotive and encouraged the ecstatic experience of the baptism in the Spirit. The Azusa Street model of unsegregated worship meant Pentecostal worship services were open to all, making them attractive to those whom modern society had marginalized.[53] The dislocation and rejection, social status, and economic deprivation felt by this group helped define the manner with which they heard and interpreted Scripture.

Involvement was also a key component of Pentecostal worship; therefore, ordinary, untrained people were able to participate in public worship in a variety of ways including the exercise of spiritual gifts, and personal testimony. These testimonies were a type of community involvement in hermeneutics for they often contained an individual's understanding and application of particular passages of Scripture. This newfound identity gave fresh meaning and purpose to life for many, and people were affirmed and encouraged, and, if even only while in the worship setting, to feel self-worth and affirmation. This reality added to the appeal of Pentecostalism, and impacted the way Scripture was understood and gave the community, through charismata and testimony, a place in the hermeneutical process.

The degree to which early Pentecostalism is comprised of the socially marginalized could be debated, however, Pentecostalism then and now is open to individual participation irrespective of social, economic, or

---

53. Anderson, *Introduction To Pentecostalism*, 122. He claims that Pentecostalism's "contextualized Christianity" provides hope, dignity, identity and fulfillment of aspirations. He argues that this contextualization appeals to Africans precisely because they are generally a marginalized society.

Defining Pentecostalism and Its Early Hermeneutic

scholastic status. This openness results in Pentecostalism's attractiveness to the marginalized as well as those from the upper levels of social status. This openness also encourages communal participation in the interpretation of Scripture through testimonies, operation of spiritual gifts, public prayer, and the "Amen." Pentecostalism's diversity is an important part of its ethos and identity.

Restorationism[54]

The New Testament bears witness that charismata were a common feature of first-century worship; however, the frequency of tongues, healings, prophecies, etc. within the worship of the first-century church cannot be established with certainty. On this issue there would be wide variance of opinion among scholars, but the Pauline instructions regarding charismata in 1 Corinthians chapters 12 and 14 would suggest, at least in Corinth, that charismata were very common. It further suggests the charismata were sometimes exercised to the point of overuse and abuse, in public worship, but we can only speculate as to how normative the Corinthian situation might be. The emergence of the Montanists in the second century intimates a serious decline of charismata in public worship in the late first or early second century. Perhaps it was the excesses of Montanism that contributed to the cessationist view that dominated the Western church after the time of Origen.[55] Although there are evidences of individuals and certain groups

---

54. Blumhofer, *Restoring the Faith*, 12. She defines restoration as, "the impulse to restore the primitive or original order of things as revealed in Scripture free from the accretion of Church history and tradition." Hughes, *The American Quest for the Primitive Church*, 243: "The Holiness tradition emphasized an *ethical primitivism*, concerned with a sanctified life, the Pentecostals sought an *experiential primitivism* directed toward recovery of the apostolic gifts of the Spirit, especially glossolalia and healing. Indeed, Pentecostals sought nothing less than a restoration of the Jerusalem Pentecost." The following quote appeared in the October 1906 issue of *The Apostolic Faith* by William Seymour: "All along the ages men have been preaching a partial Gospel. A part of the Gospel remained when the world went into the dark ages. God has from time to time raised up men to bring back the truth to the church. He raised up Luther to bring back to the world the doctrine of justification by faith. He raised up another reformer in John Wesley to establish Bible holiness in the church. Then he raised up Dr. Cullis who brought back to the world the wonderful doctrine of divine healing. Now He is bringing back the Pentecostal Baptism to the church."

55. Rudd, *When the Spirit Came Upon Them*, 21. Many Pentecostals would identify the conversion of Constantine as the point of the "Great Apostasy." They would point to this as the time when the church deserted its apostolic faith. The division between

experiencing charismata scattered throughout church history, a cessationist view clearly dominated the Western church after the break between East and West until the Pentecostal Revivals of the twentieth century. The experience of the Eastern church is quite different where "pneumatology has always been at the centre of their theology and they have always been open to the charismata."[56] Consequently, early Pentecostalism was in essence a restorationist, revivalist, and eschatologically oriented movement.

Early Pentecostals were shaped by their belief that the experience of the apostles was available to them, and their experience of the charismata confirmed this belief. They rejected cessationist teaching, continued to proclaim the Holiness (Wesleyan and Keswickian) message of renewal and sanctification, and promoted the baptism in the Spirit with evidence of speaking in tongues for every believer. Ultimately, the second (and/or third) blessing theology developed into the doctrine of the baptism in the Holy Spirit with evidence of speaking in tongues. Pentecostal theology and experience promoted the view that God was restoring the apostolic experience and power to the church. The Latter Rain motif along with charismatic experience informed their interpretation of Scripture that fuelled their proclamation of the "full gospel," and the "full gospel" message became uniquely identified with the Pentecostal movement by the end of the second decade of the twentieth century.

Since early Pentecostals approached Scripture from a restorationist point of view their reading of Acts presented the depiction of a possible, present reality. The Gospels and their miracles were promises of what could happen in any Pentecostal worship service. Their numbers grew rapidly as their preaching, accompanied by signs and wonders, found favor with multitudes. For Pentecostals, the Gospels and Acts were central to their interpretation of Scripture,[57] and Acts offered a picture of what ought to be normative Christianity; therefore, they were at odds with liberal theology, Protestant orthodoxy, modernity, and mainline Christianity.[58] It is

---

Eastern and Western Christianity marks the time when Pentecostals suggest the apostasy was complete.

56. Anderson, *Introduction To Pentecostalism*, 21.

57. Donald Dayton claims that Pentecostals read Scripture "through Lukan eyes especially with the lens of Acts." They read Old and New Testament alike through Acts. Dayton, *Theological Roots of Pentecostalism*, 23.

58. See Ewart, *The Phenomenon of Pentecost*, 39. Ewart was an early leader in the Pentecostal movement. He claimed that Pentecostalism had no affiliation with modern theology but was based firmly on Scripture.

Defining Pentecostalism and Its Early Hermeneutic

restorationist, revivalist experientialism that produced the critical aspects of Pentecostal identity and ethos that shape their hermeneutics. More than a century has passed since Azusa Street, and yet restorationism, revivalistic experientialism, signs and wonders, the supernatural, tongues, and an eschatological perspective continue to shape the Pentecostal self-understanding. They are essential elements of the Pentecostal ethos, and a distinct Pentecostal hermeneutic must take this into account since "community narrative" is an important element in any hermeneutic.

The "Latter Rain" Motif

As noted, the Latter Rain motif[59] is an important aspect of early Pentecostalism because it provides the primary organizational structure for the Pentecostal narrative tradition.[60] As Archer points out, "The Latter Rain motif enabled the early Pentecostals to interpret the Old and New Testament according to a promise-fulfillment strategy."[61] This motif provided early Pentecostals with a means to explain the Holy Spirit's outpouring at the turn of the twentieth century. To fully understand Pentecostalism's ethos and identity we must understand the Latter Rain motif and we now turn our attention to this task.

The Latter Rain motif is based on the typical weather cycle in Palestine. Yahweh promised Israel that the early and latter rains necessary for a bountiful harvest would adequately occur if they remained faithful to the covenant (Deut 11:10–15). Pentecostals spiritualized this natural phenomenon seeing the early rain as representing the Acts 2 Pentecost, and the Latter Rain representing the Pentecostal outpouring of the early twentieth century. The time between the early and latter rain was "a time of drought caused by the 'great apostasy' of the Roman Catholic Church."[62] The Latter Rain motif predates the Pentecostal outpouring at the turn of the twentieth century as some within the Holiness movement, like A. B. Simpson

---

59. The Latter Rain motif is based on Deut 11:10–15; Job 29:29; Prov 16:15; Jer 3:3, 5:24; Hos 6:3; Joel 2:23; Zech 10:1; and Jas 5:7. Of these Deut 11:10–15; Joel 2:23; and Jas 5:7 were the more important. The Latter Rain motif holds a central role in the early Pentecostal self-understanding. The Latter Rain motif provided Pentecostals with a credible explanation for their existence. See Archer, *A Pentecostal Hermeneutic*, 100–110.

60. Faupel, *The Everlasting Gospel*, 19–43. Faupel effectively argues this position.

61. Archer, *A Pentecostal Hermeneutic*, 100.

62. Ibid., 102.

A Distinct Twenty-first Century Pentecostal Hermeneutic

(founder of the Christian Missionary Alliance), also referred to the Latter Rain concept.[63] Those in the Holiness movement who were not cessationist expected, even prayed for, a latter rain outpouring that would restore apostolic signs to the church. Early Pentecostals, with their roots deeply imbedded in the Holiness tradition, seized on this motif as an apologetic for the significance of Pentecostalism.

Faupel states that early Pentecostals saw themselves as the people of the prophetically promised Latter Rain,[64] and the Pentecostal outpouring meant that apostolic faith, power, authority, and practice had been recovered and restored to the church. The Latter Rain motif gave early Pentecostals an organizing center for their self-understanding, and provided a distinctive narrative story within which they applied the Bible Reading method of interpretation. The result of this was that Pentecostals were enabled to see themselves as the representation of *authentic* Christianity.

D. Wesley Myland's lectures at Stone Church, Chicago in 1909 became the foundation for the definitive apologetic of this Pentecostal outpouring as fulfillment of the Latter Rain.[65] This motif is a critical element in early Pentecostalism's self-understanding and interpretive methodology. To understand Pentecostalism we must take into account the Latter Rain motif and how it informed the Bible Reading method of interpretation, and helped shape the early Pentecostal self-understanding. Pentecostals continue to see themselves as the end times people who have restored apostolic faith and power with a focus on bringing in the harvest before Jesus returns remaining a central belief and practice. As such, Pentecostals continue to read Scripture through a Latter Rain motif and Lukan lens.

---

63. Ibid., 101. Archer quotes A. B. Simpson as writing, "We may . . . conclude that we are to expect a great outpouring of the Holy Spirit in connection with the coming of Christ and one as much greater than the Pentecostal effusion as the rains of autumn were greater than the showers of spring. . . . We are in the time . . . when we may expect this Latter Rain."

64. Faupel, *The Everlasting Gospel*, 39.

65. Myland was a featured speaker at a Pentecostal convention held at Stone Church, Chicago, May to June of 1909. These lectures were homiletical in nature and were an exposition of the Old and New Testament through the Latter Rain lens. Myland is a significant individual in early Pentecostal hermeneutics. It is important to note that he spent four years training as a Methodist minister. Myland maintained his Methodist credentials throughout his ministry.

Defining Pentecostalism and Its Early Hermeneutic

Early Pentecostal Worldview

The early Pentecostal worldview in many respects reflected the broader Christian worldview. Early Pentecostals held to the doctrines of the patristic fathers, and they adhered to much of what the Wesleyan Quadrilateral identifies as "Tradition." Pentecostals from the beginning are adherents of orthodox theology, and embrace the core Christian beliefs in the incarnate, crucified, risen Christ. Like all Christians they embrace the belief that Jesus of Nazareth is the Son of God. They believe humanity is fallen and in need of a savior, and that salvation is through Christ and his cross. Basically it could be said the early Pentecostals shared beliefs in common with Holiness, and other, Christians with the major difference being Pentecostalism's embrace of, and emphasis on, divine healing and the baptism in the Holy Spirit evidenced by speaking in tongues. These are core elements in their worldview and for Pentecostals the supernatural and charismata are a normative and essential part of reality.

As already noted, early Pentecostal culture embraced unsegregated worship, revivalist preaching, and community involvement in worship, and their theology embraced Spirit Baptism evidenced by tongues and the imminence of the second coming of Jesus. Emphasis on the supernatural was central to the Pentecostal worldview, and ecstatic experience, signs and wonders, healings, and other supernatural phenomena were regular occurrences in Pentecostal worship. This helped shape their worldview in opposition to the dominant modernistic, naturalistic worldview of the twentieth century. Wacker identifies this supernaturalistic worldview as the primary explanation for early Pentecostalism's phenomenal growth.[66] Scripture was heard, understood, interpreted, and proclaimed out of a supernaturalistic worldview.

The Pentecostal "full" or "four square" gospel proclaims Jesus as Savior, Healer, Baptizer, and Soon Coming King, and the soteriological and christological emphasis in Pentecostal theology has both a pneumatological and missiological dimension.[67] "Jesus Christ is 'Baptizer in the Holy Spirit'

---

66. Wacker, "The Functions of Faith," 360.

67. Miller, *Canadian Pentecostals*, 219–43. Miller gives an interesting survey of the Canadian Pentecostal missionairy activity from 1907–1940. He writes, "In Toronto, the Hebden Mission witnessed a similar spontaneous move to reach the masses with the full gospel. These attempts were made, it must be remembered, in the complete absence of any form of ecclesiastical structure or regular financial support. Overseas missions was entirely 'a faith work'" (219). For Pentecostals baptism in the Spirit is for the purpose of

A Distinct Twenty-first Century Pentecostal Hermeneutic

who empowers ordinary people to witness to the ends of the earth."[68] For the Majority World that experiences poverty, poor health services, abusive government, etc. the full gospel of Pentecostalism offers socio-economic and political promise and liberation. For Pentecostals the Bible holds the answers to the problems of poverty, trouble, sickness, evil spirits, witchcraft, oppression, etc., and for some this explains Pentecostalism's phenomenal growth worldwide.

Pentecostals expect a "reciprocal relationship between the Bible and the Spirit."[69] For Pentecostals the Bible explains the experience of the Spirit and the experience of the Spirit enables people to better understand the Bible, a position Archer refers to as the Holy Spirit being drawn into the process of hermeneutics.[70] The Latter Rain motif enables Pentecostals to engage in a hermeneutic that filtered Scripture through their revivalist, restorationist, eschatological, supernaturalistic worldview. They saw the world as lost and in need of a savior, but once saved individuals could enter into a life with God as seen in Acts. Their preaching, praxis, hermeneutics, and self-understanding were governed by this worldview.

The African Context

No credible historian would deny an important place for African Americans in the early formation and continuing development of Pentecostalism.[71] As noted, William Seymour, an African American, holds a significant place in the early formation and promotion of Pentecostalism, and one of the criticisms of early Pentecostals was the unsegregated nature of their worship services. Indeed the African American presence contributed significantly to the liveliness and style of Pentecostalism's worship form.[72] A full discussion of the extent of the African American influence upon Pentecostal

---

power to witness. Since they believed Jesus would return in their generation taking the gospel to the whole earth was a must. Their missionary zeal was energized by their belief in the near return of Jesus.

68. Anderson, *Introduction To Pentecostalism*, 230.

69. Ibid.

70. Archer, *A Pentecostal Hermeneutic*, 77. This will be dealt with in greater detail in chapter 4 under the discussion of the Spirit's role in the hermeneutical process.

71. Archer, *A Pentecostal Hermeneutic*, 10 n. 7. Land, *Pentecostal Spirituality*, 35.

72. Leonard Lovett, "Black Holiness Pentecostalism," 76–77.

Defining Pentecostalism and Its Early Hermeneutic

ethos is far beyond the boundaries of this book, but we must recognize that Pentecostalism contains within it aspects of African American influence.

The African influence is not limited to African Americans but extends to the continent also. John Graham Lake began his ministry as a Methodist preacher, and in 1907 Lake received the baptism in the Spirit at "Zion City," near Chicago under the ministry of Charles Parham.[73] In answer to a lifelong call to minister in South Africa, he led a missionary party to Johannesburg in April 1908. Synan emphatically states: "The work of Lake was the most influential and enduring of the South African Pentecostal mission endeavors."[74] He planted the Apostolic Faith Mission in 1910 and the renowned David duPlessis (often referred to as "Mr. Pentecost") came from this church. This suggests that early African Pentecostalism has indirect connection with both Parham and Azusa Street, and points to an African influence upon Western Pentecostalism. From those early days Pentecostalism has spread throughout Africa until the number of Pentecostal believers in Africa is multiple times larger than those in North America. Lowenburg says,

> In the twenty-first century, the Church of Africa, empowered by the Spirit and grounded in the Word of God, will reach out holistically to the world with a fresh excitement and with spiritual, contextual flexibility that will astound and instruct Western pastors, missiologists, biblical scholars, and theologians as African Pentecostal practitioners joyfully work and bleed in the harvest fields of the unengaged peoples, glorifying God and making disciples while they faithfully await His return.[75]

This statement points to an ongoing African impact upon the DNA of Pentecostalism. African Pentecostals will bring a fresh impetus to Pentecostal self–understanding and ethos in the twenty-first century. African Pentecostals may well revive the restorationist, eschatological urgency of Latter Rain theology within the Pentecostal movement worldwide during the next quarter century.

A twenty-first century Pentecostal hermeneutic must be open to, listen to, and be informed by this important African Pentecostal voice. Unfortunately the proposals of Archer and many others are weakened because they all but ignore the African (and other Majority World) context. Vinson

---

73. Synan, "The Origins of the Pentecostal Movement," lines 317–20.
74. Ibid., 321ff.
75. Lowenburg, "A Twenty-first Century Pentecostal Hermeneutic," 31.

A Distinct Twenty-first Century Pentecostal Hermeneutic

Synan demonstrates that Pentecostalism from its very beginnings had an African component, and because of the missionary activity of Pentecostal denominations such as Assemblies of God, Pentecostal Assemblies of Canada, and Church of God, plus the African homogeneous growth Pentecostalism has experienced phenomenal growth on the African continent. Pentecostalism both historically and currently is significantly impacted by African Pentecostals who contribute much to the shaping of the Pentecostal community. This must be taken into account in developing a distinctive twenty-first century Pentecostal hermeneutic.

The Early Pentecostal Hermeneutic

Whether one adopts Robert Funk's "watershed"[76] or Thomas Kuhn's "paradigm shift"[77] imagery, the reality is that a major shift in biblical scholarship was occurring around the same time Pentecostalism was developing, and the hermeneutics of the early Pentecostals was partly shaped by this radical shift. Traditional biblical scholarship was profoundly impacted by German higher criticism, and the concept of a neutral, scrupulously objective hermeneut began to dominate.[78] This shift moved the Bible out of the hands of ordinary people and into the hands of highly trained professionals resulting in the eruption of a firestorm around the source and authority of Scripture.[79] Prior to this shift the idea of common sense reasoning in interpretation dominated, and it was held that anyone, using the inductive method, could interpret Scripture. Conservative Protestants saw the Bible as a book of propositions, truth, and fact all of which could be comprehended and apprehended by ordinary persons. As higher criticism gained ground among the academies the idea that the common person could interpret Scripture lost ground.

Common sense realism implied that truth is static rather than culturally derived or conditioned, but the view of a static truth was being shattered by German higher criticism and evolutionary theory.[80] Marsden

---

76. Funk, "The Watershed," 4–22.
77. Weber, "The Two-Edged Sword," 104.
78. Archer, *A Pentecostal Hermeneutic*, 36.
79. Wacker, "The Demise of Biblical Civilization," 123.
80. In postmodernism the idea of a static truth has been expelled. Truth is relative within this philosophical framework. Truth is also culturally (the term community is sometimes used) conditioned. Contemporary Pentecostalism exists within this

Defining Pentecostalism and Its Early Hermeneutic

argues that American Protestants moved in one of three directions as a result of this shift.[81] Liberals argued that the Bible's authority rested on personal experience, and Fundamentalists reaffirmed the factuality and authority of Scripture with truth linked to historicity. They employed the Baconian common sense model[82] of interpretation and held firmly to the idea that the common person could know truth. The Wesleyan Holiness movement and Pentecostals forged a third route affirming the objective nature of Scripture and the importance of personal experience. Pentecostals and the Wesleyan Holiness movement understood "the inspirational work of the Holy Spirit in both"[83] as the written documents *of* Scripture and the present experience *with* Scripture. Consequently, Pentecostals, past and present, easily flow from experience to Scripture and vice versa in their interpretive strategy.

The great concern of Pentecostals, as with the Holiness groups, was living faithfully in relationship with God. Living out the gospel in every day life was of primary importance; therefore, they were far less interested in the cognitive intellectual *understanding* of God than with a personal *relationship* with God. They did not give much attention to the academic pursuits of biblical intellectuals and the debates of the academies, but like the liberals, Pentecostals were concerned about religious experience, and it was their experience in the Holy Spirit that authenticated Christianity. The supernatural occurrences in their worship (tongues and healing primarily) validated their faith and understanding of Scripture. For Pentecostals, both experience and Scripture were authoritative with Scripture informing experience and experience interpreting Scripture in something of a creative tension. Thus the hermeneutics of early Pentecostals operated from a

---

philosophical environment and a distinct twenty-first century Pentecostal hermeneutic must speak to this reality. That does not mean they must accept truth as relative but they must be able to speak effectively to those (scholar and non-scholar alike) who hold such a view. Some postmodern shifts resonate with the way early Pentecostals approached Scripture, and also resonate with Pentecostal ethos and interpretive strategies that recognize meaning as not anchored to the text and original intent.

81. Marsden, "Everyone One's Own Interpreter," 92.

82. Murphy, *Beyond Liberalism and Fundamentalism*, 61.

83. Archer, *A Pentecostal Hermeneutic*, 40. For early Pentecostals inspiration was *not limited* to the Scripture in the sense that it was a past document containing no errors. In time Pentecostals adopted a verbal plenary theory of inspiration. However, Pentecostals continued to interpret Scripture from the early Pentecostal stance that inspiration is operative in both the text and one's experience with the text. This early Pentecostal stance resonates with the stance proposed in this book.

A Distinct Twenty-first Century Pentecostal Hermeneutic

common sense platform and flowed with a creative dance between Scripture and experience.[84]

Although early Pentecostals employed the Bible Reading method[85] they also recognized that cultural and historical background, context, etc. were important in determining the meaning of a text. They were not engaged in higher criticism's interest in the world behind the text because it was the world of the text that mattered. However, Pentecostals did recognize that in some cases interpreting the text required an understanding of historical and cultural issues as well as the context. Occasionally early Pentecostals would refer to the original languages in order to understand and interpret a text, but the world of the text was the primary concern. When necessary to understand the text Pentecostals would consult history, context, original language, or any other information that was helpful, thereby operating a somewhat eclectic methodology with the Bible Reading method holding first place.

The early Pentecostals also engaged the Bible Reading method's strategy of allowing Scripture to interpret Scripture, but did so from a uniquely Pentecostal stance. This meant the Pentecostal narrative, worldview, and Lukan lens governed their use of the Bible Reading method.[86] For Pentecostals the book of Acts was the controlling biblical narrative and all

---

84. After 1920 Pentecostals moved away from this mode of understanding Scripture. They attempted to follow the route of Fundamentalism. They embraced the ideas of verbal inspiration and inerrancy, some aspects of dispensationalism as well as the other fundamentals. They were unwilling to change their stance regarding Spirit Baptism and tongues. Inevitably, the Fundamentalist camp never embraced the Pentecostals. However, Pentecostals continued down the path of education as it was laid out by the fundamentalist academics. They embraced the historical-grammatical method of biblical interpretation.

85. This method strings all the scriptures dealing with the same subject or word together to ascertain what Scripture says on that subject. In this way one can obtain God's truth on a matter. The Bible Reading method relied upon inductive and deductive interpretative reasoning skills. The Holiness movement employed the Bible Reading method prior to the Pentecostal explosion. The early Pentecostals used this method but did so from a Pentecostal perspective. Frank Ewart, one of the early Pentecostal writers, described the hermeneutical approach of Charles Parham: "Their adopted method was to select a subject, find all the references on it, and present to the class a scriptural summary of what the Bible had to say about the theme" (Ewart, *The Phenomenon of Pentecost*, 60). This description is typical of the Bible Reading method. Archer refers to this method as a pre-modern hermeneutical methodology. Archer, *A Pentecostal Hermeneutic*, 65.

86. Archer, *A Pentecostal Hermeneutic*, 46–48, 72–80, 93. The Bible Reading method is an adaptation of the proof-text method. Pentecostals used the Bible Reading method as Pentecostals.

Defining Pentecostalism and Its Early Hermeneutic

other texts were harmonized with, and subservient to it. Their acceptance of the authority of experience as well as the authority of Scripture also modified their use of the Bible Reading method.[87] Spittler points out that Pentecostals employed a literalist, Bible Reading method of interpretation, and that Pentecostal interpretation and theology always has the function of strengthening faith, hope, and love for both the individual and community.[88] He says that for Pentecostals "biblical understanding is held to be *subordinate* to and *necessary* for the preaching of the Gospel."[89] Early Pentecostals interpret Scripture to promote the activities of evangelism and spiritual renewal, and this continues to be the incentive for Pentecostals to interpret the Bible.

Pentecostals do not read the Bible only as an ancient revelatory document, but understand Scripture to be a presently inspired story, alive and quick like a two-edged sword. Consequently, texts like Mark 16:9–20 and 1 Corinthians 12 and 14 describe the way things ought to be not how they once were.[90] Pentecostals read Scripture, including its supernatural elements, with the expectation that such is the contemporary possibility. To say that this interpretive stance was taken to extremes at times is an understatement,[91] but most often it was/is employed with sanity, balance, and realism. Pentecostals saw themselves as restoring the supernatural elements of the apostolic age, and to some extent the entirety of Scripture, to the contemporary church. The presence of signs and wonders in their worship services was evidence, at least in their minds, that they were cor-

---

87. Ibid., 63.

88. Spittler, "Are Pentecostals and Charismatics Fundamentalists," 103–16. Unlike Spittler, many scholars refer to early Pentecostal interpretation as "literal" or "ahistorical" in a negative manner. However, stating that Pentecostals employed a literalistic hermeneutic only provides part of the picture for early Pentecostal interpretation.

89. Spittler, "Scripture and the Theological Enterprise," 57; italics mine.

90. Granted an over emphasis on some aspects have led some Pentecostal groups into radical applications of these texts. One example would be the snake handling churches of the Southern U.S. However, these extremes should not be seen as typical or even illustrative of the early Pentecostal hermeneutic.

91. Some who interpreted the Sons of God and daughters of men of Genesis chapter 6 as angels having sexual relations with women went so far as to suggest such continues to happen today. According to Gordon J. Wenham the view that the sons of God in Genesis 6 were angelic beings (good or bad) is both the oldest view and also that of most modern commentators. Wenham, *Genesis 1–15*, 139–43. However, these commentators do not claim that such continues today. That some Pentecostals practice snake handling and believe angelic beings still produce children with women is evidence of an extremist group within the broader spectrum of Pentecostals.

A Distinct Twenty-first Century Pentecostal Hermeneutic

rect. They interpreted Scripture out of a lived experience that affirmed the supernatural aspects of Scripture were possible in the now.

Dual Interpretation

D. W. Myland[92] was a leading figure in early Pentecostalism,[93] and his hermeneutical addresses at Stone Church in Chicago in 1909 significantly influenced early Pentecostal hermeneutics. He believed the preacher's message should be evaluated by the word of God, and taught that Scripture should be interpreted through a twofold, and at times a threefold lens. First, Scripture should always be interpreted literally. Second, Scripture should be applied spiritually or typologically. Third, some Scripture should also be interpreted prophetically through the Latter Rain Covenant motif.

In this third hermeneutical tool, Myland is raising the subject of "revelation knowledge." In Myland's thinking, and among early Pentecostals, revelation knowledge meant experiential knowledge. Comprehension comes through an experience with the Holy Spirit, what some would refer to as illumination. Myland recognized the inherent danger in an open-ended allowance for revelation knowledge; therefore, he insisted that Scripture must validate experience. He said, "Every Scripture must be interpreted by Scripture, under the illumination of the Holy Spirit, to get its deeper sense."[94] His statement indicates that Pentecostals are open to, even expect, a deeper sense to emerge from the text *via* the Holy Spirit's illumination. This was an important part of the early Pentecostals' hermeneutical strategy and plays a role in our strategy for a distinct Pentecostal hermeneutic for the twenty-first century[95] that includes a place for the Holy Spirit's involvement.

Myland was trained as a Methodist pastor; therefore, it is reasonable to assume he was familiar with the Wesleyan Quadrilateral.[96] A close ex-

---

92. Myland was trained as a Methodist minister. It is important to note that there were a number of well trained individuals that held positions of influence and leadership within the early Pentecostals. Archer's thesis would leave the impression that early Pentecostalism was comprised of marginalized, uneducated, and lower class persons. Though not in the majority, there were many well qualified individuals who made significant contributions to the development of early Pentecostal belief and practice.

93. Robinson, "Myland, David Wesley," 632–33.

94. Myland, *The Latter Rain Covenant*, 107.

95. More will be said about this in chapter 3.

96. The Wesleyan Quadrilateral is an interpretive method that engages Scripture,

Defining Pentecostalism and Its Early Hermeneutic

amination of Myland's approach, insisting on Scripture's dominant role, and the active engagement of the Holy Spirit in interpretation suggests he is at least influenced by the Wesleyan Quadrilateral. To date this writer's research has not uncovered any reference to the Wesleyan Quadrilateral in the lectures of Myland or those who write about him;[97] however, the significant Holiness roots of early Pentecostalism and Myland's training as a Methodist minister make it reasonable to conclude there is some influence of the Wesleyan Quadrilateral on his interpretive approach. At the very least, early Pentecostals shared the Quadrilateral's position that Scripture holds the principal place in the interpretive process. The "Tradition," and "Reason" components of the Wesleyan Quadrilateral hold promise as controls for the unrestrained imaginative interpretation that exists among some Pentecostals.

Conclusion

We have seen that the twentieth century Pentecostal revival occurs at a time of social and spiritual change, and amid the heat of revivalism. Pentecostalism's Holiness background provided a foundation for understanding the baptism in the Spirit as a post conversion experience with the purpose of giving power for witness. The Bible Reading method and pietistic approach to Scripture provided an interpretive approach with the Latter Rain motif providing a specific, distinct lens through which the Bible Reading method was employed. We also noted that Luke–Acts served as the interpretive lens through which all Scripture was read, enabling Pentecostals to see themselves as restoring the apostolic power and faith to the church so the world could be evangelized prior to the return of Christ. Pentecostalism's worldview, ethos, metanarrative and identity are shaped by these contributing factors until it emerges as a distinct expression of Christianity.

Pentecostalism has evolved during the decades of the twentieth century, and obviously the early Pentecostals were not the generation that would see the return of Jesus. The passing of time may have caused some loss of urgency among Western Pentecostals, but this cannot be said of Africa and perhaps much of the Majority World; therefore, it may be that

---

Tradition, Experience, and Reason in the interpretive process. Wesley gave Scripture the greatest weight in the process of interpretation.

97. In fact research for this book has uncovered no mention of the Wesleyan Quadrilateral in the hermeneutical debate and discussion among Pentecostals.

A Distinct Twenty-first Century Pentecostal Hermeneutic

Majority World Pentecostals will re-energize Pentecostalism. However, the fundamental core concepts of early Pentecostalism remain within the general ethos of twenty-first century Pentecostals, even if twenty-first century Pentecostals use different language, and have a slightly different approach. In essence contemporary Pentecostals are not far different from those in the early decades of the twentieth century, and it is extremely diverse, multicultural, and worldwide in scope as is clearly seen in the *Dictionary of Pentecostal and Charismatic Movements*.[98] Diversity rises from Pentecostalism's origins[99] and its effective growth worldwide. Pentecostalism's background provided them with a worldview, a theological framework, and a distinct hermeneutic, and contemporary Pentecostals continue to hold a worldview, theology, and approach to Scripture similar in most respects to that of early Pentecostals; therefore, our proposed interpretive method and strategy takes these into account. We do not propose a unique, innovative or mystical methodology. The distinctive aspect of the proposed hermeneutic is the manner in which common methods are used and the particular strategy employed. Having presented a description of Pentecostalism's distinctiveness, background and identity we now turn our attention to the important task of considering the scriptural background to a distinct twenty-first century Pentecostal hermeneutic.

---

98. Though this resource is now somewhat dated it is a clear testimony to the complexity and diversity of contemporary Pentecostalism. Pentecostalism has significantly expanded, especially in the Charismatic and Independent categories since 1988.

99. Synan, *Aspects of Pentecostal-Charismatic Origins*, 1975. This volume traces the diverse origins of Pentecostalism. This examination is very helpful in identifying the varied backgrounds that formed the early Pentecostal movement.

CHAPTER 3

BIBLICAL FOUNDATIONS FOR A TWENTY-FIRST CENTURY PENTECOSTAL HERMENEUTIC

Introduction

As we have shown, Pentecostalism has always been a clearly identifiable community with specific beliefs, practices, worldview, and self-understanding. This distinctiveness informs Pentecostal interpretation, and Pentecostal bibliology calls for a biblical foundation for its interpretive method and strategy. An examination of Acts 2 and 15 provides the primary biblical foundation for the proposed hermeneutic presented later, while a consideration of Matthew 1:23 and Jude 14–15 adds to this biblical foundation. As we shall see, the scriptural examination that follows calls for a hermeneutic that moves beyond a modern approach to meaning, and the exclusive use of historical-grammatical method.

As noted in chapter 1, there has been an energetic hermeneutical discussion going on among scholars in recent years. In 1993 Arden Autry presented an argument suggesting that an authentic Pentecostal hermeneutic consisted of five elements: History, Language, Existence in Time, Transcendence (some would call this Spirit), and Community.[1] Later Thomas, Archer and Yong argued for a tridactic hermeneutical method and strategy with interaction among Scripture, Spirit, and Community.[2] Paul Achtemei-

---

1. Autry, "Dimensions of Hermeneutics," 30.
2. They each argue for a model which includes Scripture, community, and Holy

A Distinct Twenty-first Century Pentecostal Hermeneutic

er argues for a place for the Holy Spirit and Scripture in the hermeneutical process,[3] stating: "Without the internal testimony of the Spirit, Scripture remains mute in its witness to the truth."[4] Douglas Lowenburg has recently proposed a pentadactic model for Pentecostal interpretation.[5] What we can observe from these proposals is whether we speak of Pentecostal identity, the Pentecostal story, or Pentecostal interpretive method, Scripture always appears as a significant (indeed the leading) component because an essential aspect of the Pentecostal ethos is a high view of Scripture. Pentecostals look to Scripture when they want to defend and/or critique their beliefs or practices, find direction in life, and provide answers to life's problems. For Pentecostals Scripture is the source of understanding, knowledge, truth, and spiritual-life; therefore it is legitimate, if not necessary, to establish a biblical foundation for a distinct Pentecostal approach to interpretation.

It has also been noted that Pentecostals interpret Scripture from a Gospel–Acts perspective; more specifically they view Scripture through a Lukan lens. Further, Luke's presentation of Jesus' ministry, beginning with his exit from the wilderness temptation, as being empowered by the Holy Spirit (Luke 4:4) is foundational for Pentecostal ministry since Pentecostals understand the baptism in the Spirit's purpose as *power* for *mission* (Luke 4:4; 24:46–49; Acts 1:7–8). Consequently a biblical foundation for a Pentecostal hermeneutic is most effective if it is rooted in the Lukan material, especially the book of Acts; therefore, Acts 2 and 15 form the centerpiece of our investigation to establish a biblical foundation, and a basic understanding of a legitimate and distinct Pentecostal interpretation of Scripture.

For the purpose of this study it is assumed that Peter and James are Pentecostals in experience, and that Acts 2 and 15 accurately present the church's response to the respective current events. We also take Luke's account of Peter's Pentecostal sermon (Acts 2), and James' speech that draws on Amos 9 (Acts 15) as accurate. Based on these assumptions James and Peter, operating as hermeneuts, provide us with an interpretive model we can draw on. In addition to Acts 2 and 15 we examine other New Testament

---

Spirit although each has a different understanding of how the three interact. Archer, *A Pentecostal Hermeneutic*; Thomas, "Women, Pentecostals and the Bible"; Yong, *Spirit—Word—Community*.

3. Achtemeier, *Inspiration and Authority*, 122–26.

4. Ibid., 123.

5. Lowenburg, "A Twenty-first Century Pentecostal Hermeneutic," 1–41. Lowenburg wants to add individual and theophany to Archer's Scripture, Spirit, and community as components in the hermeneutical process.

Biblical Foundations

passages, giving attention to the New Testament's use of the Old Testament, and other related issues, as additional support for a firm biblical foundation for a distinct twenty-first century Pentecostal hermeneutic. Our study will also show an interaction between Scripture, Spirit, community, and trained leader as the essential elements in the hermeneutical strategy.

Acts 2

We now turn our attention to Acts 2 that begins by describing the outpouring of the Holy Spirit on the day of Pentecost (Acts 2:1–13). Witnesses of this event react by either asking what it meant or ridiculing the participants. In this way Luke presents us with an urgent spiritual issue, initiated by the Holy Spirit, that demands the church community's immediate apologetic. In response Peter stands with the other apostles and offers an explanation of the witnessed phenomenon, and in his explanation Peter presents an interpretation of Joel 2:28–32. His handling of the Joel text offers insight into first century Pentecostal biblical interpretation, and aids in providing a foundation for the same in the twenty-first century.

The events of the upper room experience need no detailing here, but we should note that the particular phenomenon that attracts attention is the *glossolalia*. Whether some or all of the 120 exit the upper room and appear in an ecstatic state in public is not clear. However, it is clear that the general public in the vicinity observe and react to the glossolalia in particular by asking, "What does this mean?" The question Peter responds to comes from non-Pentecostals (what may now perhaps be called non-believers) who witness the event, and it is this experience that initiates Peter's response under investigation here.

It should also be noted that though Peter is the spokesperson the other apostles stand with him. At this point in time the apostles would be seen as authoritative figures (leaders) within the community of faith. It can also be argued that after three years with Jesus the twelve were well-trained leaders; therefore, Peter qualifies as a well-trained leader, capable to interpret Scripture. It is not just any member of the newly formed church that speaks, it is Peter and he speaks authoritatively for the church. The entire community of believers are also involved in the interpretive process for it is their activity (glorifying God through the exercise of glossolalia) that supports Peter's interpretation.

A Distinct Twenty-first Century Pentecostal Hermeneutic

As part of the apologetic Peter quotes (or perhaps more correctly misquotes) Joel 2:28–32. *Scripture* stands front and center in Peter's apologetic as he uses the Joel text to explain a contemporary event. The actual event, the believing community and Peter (trained leader) function together with, and subject to, Scripture in the interpretive activity. This leads us to conclude that there is a critical role for Scripture in the important task of establishing theology, validating experience, and clarifying God's purpose(s) active in specific historical events. Further, as an example of intertextuality (a later biblical author importing a passage from an earlier inspired writer to explain a recent event), Luke's account of Peter's use of Joel provides insight into how biblical writers sometimes handled Scripture. As a foundational text Acts 2 suggests that Scripture hold a primary position in an interpretive methodology for twenty-first century Pentecostals, and that meaning in a text can, at least in some cases, lie beyond authorial intent.

Our study of Acts 2 also establishes that the Spirit is involved in several ways. First, it can be argued that the Holy Spirit orchestrates and superintends the events that require a community response. Second, the Spirit promotes a missional purpose through the entire episode,[6] for it is the Spirit who fills each believer enabling them all to speak in tongues (Acts 2:4) which culminates in the addition of 3000 new believers to the church (Acts 2:41, 47). Third, Peter is "full of the Holy Spirit" as he addresses the crowd using Joel 2:28–32 as the biblical support for his explanation. Fourth, the Holy Spirit, via the act of inspiration, was involved in the writing of both Joel and Acts. Fifth, Peter is at least guided by the Spirit in his choice and use of the Joel text; therefore, we can take direction from Luke's record of Peter's use and interpretation of Joel for our purpose here. The witness to the Spirit's involvement in Acts 2 supports our position that the Spirit is an integral part of a legitimate hermeneutic.

As noted the *community* of believers is also present, and active in the Acts 2 account. Their involvement is somewhat peripheral, and yet it is present as their experience serves as a witness, or testimony, to Peter's preaching. They testify to Peter's interpretation by means of the glossolalia; however, they are not directly involved in the interpretation of Joel.

---

6. Lowenburg, "A Twenty-first century Pentecostal Hermeneutic," 23. Paul Mumo Kisau writes, "There is a play on the word 'tongues' here, with the contrast between 'tongues of fire' and speaking 'in other tongues.' The Holy Spirit came in the physical form of tongues of fire to bring a transformation of the tongues of the disciples so that they would be able to witness to those present who would not have understood the gospel without this miracle" (Kisau, "Acts of The Apostles," 1328).

Biblical Foundations

Their activity may be understood as illustrating what Thiselton calls "the *formative* impact of Scripture in thought, life and action."[7] The glossolalia, through which the community expresses praise to God, may be considered an "Amen" to Peter's interpretation of Joel. The community's involvement is twofold: first, their action initiates the need for interpretation, and second, their activity affirms the interpretation. In Acts 2 Scripture, Spirit, community and trained leader interact to reveal God's will that points to a new understanding for the future.

An investigation of Peter's use of Joel provides insight into the very first Pentecostal's interpretive methodology providing helpful insight into how the contemporary Pentecostal hermeneut should operate. An initial, somewhat surprising observation is that Peter alters the inspired words of Joel in several ways.[8] First, he makes additions ("God says" and "they will prophesy"). Second, he replaces "afterwards" with "last days." Third, Peter reverses the order of "old men will dream dreams/young men will see visions," and he eliminates the final phrases of Joel 2:32.[9] This could be explained as poor memory on Peter's part; however, our understanding that the Holy Spirit inspires the writing of Scripture, and Luke's opportunity as writer to correct the inconsistencies, forces us to consider other possibilities. One Possibility is that Peter has access to a version of Joel 2:28–32 that we no longer have access to.[10] It is also possible that the text of Scripture is not as static as a verbal plenary theory of inspiration would propose. Another possibility is that the Spirit directed Peter to paraphrase[11] Joel so

---

7. Thiselton, "Hermenetical Dynamics," 17; italics his.

8. It must be acknowledged that Luke, as author of Acts, may be the one who alters the text of Joel. The assumption here is that Luke presents an accurate, though summarized, account of Peter's actual sermon. We attribute the alteration of Joel to Peter rather than Luke based on the biblical account. It must further be noted that Peter's alteration of Joel is not license for the contemporary interpreter to do the same since the contemporary preacher is neither writing nor contributing to the writing of Scripture as in this case.

9. Max Turner suggests that Acts 2:39b is the citation of the last part of Joel 2:32 (Turner, "Luke and the Spirit," 278–79).

10. There is no evidence to support this idea. I've not found this perspective raised in any of my research. I mention it here only because it is a possible explanation. Evidence to date would lead us to conclude this is a very remote possibility.

11. Lowenburg, "A Twenty-first Century Pentecostal Hermeneutic," 24. Lowenburg uses the word "paraphrase" in reference to Peter's alteration of Joel. Much of what Peter does could be classed as a paraphrase, but the addition of the phrase "they will prophesy" seems to be more than a paraphrase.

A Distinct Twenty-first Century Pentecostal Hermeneutic

the ancient text could effectively address a new context. It is not possible to provide a definitive explanation of what, or why Peter handles Joel as he does, but it is clear that Scripture as a "living word" spoke effectively in a contemporary context. We can also note that Scripture's use of Scripture in Luke's recounting of Peter's sermon portrays the interpreter (Peter) as involved in manipulating the text and the creation of meaning. Peter's use of Joel to explain the current event is an example of *pesher* interpretation, and suggests that meaning is partly controlled by the contemporary context in which a text is employed. Joel was speaking to a completely different context than Peter yet the text had meaning in both instances. Acts 2 implies that the interpreter's context as well as the author's is involved in the creation of meaning.

Peter's alteration of the Joel 2:28–32 text points to the creative inspiration of the Holy Spirit working in Peter. The Spirit enabled Peter to take an Old Testament text and creatively deliver a new contextualized meaning and message providing support to a Pentecostal hermeneutic that recognizes, even encourages, the interpreters role in the creation of meaning. Lowenburg states, "Considering both the author-text and the text-reader aspects of hermeneutics implies that there is no communication without understanding and there is no understanding without a person reading or hearing the message followed by an active deciphering of language in order to grasp what has been conveyed."[12]

Peter did more than discover a static meaning in Joel for he was creatively engaged in the creation of new meaning. This provides a biblical foundation for a twenty-first century Pentecostal hermeneutic whereby the Spirit and reader are actively engaged with the text in the creation of meaning. Meaning does not reside *exclusively* in the text and the Spirit is able to illuminate a text so as to produce a meaning that goes beyond what authorial intent would support or allow. The reader is also actively engaged in the creation of meaning in the interpretive process, and the community renders its assessment of the offered interpretation. It would appear that Acts 2 points to a hermeneutic that involves interaction between, Spirit, Scripture, trained leader(s) and community in the interpretive process and creation of meaning.

---

12. Ibid., 5.

Biblical Foundations

Acts 15

Having examined Acts 2, the birth of the Pentecostal church, we now look at Acts 15's record of the first Pentecostal community's struggle with a significant internal crisis revolving around the issue of how to incorporate Gentile believers. This is both a theological and practical issue with numerous implications. Acts 15 is Luke's account of this momentous event that is generally recognized as the first church council. The Pentecostal nature of the church in Acts 15 is widely, if not universally, acknowledged; therefore, we can legitimately look there to find scriptural direction and foundation for developing our hermeneutic proposal.

The crisis, as noted, arises since the community of faith is divided over the issue of how to respond to the great influx of Gentile believers. Some (generally those of the Pharisee sect) demanded Gentiles be circumcised and live Jewishly, while others argued against this requirement. The Jerusalem council is convened in an effort to resolve the issue, and Acts 15 provides the only known record of the proceedings. Including James' use of Amos 9, Luke's account of the council proceedings provides another biblical example of Scripture's interpretation and use within the context of a Pentecostal community. Acts 15 invites us to observe the first Pentecostals struggling with a theological problem, resolving a community conflict, and practicing the art of interpreting Scripture to solve a life problem. Responding to that invitation we now probe Luke's account to discover direction for, insight into, and a biblical foundation for a legitimate, distinct Pentecostal hermeneutic.

We begin with Acts 15:1–5 as it sets out the problem informing us that individuals reportedly from Jerusalem have come to Antioch and are teaching that Gentiles must be circumcised and live Jewishly. We further learn that Paul and Barnabas have been dispatched from Antioch to Jerusalem to seek a verdict from the Jerusalem church on this matter. (This clearly indicates that the authority of the Jerusalem church is widely recognized by the broader church at this point in history.) The seriousness, and potential for division, of this issue is heightened by the report that Pharisees in Jerusalem are also calling for the Gentiles to be circumcised and live Jewishly (Acts 15:5). From this we can conclude that the council meeting included all sides of the issue, and the debate was likely lively and comprehensive; therefore, the passage offers foundational, instructive, and important help for our purpose.

A Distinct Twenty-first Century Pentecostal Hermeneutic

As Acts 15:1–5 sets the stage, Acts 15:6–35 gives the details of the first church council as it moves to resolve the crisis. The text identifies those who were involved in the debate as the apostles, church elders, Judaizing Pharisees, Paul and Barnabas, and "some others" (1:3). This along with the "whole assembly" of verse 12 (including apostles, elders, and others) identifies the *community's* presence at the proceedings. The apostles, elders, Paul, Barnabas, and James are leaders in the early church, and this tells us that *trained leaders* play a leading role in resolving the issue. The community is present and engaged, but a leading role in the interpretive activity is given to trained leaders, and ultimately it is these leaders who speak authoritatively on this critical issue.

Initially Paul, Barnabas, and Peter present testimonial evidence to the gathering. Peter reports his experience at Cornelius' house and concludes that Gentiles should not be required to live Jewishly and be circumcised. Peter's position is based entirely on experience indicating that the initial suggestion of the ultimate solution is experientially based. Paul and Barnabas report what God has been doing among the Gentiles throughout the Roman Empire adding the weight of their experience to that of Peter's. Peter addresses the group passionately asking that no yoke be put on the Gentiles' neck that the Jews themselves have not been able to wear. He further argues that both Gentiles and Jews are saved by grace (v. 11) and points to the accounts of signs and wonders among the Gentiles as reinforcing the claim that God is at work among them. The weight of *testimony* and *experience* evidenced in this pericope is significant, yet not even the testimony and experience of Paul and Peter is sufficient to conclude the matter.

James first draws attention to the experiential dimension by referring to the testimonies of Peter, Paul, and Barnabas and then he stands and offers a scripturally based solution. James turns their attention to Scripture by quoting Amos 9:11–12, a passage that seems to refer to the Davidic dynasty being restored, and possibly a restored temple so that a remnant of people (Israelites) would seek God. The Jewishness of the Amos text is amplified as James uses a very specific Greek word, (λαός) translated "people" in Acts 15:14, that was used by Jews to refer to fellow Jews but never to Gentiles.[13] Although this term, in its usage, specifically refers to Jews, James asserts the prophecy in Amos 9:11–12 is being fulfilled as Gentiles are coming to Christ. In his interpretation James moves beyond the bounds of authorial and original intent as he re-presents and gives new meaning to this ancient

---

13. Kisau, "Acts of the Apostles," 1353.

text to identify God's will in a new context. A further point, important to the proposal here, is to note that James' interpretive process moves from the present context (experience) to the Scripture and then from Scripture to a new understanding of experience.

This observation suggests that Acts 15 points to the meaningful role experience plays in interpretation since it is the church's current *experience* of Gentile conversions, and the response of a *particular* Jewish-Christian group to it, that initiates the interpretive process. All will agree the church began as a Jewish entity, but the Holy Spirit "outside of the church and without her endorsement"[14] quickly embraced Gentiles such as Cornelius' household and added them to the church. Through the missionary ministry of Paul and Barnabas the Spirit continued *his* mission of bringing in a Gentile Harvest, thereby creating the division and crisis. It is experience initiated by the Spirit that instigates the interpretive process reversing the order observed by the historical critical method.[15] Moving from experience to Scripture is not unique to Acts 15, but was observed in Acts 2 and is evidenced by the fact that the New Testament epistles are often referred to as "occasional" because their writing is *occasioned* by some current situation in the life of a particular congregation. Frequently, as evidenced by Paul's numerous references to the Old Testament, the epistles offer scriptural responses to these occasions providing correction, edification, teaching, etc. directly linked to the interpretation of Scripture. The evidence of Acts 15 supports a conclusion that experience may initiate and play a role in the interpretive event; however, it is Scripture that holds the ultimate place of authority. A legitimate Pentecostal hermeneutic for the twenty-first century must operate from a stance of Scripture's primacy while allowing a place for experience in the interpretive process.

We also note Acts 15 suggests an important place for trained leaders in the interpretive activity with attention drawn to Paul, Peter, James, and Barnabas as critical players in the action. Peter and the apostles as disciples of Jesus would seem to qualify as *trained* leaders and Paul, a student of Gamaliel, was highly trained. It is reasonable to assume Barnabas, a companion of Paul (along with Timothy and Titus), received training from Paul; therefore, we can reasonably argue that he qualifies as a trained leader.

14. Lowenburg, "A Twenty-first Century Pentecostal Hermeneutic," 24.

15. Archer, *A Pentecostal Hermeneutic*, 145; Thomas, "Women, Pentecostals and the Bible," 41–56. Archer and Thomas both draw attention to this point. From this they argue that the role of historical critical methodology in a Pentecostal hermeneutic, if present at all, is extremely limited.

A Distinct Twenty-first Century Pentecostal Hermeneutic

The training of James cannot be clearly established, and his leadership role may have been based on his sibling relationship to Jesus; however, his use of Scripture suggests some level of training. The level of training among the elders and Pharisees present is beyond investigation but their presence, however, points to the involvement of the community in the council meeting and ultimately in the interpretive action.[16]

Along with trained leaders and community Scripture is evident in Acts 15 since James does not merely pronounce a council edict, but draws upon Amos 9:11–12 to arrive at the decision that Gentiles will not be required to be circumcised or live Jewishly. James' use of Amos illustrates the application of an ancient text to a contemporary context that has no affinity with the original context or original intended meaning. In this passage we observe a (trained) leader inspired by the Holy Spirit bringing meaning to a text that is beyond what could be called original intent suggesting that meaning is created through an interaction between community experience, text, and reader under the superintendence of the Holy Spirit.[17]

Interestingly the Old Testament witness concerning the place of Gentiles is divided; therefore, council participants could have offered many Old Testament Scriptures that pointed to Yahweh's rejection of Gentiles. Many Old Testament Scriptures support the view of Yahweh's rejection of Gentiles, but some offer a place for Gentiles within the people of God. Numbers 15 would allow Gentile inclusion in the people of God but require them to be circumcised and live Jewishly. Interestingly, the Holy Spirit illumines James' understanding and interpretation of Amos 9:11–12 enabling him to overcome those Old Testament texts that reject Gentile inclusion in God's covenant community and those that would admit them but require them to live Jewishly. The Holy Spirit, using testimony and experience,[18] guides

---

16. Archer, Thomas, and Yong each point to Acts 15 as biblical support for identifying "community" as one of the three elements in their respective approaches. Archer, *A Pentecostal Hermeneutic*, 145ff.; Thomas, "Women, Pentecostals and the Bible," 41–56; Yong, *Spirit-Word-Community*.

17. This point is merely noted here but more will be said on this issue in chapter 6.

18. Stronstad, "Pentecostal Hermeneutics," 215–22. He refers to the experience as "historical precedent." He contends that the selection of Scripture is determined by Peter's testimony of Cornelius' conversion. Peter's proposal that Gentiles be accepted without circumcision or living Jewishly is based on his Cornelius encounter. Stronstad says, "Peter's argument for the conversion of the Gentiles apart from the necessity of circumcision is based on historical precedent and James supports Peter's position on the basis of the same historical precedent . . . this proof from historical precedent is prior to, and superior to, the proof from Scripture, for it is Scripture which agrees with historical

Biblical Foundations

the community through the valley of conflicting scriptural positions and a new understanding emerges yet this new understanding is still rooted in Scripture. The Spirit, in this instance, speaks to the church through more than the text using community experience, testimony, trained leaders, and Scripture in cooperative interaction to express God's will on a specific issue.

We should note that the Spirit's activity recorded in Acts 15 is multivalent. First, the Holy Spirit's involvement is seen in that he creates the crises by bringing Gentiles into the church. Second, the Spirit further complicates matters when Gentiles are baptized in the Spirit with the evidence of tongues without their being circumcised (i.e., Cornelius' household). Third, the letter the council sends to the Gentiles clearly invokes the involvement and authority of the Holy Spirit in the final decision (15:28). Fourth, by extension James' statement "It seemed good to the Holy Spirit and to us" suggests the Holy Spirit's involvement in the *choice* and *interpretation* of Amos 9:11–12 resulting in the Amos text becoming the *prophetic pronouncement* on the issue. Although the activity of the Spirit is impossible to quantify or fully examine, he is clearly at work in the interpretive event as it is described in Acts 15.

Community also has a place in the interpretive activity for Acts 15:22 states, "Then the Apostles and elders, with the whole Church, decided." The community's involvement is also seen in that the crisis affects the whole church. The voice of the community has been present, to some extent at least, via the apostles and elders as they participate in the process.[19] Lastly, in the choosing of those who would deliver the written decision is at least giving their "Amen" to the decision. Again, the text does not allow us to clearly determine the extent of larger community involvement but, in various ways, points to the community's involvement.

An examination of Acts 15 also raises the thorny issue of the place for historical precedent in establishing doctrine. Many evangelicals, and some Pentecostals such as Gordon Fee, declare a resounding no to the use of historical precedent in establishing doctrine. Acts 15 would oppose this position. The issue at hand, must Gentile converts be circumcised and live Jewishly to be fully saved, is a doctrinal issue. The answer to this question has soteriological and ecclesiological implications. In Acts 15:7ff. Peter reports how God used him to bring the gospel to Cornelius' household and Acts 15:12 gives Paul and Barnabas' report of signs and wonders God

---

precedent and not the other way around" (ibid., 218).

19. Lowenburg, "A Twenty-first Century Pentecostal Hermeneutic," 24.

71

A Distinct Twenty-first Century Pentecostal Hermeneutic

did through them among the Gentiles. When James speaks (Acts 15:14) he reminds the audience of what Peter has just said. In this way James applies historical precedent, along with the application of Scripture, in the ultimate decision that is doctrinal in nature. Here we would agree with Stronstad who states, "This Lukan report of the use of historical precedent at the Jerusalem Council is the biblical precedent for the contemporary use of historical precedent."[20]

Acts 15 shows how God revealed his will to the church concerning the acceptance of Gentile converts. The great question, "Must Gentiles become Jews and live Jewishly?" is resolved in the negative. The requirements imposed on Gentiles are restricted to those that enable table fellowship between Jew and Gentile, and this decision radically alters the understanding of the nature of the church. As we investigate this passage we discover a creative, dynamic interaction among the Holy Spirit, community, trained leaders, and Scripture in the interpretive process, and the discovery of God's will for the church as it moves forward to fulfill its mission. This interactive engagement in the interpretive process results in a new understanding of God's salvific plan and purposes. Our investigation of this text points toward a biblically sound foundation for a Pentecostal interpretive methodology and strategy for the twenty-first century that involves a creative interaction between Scripture, Spirit, community, and trained leaders with Scripture taking the place of primacy.

Acts 2 and Acts 15 support the inclusion of community as part of the interpretive process but challenge the way Archer and others seem to want to include community. Archer and others seem to include the community without any restriction or clear description of how its involvement works and they give no recognition to the significant role of leaders, trained or otherwise, as Acts 2 and 15 suggest. The proposal in this book, rooted in our investigation of Acts 2 and 15, attempts to address these shortcomings by identifying community's role and recognizing a considerable role for trained leaders. Chapter 6 will develop the role and place for Scripture, Spirit, community, and trained leader in the distinct hermeneutic proposed in this book.

---

20. Stronstad, "Pentecostal Hermeneutics," 218.

Biblical Foundations

Matthew 1:23, John 10:34–36, and Jude

Matthew 1:23 provides an excellent example of Scripture's use of Scripture that is helpful to our purpose. Matthew quotes Isaiah 7:14 and identifies the events of Jesus' birth as fulfilling this prophecy. In referring to this text the author of Matthew is obviously ignoring authorial or original intent since the Isaiah text, to make sense at all, must have referred to a male child to be born in the near future.[21] The birth of Jesus could not be a sign to Ahaz for he had been dead for several centuries. The author of Matthew under the guidance of the Holy Spirit gives meaning to Isaiah 7:14 that moves beyond authorial intent. The text is wrestled out of its original context and given new meaning. Matthew's author finds a *deeper* meaning in the ancient text of Isaiah 7:14. As Glenn Wooden points out, New Testament writers clearly "violate the plain meaning of the text."[22]

Scripture's use of Scripture, as exemplified in Matthew 1:23, supports the view that a text is not restricted to a singular meaning and suggests, contrary to Fee and others,[23] that the interpreter, *led by the Spirit*, is not limited to original or authorial intent in determining meaning. It would seem meaning in the biblical text is not static but is somewhat fluid. In view of this reality the Qumran community, Philo, Josephus, and at least some New Testament writers employed a Hebrew interpretive method called *Pesher* that enabled the discovery of meaning beyond the "plain meaning." Following this example the twenty-first century hermeneutic ultimately proposed here seeks to enable, or at least allow for, the discovery of deeper meaning without giving unlimited license to create meaning.

The reality of the state of what we call Scripture also speaks to the issue of interpretation and meaning. The Christian church from its very beginning has dealt with a translation rather than an original text. The Septuagint (LXX), a translation, was the primary Scripture for the early church and is the text most frequently cited in the New Testament. The Masoretic

---

21. This is not the place to debate whether the promised child would be a son of Isaiah or Ahaz. The relevant issue is that the child to be born would be a sign to Ahaz, something Jesus' birth could not be.

22. Wooden, "Guided By God," 103.

23. Oleka, "Interpreting and Applying the Bible," 108. He states, "There is only one interpretation to every Scripture text but there could be several application to it." See also, Anderson, "Pentecostal Hermeneutics: Part 2," 13–22. Anderson argues that a text has a fixed, objective meaning. He would argue that all, even the unregenerate, can equally access the meaning of a text. He goes on to argue that it is the "significance" of the text that eludes the unregenerate.

A Distinct Twenty-first Century Pentecostal Hermeneutic

Text (MT) was available to at least some of the New Testament writers as is evidenced by the fact that it is occasionally quoted. Why New Testament writers favored the LXX is a discussion beyond the parameters of this book; however, as in the case of Matthew 1:23, it seems to be selected at times because of its particular wording. The LXX enabled the writer of Matthew to highlight the supernatural conception of Jesus in a way not possible from the MT.

Although the canon has been closed for centuries the actual words within the canon are not fixed as scholars continue to engage in textual criticism in an effort to produce a text that best represents the original.[24] At best we have a highly reliable, reasonable facsimile of an original text. This reality suggests at least some element of fluidity in meaning continues to reside in the text and must be allowed in the process of interpretation.

John 10:34–36 provides another biblical example of interpretation that moves beyond the parameters of authorial or original intent. The context of John 10:34–36 is that Jesus' opposition (The Jews) have taken offense to his claim of being one with the Father. In responding to their anger Jesus quotes Psalm 82:6 that begins by saying "You are gods" and he takes the "you" as referring to Israelites. In discussing this text Peter Enns states: "What is interesting here is that Jesus says 'the scripture cannot be annulled' but he seems to bend the particular scripture in question, Psalm 82, beyond its breaking point."[25] Psalm 82 is set in the "divine council" and in its original context the "you" refers to the rulers of the nations who are "sons of God"; therefore, "You are gods" is "not a proof text that Israel was 'divine' but a nod to ancient royal ideology."[26] As Enns observes there is some disconnect between what the psalm means and the meaning Jesus gives to it, therefore, we again find biblical support for a hermeneutic that allows for meaning that moves beyond authorial or original intent.

A creative handling of Scripture to support one's views had been, by Jesus' day, a longstanding method of Jewish interpretation. One of the creative techniques frequently used was to "deliberately isolate a few words or a verse from its surrounding context and work it to make a point."[27] Enns notes that Jesus seems at home with this type of creative use of the Bible as he employs it here in John 10:34–36 and "elsewhere in his debates with the

---

24. Wooden, "The Role of 'the Septuagint,'" 136.
25. Enns, "Would Jesus Get Hired," lines 38–40.
26. Ibid., line 47ff.
27. Ibid., line 91.

Biblical Foundations

religious leaders."[28] The hermeneutics taught in most Bible colleges today would label this approach as *eisegesis* and reject it as a legitimate interpretation. Neither modernity nor historical-grammatical method would approve of this creative approach to meaning in a written text—especially Scripture. However, the New Testament writers and Jesus seem very comfortable with this creative model of interpretation that moves significantly beyond authorial or original intent. Enns' closing remark presents us with a challenge and also a support for the hermeneutical approach being proposed in this book: he says, "If how we are taught to handle the Bible 'properly' can't account for the Bible's own inner interpretive dynamic, and if we claim to 'follow the Bible,' we probably need to think about whether we actually are."[29]

In addition to Matthew and John we also have Jude's quotation of 1 Enoch 1:9 that illustrates some very interesting points. First, Jude adds the word *kurios* as the subject, while in 1 Enoch 1:9 God is the subject, and it is Jude's addition of *kurios* that provides a christological interpretation so that 1 Enoch 1:9 may be applied to the Parousia.[30] Bauckham says of Jude, "he has deliberately adapted the text to suit the interpretation he wishes to put on it."[31] Second, Jude's use of "prophesied" indicates he considered the prophecies in 1 Enoch inspired but does not necessarily indicate he considered the book canonical.[32] Jude's use of the Enoch material is similar to Peter's use of Joel seen in Acts 2 and is another example of a New Testament writer creatively interpreting older text. We cannot firmly establish if 1 Enoch was or was not canonical for Jude but clearly it is not for Pentecostals; however, his use of material that he seemingly considered inspired helps provide a biblical foundation for a hermeneutic that is open to the creation of meaning clearly beyond the limits of authorial and original intent. Matthew, John, Jude, James, and Peter use inspired material in a manner that illustrates interpretive methodology and, at least in these instances, Scripture supports interpretation that goes beyond original meaning. Jude's use of 1 Enoch also suggests the Holy Spirit speaks beyond Scripture and that revelation may come through extrabiblical means.

---

28. Ibid., line 83.
29. Ibid., line 110.
30. Bauckham, *2 Peter, Jude*, 93.
31. Ibid., 94.
32. Ibid., 96.

A Distinct Twenty-first Century Pentecostal Hermeneutic

Conclusion

Many other Scriptures could be drawn upon but these suffice to establish a biblical foundation for a distinct twenty-first century Pentecostal hermeneutic. Acts 2 and 15 point to the interactive role between Scripture, Spirit, community and trained leader in the interpretive process.[33] Matthew, John, and Jude suggest that a biblical model of interpretation allows for meaning beyond authorial intent and that the interpreter is manifestly involved in the creation of meaning. It has also been noted that there is a creative interface between experience and Scripture in the process of interpretation and the creation of meaning. The possibility that the Holy Spirit might decontextualize Scripture to produce a new understanding of God's will in the world also finds support in the biblical record presented here.[34] The biblical foundation laid here points toward a distinct Pentecostal hermeneutic that engages Scripture, Spirit, community, and trained leader while being open to meaning that goes beyond authorial intent and allows for the discovery of deeper and/or multiple meaning in the text.

As well as presenting a biblical foundation there is a need to identify the starting point for the proposed hermeneutic; therefore, the next chapter discusses the role of hermeneutics, early Pentecostal hermeneutical practices—especially those of Myland—as the starting point for our task. The starting point discussed in the next chapter also attempts to establish certain community specific issues that are operating in the interpretation of Scripture by Pentecostals. Therefore we now turn our attention to this task.

---

33. Lowenburg wants to add theophany to the interpretive process. His claim that theophany is always present in the interpretive activity seen in Acts is, in my view, not supported by the evidence. There is clearly no theophanic activity in Acts 15. Depending on how one defines theophany it could be argued that theophany is present in Acts 2. However, the broader examination of interpretation seen in Acts and other New Testament texts does not support Lowenburg's claim. See Lowenburg, "A Twenty-first Century Pentecostal Hermeneutic," 24–30.

34. This author recognizes the inherent danger of this position. A distinct twenty-first century Pentecostal hermeneutic, while allowing for creativity in interpretation and the establishment of meaning, must also limit creative imagination. More will be said on this matter.

CHAPTER 4

A DISTINCT TWENTY-FIRST CENTURY PENTECOSTAL HERMENEUTIC

The Starting Point

Introduction

THE PREVIOUS CHAPTER ARGUES for a particular biblical foundation for a Pentecostal hermeneutic that points to a methodology and strategy that embraces an interpretation that is textually anchored, but also allows the interpreter's involvement in the ultimate creation of meaning. Now we turn our attention to the starting point for the hermeneutic ultimately proposed in this book. Since Pentecostalism has existed for over a century understanding the role of hermeneutics and the early Pentecostal hermeneutical practices is the proper starting point.

The role of hermeneutics is the launching pad for this discussion. This may seem unnecessary but the multitude of hermeneutic strategies and the vociferous debate on the subject suggests that an important starting point is establishing how Pentecostals understand the role of hermeneutics. For Pentecostals, hermeneutics is anchored to Scripture and serves the purpose of interpreting the text consequently interpretation is not wrestled from the grip of Scripture and placed solely in the hand of the hermeneut. The role of hermeneutics is to enable the interpreter to offer a legitimate and understandable meaning of a biblical text to the faith community, and enable them to fulfill their mandated mission.

A Distinct Twenty-first Century Pentecostal Hermeneutic

Arguing for a distinct twenty-first century interpretive approach does not mean Pentecostals have not been practicing hermeneutics for indeed they have. We consider the early Pentecostal approach to gain helpful insight into the nature of Pentecostalism since community identity operates at the presupposition level in the interpretive process. The better we understand the interpreting community the more equipped we are to offer a legitimate, effective and distinct interpretive strategy. As part of this investigation we examine the hermeneutical method of Myland because he was an influential early Pentecostal leader and one of the few who actually wrote about biblical interpretation from a methodological perspective. His methodology is very helpful and provides support for certain aspects of the direction proposed in this book for a twenty-first century Pentecostal interpreter to follow.

The Role of Hermeneutics

The definition of hermeneutics I was given at Bible college in the 1970s was, "the art and science of interpretation," which, in light of recent debates, is a helpful definition. Hermeneutics is a science in that it is the application of rules in accordance with a particular hermeneutical methodology. The term "art" in this definition captures the current openness to multiple dimensions in the interpretive process. Lowenburg identifies hermeneutics as: "the pursuit of a holistic understanding of the divine author of the Book, who reveals himself through the historical particularities of Scripture in order that people will be changed by the Spirit to be more like Jesus and serve His Kingdom purposes."[1] This definition captures the "art" and "science" elements of hermeneutics within the context of a Pentecostal ethos and adds the element of purpose stating, "that people will be changed."

One task of hermeneutics is to conquer the gap between the past and present. This gap is cultural, linguistic, philosophical, and psychological. God's self-revelation and the record of his redemptive activity occurred in an agrarian context within an ancient Near Eastern Hebrew culture. The contemporary context in the Western world is a postmodern, technological environment that has little consonance with this ancient Near Eastern reality. Little of the Western world is agrarian in the sense of the biblical world while certain parts of the African continent share a far greater

---

1. Lowenburg, "A Twenty-first Century Pentecostal Hermeneutic," 8.

A Distinct Twenty-first Century Pentecostal Hermeneutic

correspondence with the biblical world.[2] However whether we speak of the Western or Majority World the contemporary context is generally vastly different from the biblical context and hermeneutics must span this gap to answer the questions: What does the text mean? How does this effect the way the church functions to fulfill its mandated mission? How does the individual believer live out their faith in the world? How do we, as the people of God, live in the world? The task of the hermeneut engaging interpretive methodology and strategy is to provide scriptural answers to these and many other questions.

In light of this Carl Braaten's definition of hermeneutics is helpful. He defines hermeneutics as, "the science of reflecting on how a word or an event in a past time and culture may be understood and become existentially meaningful in our present situation."[3] Hermeneutics in the plural refers to the broad activity of applying rules of interpretation to gain understanding and these rules and methods are universally applicable. However, the singular "hermeneutic" generally refers to a particular frame of reference from which to proceed to interpretation. This distinction is important since we are suggesting a distinct Pentecostal hermeneutic for the twenty-first century. Ferguson states, "A given hermeneutic is essentially a self-consciously chosen starting point containing certain ideological, attitudinal, and methodological components designed to aid the work of interpretation and facilitate maximum understanding."[4] This implies there is no singular interpretation and/or understanding; therefore, a Pentecostal interpretation and understanding may differ from an Episcopal interpretation yet both are legitimate. The issue for Pentecostals then is to self-consciously choose an appropriate strategy that is commensurate with the

---

2. This suggests that African theology and hermeneutics, which is just now coming into its own, has much to offer the contemporary Christian world. As Africans write more we will see their impact on biblical interpretation continue to grow. It is quite possible that within the next quarter century the African voice will take a leading role in some aspects of theology and hermeneutics. This will prove interesting, if not challenging, since the African church is predominantly Pentecostal. It is interesting to note that the Bible Reading method, harmonization, and experiential orientation of early Pentecostals resonates well within the African culture. (It may with other Majority World cultures also but I am most intimately acquainted with African Pentecostalism and culture.)

3. Braaten, *History and Hermeneutics*, 131.

4. Ferguson, *Biblical Hermeneutics*, 5. Note Ferguson's idea that a hermeneutic has a "self-consciously chosen starting point." A community's hermeneutic is deliberately chosen by the community. A hermeneutic is not something imposed from the outside. Each community deliberately decides the framework of their hermeneutic.

A Distinct Twenty-first Century Pentecostal Hermeneutic

Pentecostal community in the twenty-first century. Archer says, "Because Pentecostals are also a part of the broader Christian community, they must be concerned with the interpretation of its most authoritative text—the Bible. However, Pentecostals will engage Scripture and reality from their own community and narrative tradition."[5] In this way Pentecostals are able to offer a distinctive interpretation of Scripture and offer it for the rest of Christendom to consider.

Ferguson's statement also implies that a hermeneutic is more than method and/or the exegetical process. Since Schleiermacher, hermeneutical theory has become concerned with how the reader understands (epistemology).[6] The interpreter's encounter with the text is now part of most hermeneutic theories, and community is recognized as an important and essential element in the hermeneutical process.[7] Thus the interpretive model proposed here must involve more than merely arguing for one methodology over another since there are non-methodological elements that must also be considered, and how these non-methodological elements should operate must be carefully thought through. In fact, what is distinct about a Pentecostal hermeneutic is not a unique method, rather it is the particular way in which Pentecostals employ commonly used methods.

The work of Hans-Georg Gadamer and Paul Ricoeur have furthered understanding of the hermeneutical task. Ricoeur gives attention to the revelatory role of language and how the interpreter must assume a posture of "second naivete" which allows the text to reveal and enlighten. From Gadamer's perspective hermeneutics is concerned with the experience of truth. All of this points to an existential element in the hermeneutical process. The hermeneut is attempting to hear an ancient text so that it may inform the present and point the way to the future. This is how Pentecostals, early and contemporary, approach Scripture.

Experience, as in the Wesleyan Quadrilateral, is a dimension of Pentecostal interpretation as it has been practiced from the beginning. The examination of Acts 2 and 15 points out how current experience initiated an interpretive action and Scripture provided the explanation and understanding that was needed for a current event in the life of the community.

---

5. Archer, *A Pentecostal Hermeneutic*, 98.

6. Autry, "Dimensions Of Hermeneutics," 30.

7. Ibid., 31. History, language, existence in time and transcendence are the other four dimensions Autry identifies. Many working in hermeneutical theory today would agree that community is an important component of how one interprets texts.

A Distinct Twenty-first Century Pentecostal Hermeneutic

The crisis pushed the church to address what "they recognized as God's initiative at work within their social milieu."[8] Scripture explained the experience and also provided a future direction, especially in the case of Acts 15, for the community. Experience frequently motivates Pentecostals to seek understanding and Scripture, through interpretation, provides the definitive response.

If God's word is heard through reading the Bible then it is possible to have *fellowship* with God through Scripture. It is also possible to gain *insight* that enables growth toward spiritual maturity. If God's word is heard through Scripture then it is possible to find *direction* for daily living as a member of God's kingdom through the Scriptures. The Pentecostal hermeneut is seeking to discover the meaning and significance of Scripture so that the people of God can be trained in righteousness and mission. Russell Spittler effectively illustrates that Pentecostals interpret Scripture to instruct believers how to live and to support missionary effort.[9] Pentecostals practice hermeneutics for the purpose of preaching the Gospel and their interest in hermeneutics is missional; therefore, a proposed Pentecostal interpretive model must be in alignment with mission. The role of hermeneutics for Pentecostals is to enable understanding and application of Scripture so they are able to fulfill the mission of Christ articulated in the great commission.

The Early Pentecostal Hermeneutic

As established in chapter 1, the early Pentecostals engaged in a distinctive hermeneutical strategy; therefore, a first step in establishing a distinct, twenty-first century approach is understanding and possibly renewing some aspects of this strategy so that it fits within a twenty-first century context. This is not to suggest Pentecostals return to the Bible Reading method but does propose that Pentecostals employ interpretive methods from a Pentecostal stance using the Lukan lens as was the case for early Pentecostals. It is certainly essential to understand how this early hermeneutic helped shape the Pentecostal ethos even though a twenty-first century strategy will require the application of some postmodern methodological approaches. The early Pentecostal strategy (not method)[10] provides a platform from which

---

8. Lowenburg, "A Twenty-first Century Pentecostal Hermeneutic," 23.
9. Spittler, "Scripture and the Theological Enterprise," 57.
10. For our purposes here "method" refers to interpretive methods such as "narrative

A Distinct Twenty-first Century Pentecostal Hermeneutic

to launch the development of a distinct twenty-first century Pentecostal hermeneutic.

Although Pentecostals used a literalist approach and held a high view of Scripture as did the Fundamentalists there was a significant difference in their strategy and approach. Spittler claims, "there is a profound difference between the cognitive Fundamentalist and the experiential Pentecostal."[11] According to Spittler, Fundamentalists mounted their arguments in the form of creeds while Pentecostals used testimonies. The early Pentecostal approach to Scripture was pre-critical[12] and this pre-critical approach continues to be how Pentecostals, perhaps even most people, read Scripture. The postmodern context, as will be seen later, has some affinity with the pre-critical stance of Pentecostals;[13] therefore, the following thesis retains the early Pentecostals' high view of Scripture and certain aspects of their strategy while moving away from the methodology and positioning of early Pentecostals.

There is both a positive and a negative side to such a pre-critical reading of Scripture. The positive is that this method implies Scripture is relevant, understandable, and accessible to everyone. It takes the Bible out of the exclusive hands of experts and places it back in the hands of ordinary individuals and, at the same time, does not negate the important role of trained leaders. The negative is that it fails to recognize that language is embedded in culture and provides no direction as to determining which

---

criticism," while "strategy" refers to the particular way Pentecostals use these methods. The methods used by Pentecostals will not differ from other hermeneuts but the Pentecostal strategy will be distinctive.

11. Spittler, "Are Pentecostals and Charismatics Fundamentalists?," 106.

12. Pre-critical refers to an approach to Scripture that understands the text to be transhistorical and transcultural. Joel Green writes, "the Bible reading conducted by many people today can be characterized as 'pre-critical' insofar as it advances on the basis of the examined presumption that a New Testament text written, say, in the late first century CE continues to possess an immediate and straightforward relevance in new times and situations" (Green, "Hermeneutical Approaches," 972–88). It should be noted that pre-critical is used by Green as one of four contemporary reading approaches not as a temporal chronological category.

13. Noel, *Pentecostal and Postmodern Hermeneutics*, 10ff. Noel's thesis is that an affinity exists between the early Pentecostals and their hermeneutics and postmodern generation Xers and millenials. Noel states, "The blind following of evangelical hermeneutics by Pentecostals may in the end . . . lead away from the type of presentation of the Gospel that Pentecostals would wish to proclaim to this generation" (ibid., 98). In my view retrieving the Bible Reading methodology within a twenty-first century hermeneutic holds far more hazard than benefit.

A Distinct Twenty-first Century Pentecostal Hermeneutic

texts are to be taken as relevant and/or straightforward.[14] The pre-critical approach is part of Pentecostalism's ethos and resonates in some instances with our postmodern, twenty-first century context. Pentecostals are predisposed to interpret Scripture in ways outside the modernistic critical methods and this predisposition places Pentecostals in a good vantage point for the development of a distinct hermeneutic.

The early Pentecostal high view of Scripture continues to be the Pentecostal position. Whether one looks at official Pentecostal denominational statements of faith or the actual practice of ordinary Pentecostals their high view of Scripture is evident. As in the Wesleyan Quadrilateral, Pentecostals gives first place to Scripture. This understanding of Scripture informs the hermeneut which element in the hermeneutical strategy receives greatest weight and also provides an important protection against unrestrained imaginative interpretation since the text ultimately holds an authoritative position.

Outler points out that the current era is becoming increasingly post-critical.[15] Traditionally hermeneutics meant the principles that made a correct reading and application of a text possible but today the importance of a creative encounter with the text has gained a place of prominence in hermeneutic theory. Autry states, "In some quarters the focus of attention has shifted almost completely away from the correct reading toward the consciousness of the interpreter—how his or her encounter with the text affects the person or 'interprets' the interpreter."[16] It is not, in my view, necessary to choose between correct and creative reading; therefore, the proposed hermeneutic here suggests both need to be held together as effective partners in the task of interpretation.

Early Pentecostal hermeneutics are consonant to such a balance as they were obviously open to creative interpretation but also recognized that an understanding of culture and history (correct reading) were sometimes essential for interpreting a text. G. F. Taylor, a leader in the early Pentecostal movement, said, "The best way to understand the parables spoken by our Lord, is to first note the facts from which he drew them."[17] A careful read-

---

14. For example, the pre-critical approach cannot provide help in deciding if women should wear head coverings when attending church in the twenty-first century.

15. Outler, "Toward a Post-Critical Hermeneutics," 281–91.

16. Autry, "Dimensions of Hermeneutics," 30.

17. Taylor, *The Spirit and the Bride*, 112–13. Taylor points out that Jesus drew his parables from the life of the common people. He specifically refers to the parable of the ten virgins indicating it was drawn from ordinary wedding customs. These customs read-

ing of some of the early Pentecostal writings and sermons reveals they did appreciate the importance of history and culture for a true interpretation of a text and Scripture itself claims that our faith rests on events witnessed in history.[18] Christianity is based on both *timeless truth* and also *divine acts in time*. The cross–resurrection complex, an event in history, is central to Christianity (1 Cor 15:12–19) and is the historical event around which the entirety of Scripture revolves. In reality there can be no true *witness* without history; therefore, the historical-grammatical method, though inadequate for the hermeneutical task, remains relevant to it. A distinct Pentecostal hermeneutic for the twenty-first century should employ, even if to a limited degree, the historical-grammatical method for the purpose of limiting creative readings of Scripture.

Myland's Hermeneutic

Mester's speaks of a "dislocation" occurring when "common people" read the Bible.[19] This dislocation results in an emphasis on the meaning the text has for the readers rather than the meaning of the text itself. With the increased emphasis on education and academics among Western Pentecostals since the 1960s came an increased emphasis on historical-grammatical exegesis resulting in a "correct" interpretation of the text overshadowing "creative" interpretation.[20] Early Pentecostals and those outside the Western world were/are more attuned to an experiential understanding of Scripture. For them the immediacy of the Holy Spirit results in an illumination that enables understanding of the biblical text. Multiple meanings and/or deeper spiritual meaning is assigned to a text in accord with the assump-

---

historical realities must be understood if the meaning of the text is to be apprehended.

18. Cf. Acts 2:22–36; John 19:35; 1 Cor 15:12–19; and *Ign. Smyrn.* 1–3; *Ign. Phld.* 8.2; 9.2.

19. Mesters, "The Use of the Bible," 14.

20. The early Pentecostals were primarily interested in the world of the text. Historical criticism shifts the focus from the world of the text to the world behind the text. As Pentecostals increasingly engaged in a historical-grammatical hermeneutic a distinctive Pentecostal hermeneutic all but disappeared. Mark McLean accurately points out that adherence to historical-grammatical hermeneutical (especially what is sometimes referred to as "higher criticism") principles ultimately leads to a rejection of Pentecostal phenomena. McLean, "Toward a Pentecostal Hermeneutic," 37. Some Pentecostals, like Gordon Fee, ultimately reject the Pentecostal doctrine of tongues as the initial evidence of Spirit Baptism partly because of their dependence on historical criticism and the historical-grammatical method.

A Distinct Twenty-first Century Pentecostal Hermeneutic

tion that the Holy Spirit, the true author of the Bible, helps the reader/preacher understand the text. Anderson says, "most Pentecostals rely on an experiential rather than a literal understanding of the Bible."[21] Herein lies a tension for a distinct twenty-first century Pentecostal hermeneutic. How do we engage the immediacy of the Holy Spirit's activity without falling into the labyrinth of hyperactive imagination in the guise of illumination? How do we apply historical-grammatical methodology without losing the insight and power of creative interpretation aided by the Holy Spirit and postmodern methodologies? In response to these questions the following proposal suggests embracing newer hermeneutical methodologies that embrace text/reader partnership in meaning while not completely expelling the historical-grammatical method.

As mentioned in chapter 2, Myland's threefold interpretive method was influential for early Pentecostals and the way they approached interpretation. Myland's hermeneutic employed the Bible Reading method, using the Latter Rain motif as a theological grid, along with openness to the Holy Spirit in an effort to gain Scripture's deeper sense. Pentecostals in the twenty-first century continue to hold to the same basic assumptions of Myland and other early Pentecostals.[22] This means a distinct twenty-first century Pentecostal hermeneutic can embrace a Myland like approach while correcting for the obvious potential for extremism and error. Both the historical-grammatical method and the "tradition" component of the Wesleyan Quadrilateral are helpful here. The historical-grammatical method will enable twenty-first century Pentecostals to accurately determine which Scriptures might legitimately interpret other Scripture and "tradition" will connect contemporary Pentecostal interpretation with historical and orthodox Christianity. Together historical-grammatical method and tradition bring in the theological, historical, cultural and literary information that helps the contemporary Pentecostal hermeneut ascertain what the text says as accurately as possible;[23] however, literary criticism must also be engaged so the Pentecostal hermeneut might allow the world of the text

---

21. Anderson, *An Introduction To Pentecostalism*, 226.

22. One of the basic assumptions held by Pentecostals is that the spiritual realm interacts with the natural realm. Evil angels and the Devil influence the created realm. God and good angels influence and interact with the created realm. The supernatural is part of reality and miraculous events are real historical events rather than myth or legend. Their hermeneutical strategy is informed by these beliefs. Early Pentecostals rejected modernity's view that temporal reality was the only reality.

23. Myland believed we were to first understand the literal meaning of the text.

to engage, correct, challenge, illuminate and speak to the contemporary context. In this way the Pentecostal hermeneutic allows the interpreter a place in the interpretive process, the emergence of creative meaning, and retains Scripture's supremacy thereby maintaining a good balance between "correct" and "creative" meaning.

Since, for Pentecostals, the "creative" meaning is attributed to the work of the Spirit, the *appropriate* role of the Holy Spirit in human experience and in a Pentecostal interpretation of Scripture must be understood and defined.[24] The challenge is to avoid the numerous pitfalls inherent in this perspective. Lack of clarity and consistency in what text/s should be taken literally and which ones should be understood typologically or spiritualized has been, and will always be, problematic.[25] Manipulating a text, intentionally or unintentionally, to obtain a preferred message, and a tendency toward eisegesis must be avoided. Here again the historical-grammatical method can help the twenty-first century Pentecostal hermeneut avoid these dangers, and the literary method properly employed enables the textual world to address the contemporary world in powerful ways.

The distinct Pentecostal approach to interpretation will employ a wide range of methods. The Pentecostal hermeneut should use the historical-grammatical method in a limited manner along with literary critical methods such as narrative criticism, rhetorical criticism, etc. as part of their methodological toolbox. Communication theory will also aid the interpreter in effectively uncovering meaning and significance in the text. The critical and distinctive aspect of the proposed hermeneutic is the Pentecostal story and the Lukan lens that informs the Pentecostal application of methods and strategy in their interpretation of Scripture.

Conclusion

A distinct twenty-first century Pentecostal hermeneutic, like all hermeneutics, looks to interpret Scripture. The interpreter intends to identify meaning

---

24. Fee, "Hermeneutics and Historical Precedent," 122.

25. Miller, *Canadian Pentecostals*, 107. Miller notes that, "Pentecostals sometimes inclined toward an undue subjectivism in doctrine and in practice." He refers to a report of Howard Goss who indicated that in the early days of Pentecost a preacher who did not dig up a new slant on Scripture, or get some new revelation was considered slow, stupid or unspiritual. The danger of unrestrained creative (subjective) interpretation is neither new nor absent. Among Pentecostals, especially in the Majority World context, there is danger of the subjective receiving too much emphasis.

A Distinct Twenty-first Century Pentecostal Hermeneutic

and meaningfulness of the text to the community of believers. The brief discussion in chapter 3 identified four elements necessary for a legitimate, distinct hermeneutic as Scripture, Spirit, community, and trained leader interacting in the process of interpretation. In this chapter we note that the early Pentecostal use of the Bible Reading method draws attention to three critical points relating to a legitimate, distinct hermeneutic. First, Scripture is prioritized—the text stands over the interpreter. Second, Scripture is interpreted in light of Scripture. Third, Pentecostals use interpretive methods from a distinct Pentecostal perspective with the Lukan lens, Pentecostal experience and story, along with Latter Rain convictions informing their methodology. The proposal in this book embraces these same beliefs while engaging methods and strategies consonant with a twenty-first century Pentecostal context. Therefore, our attention must now turn to identifying the interpretive methods that are legitimately engaged by Pentecostals.

CHAPTER 5

TWENTY-FIRST CENTURY PENTECOSTAL HERMENEUTIC METHOD

Introduction

CHAPTER 4 IDENTIFIED THE role of hermeneutics as understood in the Pentecostal context and identified early Pentecostal interpretive practice, highlighting Myland's method, in an effort to establish a starting point. This is helpful as it provides important insight into the Pentecostal community's ethos. The following discussion of appropriate methodology is aided in that chapter 4 established that the Bible Reading method of early Pentecostals was a normative method used by other traditions but they employed the Bible Reading method from a distinct Pentecostal perspective. The way forward then is to identify which of the normative twenty-first century methodologies are consonant with Pentecostal community identity and allow interpretation to flow from the specific, distinct Pentecostal interpretive lens.

All Christians do hermeneutics in one form or another. However, there are three variables among the various methods. The first variable is the elements included in the hermeneutic. Second is the way each of those elements is constructed. Thirdly is the different emphasis that is placed on each part in respect to the other parts.[1] When we speak of a distinct twenty-first century Pentecostal hermeneutic we are not discussing a unique meth-

1. Anderson, "Pentecostal Hermeneutics: Part 1," 1.

Twenty-first Century Pentecostal Hermeneutic Method

od but a distinct way of approaching interpretation and using methods. What makes the following proposal twenty-first century is the way Pentecostals merge the concerns of traditional, conservative hermeneutics with the concerns of postmodern literary criticism. "Pentecostals uniquely use the various genre in the Bible (the historical narratives in particular), and . . . they incorporate church history, personal experiences, theological biases and other elements in their hermeneutic."[2]

Archer, Thomas, and Yong each argue for a tridactic model of interpretation. Archer argues for a twenty-first century interpretive strategy that encompasses community, Scripture, and Holy Spirit. Lowenburg proposes a Pentadactic model of interpretation that includes Scripture, Spirit, community, individual, and theophany.[3] The proposal in this book is a quadradic model that removes theophany from Lowenburg's model and adds the trained individual to Archer's. The following approach also expands, broadens and modifies Archer's proposal in some significant ways. Archer argues primarily from theoretical and philosophical positioning and works primarily from a Western perspective and platform thus his model might more appropriately be called a twenty-first century Western Pentecostal hermeneutic. Considering the twenty-first century Pentecostal context this is too narrow an approach.

The proposal in this book seeks to expand Archer's model beyond a Western context since twenty-first century Pentecostalism is largely non-Western. The largest Pentecostal congregations (also the largest congregations in the world) are in the Majority World. At least 75 percent of the twenty-first century Pentecostal church is in the Majority World. The present context of this author is Africa; therefore, this book intends to expand the discussion to at least include African Pentecostals. Further, much of the current Pentecostal community is non-denominational, independent, and/or charismatic. This is especially true in the West. Many twenty-first century Pentecostals have no direct connection, or at best a secondary connection, with Azusa Street and the early twentieth-century Pentecostal revival. Twenty-first century Pentecostalism is broader than what is sometimes referred to as *classical* Pentecostals; therefore, the following proposal strives to be inclusive of charismatic and independent Pentecostals.

Archer gives good reason to accept the view that narrative criticism effectively serves Pentecostals within a distinct twenty-first century context

---

2. Ibid., 1.
3. Lowenburg, "A Twenty-first Century Pentecostal Hermeneutic," 23ff.

A Distinct Twenty-first Century Pentecostal Hermeneutic

and interpretive approach. However, he fails to give enough attention to the broader genre context of Scripture and the useful place of other literary critical approaches that address these various genres. The following proposal seeks to include a broader literary critical methodology than Archer's singular use of narrative criticism.

Acts 2 and 15 point to a quadratic interaction in the interpretive process. Like Archer and others this author sees the presence of Scripture, Spirit, and community in the interpretive process. However, Acts 2 and 15, as seen in Chapter 3, also clearly reveal a critical role for trained leaders in the interpretive process and the Pastoral Epistles also support their place in the interpretive process.[4] Consequently the following proposal is a quadradic interaction between Spirit, Scripture, trained leader and Pentecostal community in the interpretive process. The proposed methodology also includes a modified role for the historical-grammatical method and gives a place for literary critical methodologies and acknowledges a role for linguistic theoretical approaches to interpretation.

The Historical-Grammatical Method

The first task of hermeneutics is exegesis for we must first determine what a text meant. The majority of Pentecostal scholars today practice the modified historical critical method of exegesis known as the historical-grammatical method along with emphasis on authorial intent.[5] Conservatives, including most Pentecostals, agree that the historical-grammatical method is the appropriate hermeneutical method.[6] The historical-grammatical method seeks to identify the originally intended meaning. At the level of exegesis the interpreter, Pentecostal or otherwise, must strive to filter out bias, presupposition, experience, theological perspective, etc. In a legitimate, distinct twenty-first century Pentecostal hermeneutic these will enter

---

4. This is developed later in this book.

5. Archer, *A Pentecostal Hermeneutic*, 131.

6. Anderson, "Pentecostal Hermeneutics: Part 1," 5. Anderson, representative of the majority of Pentecostal scholars, argues that the historical-grammatical method is the appropriate methodology. As African Pentecostal practitioners enter the arena the rejection of allegorization, typology, and multiple meaning approaches is being challenged. African Pentecostals are more open to these approaches than most Western Pentecostals. The full impact this will have remains to be seen. This writer is among the minority Pentecostal position that believes a distinct Pentecostal hermeneutic must move beyond the historical-grammatical method.

Twenty-first Century Pentecostal Hermeneutic Method

the interpretive strategy at some point. For now, it is helpful to acknowledge that interpretation must begin at the level of grasping the originally intended meaning. The historical-grammatical method is the appropriate tool to accomplish this goal.

Scripture, whatever else it might be, is literature and most Pentecostals, like Fee, want to employ the historical-grammatical method exclusively.[7] Some, like Archer, believe historical-grammatical method has no place in twenty-first century Pentecostal interpretation.[8] The proposed hermeneutic in this book contends the historical-grammatical method has a limited place and is a helpful protection against some of the excesses that Pentecostals are vulnerable to because of their pneumatology and openness to experiential encounter. However, historical-grammatical method in the Pentecostal context cannot operate with modern presuppositions.[9] Pentecostal presuppositions allow for, even expect, the supernatural and God's immediate intervention within history; therefore, the historical-grammatical method must operate from a Pentecostal worldview that allows for the supernatural.

Some African scholars are among those who would employ the historical-grammatical method exclusively. Oleka argues for a traditional historical-grammatical approach to hermeneutics.[10] For him hermeneutics is discovering the author's intended meaning. Samuel Ngewa says, "I advocate that the approach to the Scriptures as the source for African theology be that of first attempting to know the meaning of a text in light of what the author intended to communicate to his original readers. Only after that has been done will we, with accuracy, apply the text to our situations."[11]

---

7. Fee, *New Testament Exegesis*, 5ff.

8. Archer, *A Pentecostal Hermeneutic*, 148. Archer states, "Pentecostals have adopted the Evangelical Historical Critical methods . . . This has affected North American Pentecostal community identity—an identity that becomes less Pentecostal."

9. Historical criticism is interested in recovering the world behind the text. Some of its practitioners claim the biblical accounts are not true history. The historical–grammatical method focuses on authorial intent and static meaning in the original text. It is important to note that these critical methods were developed because people were convinced that Scripture was God's word to humankind and were deeply concerned to interpret it with integrity. Pentecostals must carefully consider how the historical-grammatical method is to be applied. As chapter three established the Pentecostal hermeneut finds inspiration and authority in the received text and historical–grammatical methodology can assist the discovery of meaning in the received text.

10. Oleka, "Interpreting and Applying the Bible," 104–25.

11. Ngewa, "The Validity of Meaning," 51.

A Distinct Twenty-first Century Pentecostal Hermeneutic

Chris Ukachukwu also argues for this approach to hermeneutics.[12] For these scholars the hermeneut is only able to contextualize the original meaning into new circumstances. If they are to speak effectively to the community and broader church in the twenty-first century Pentecostals must move beyond the exclusive use of historical-grammatical methodology. It is necessary, especially in the African context, to control creative interpretation but a *legitimate*, distinct Pentecostal hermeneutic must also engage methodology that recognizes the interpreter's involvement in the creation of meaning.

Hart's attempt to steer a course between objectivism and relativistic pluralism is a preferred position to follow.[13] Current hermeneutical theory generally accepts the idea of the world behind the text, the world in the text and the world in front of the text. Pentecostals are primarily concerned with the world of the text and the world in front of the text. The historical-grammatical method enables the hermeneut to better comprehend the world of the text. For this reason I would want to give a more meaningful place to the historical-grammatical method than Archer or Lowenburg[14] seem to intend. Archer correctly points out that historical critical methods look for the determinate meaning of the text. Archer wants to give the text an "indeterminate" meaning.[15] I prefer to recognize the text as having an underdeterminate meaning that recognizes "text inherent meaning constraints."[16] This position does not restrict meaning as Oleka, Ngewa and Ukachukwu and others want to nor does it allow meaning to be as free floating as "indeterminate meaning" might.

Pentecostals in some ways are Bultmannian, but unlike Bultmann Pentecostals would not claim the actual history to be irrelevant nor would they reject the miraculous.[17] Generally Pentecostals come to the text as

---

12. Ukachukwu, *Intercultural Hermeneutics*, 32–35.

13. Archer, *A Pentecostal Hermeneutic*, 152 ff. See Hart, *Faith Thinking*, 116–26.

14. Lowenburg, "A Twenty-first Century Pentecostal Hermeneutic," 3–8.

15. Archer, *A Pentecostal Hermeneutic*, 153.

16. Eco, *Interpretation and Overinterpretation*, 23. "Indeterminate" seems to open the text too widely to the reader's imagination. "Underdeterminate," while allowing the reader's involvement in meaning production also recognizes the text's power to restrict and guide the reader toward certain desired understandings. Eco writes, "No reader-oriented theory can avoid the constraints presented by the message" (ibid., 43).

17. Pentecostals would absolutely reject Bultmann's statement, "an historical event which involves a resurrection from the dead is utterly inconceivable" (Bultmann, "A Reply," 39).

Twenty-first Century Pentecostal Hermeneutic Method

though the textual event was the real historical event. For Pentecostals the biblical account is the one that matters. It is the biblical account that is the word of God and contains revelation not what historical reality may or may not lie behind the text. Should historical criticism establish an alternate reality the Pentecostal will likely dismiss historical criticism and embrace the biblical account. Pentecostals in practice stand with Bultmann's view that the *kerygma* is not to be sought in uncovering the historical Jesus (world behind the text) but in an encounter with the Christ of faith (world of the text). Like Gerhard Ebeling, Pentecostals believe Christianity stands or falls on the validity of certain historical facts (the cross-resurrection complex especially). Pentecostals would fall into the camp with Pannenberg who calls for an adjustment of historical presuppositions. If God is the moving factor of history rather than humanity then the mysterious/supernatural elements of Scripture are not necessarily mythological but may be factual. For Pentecostals these supernatural elements may also be experienced in the now as they were in the past.

Pentecostals should and do employ the historical-grammatical method to the extent that it enables comprehension of the text in its received form. Invaluable information is gained through this process. Details of culture, beliefs, practice, life-style, human conditions, real life issues, etc. emerge as historical-grammatical method is applied. This information often aids in the process of legitimate application of the biblical text to contemporary life. However, Pentecostals come to the interpretive task holding to a specific understanding of historical possibilities. Pentecostals understand historical possibility from a stance that sees God active in history. Because God is active in history a single event that is unlike the norm of historical action is possible. The resurrection of Jesus, rejected outright by a historical-critical approach that is anthropologically centered and rests on the foundation of a naturalistic view of history, is taken as historical fact because God could have raised Jesus from the dead. The Exodus with all its supernatural elements is embraced because God the creator can do those things. In a legitimate, distinct twenty-first century Pentecostal setting the practitioner of historical-grammatical method rejects the prejudice that precludes God from active engagement in the affairs of men.

It is also important to remember that elements of the historical-grammatical method are not immune from subjectivism.[18] The briefest of surveys will reveal a wide variance of opinion among redaction critics, form

---

18. Anderson, "Pentecostal Hermeneutic: Part 2," 19.

A Distinct Twenty-first Century Pentecostal Hermeneutic

critics, source critics, historical critics, etc. concerning the world behind most texts. This variance is evidence of subjectivity indicating that interpretation is not absent in the historical-grammatical method. The objective observer required and assumed by this method does not exist. Pentecostals in the twenty-first century can and should use the historical-grammatical method since it assists the interpreter in discovering what the text meant.[19] However, because of its inherent shortcomings and dissonance with certain aspects of Pentecostal ethos, the *Pentecostal* interpreter needs more than the historical-grammatical method.

Postmodern Literary Criticism

Since Pentecostals deliberately use the various genres of Scripture in a unique way[20] their interpretive methodology requires the use of postmodern literary criticism along with the historical-grammatical method. This is especially true of biblical narrative—especially the historical narrative of Acts. Pentecostals attribute greater didactic value to the historical narratives, namely Acts, than others. Pentecostals engage these historical narratives to a greater extent than others in the construction of doctrine.[21] Consequently, narrative criticism is an important interpretive method in a twenty-first century Pentecostal hermeneutic.

Many evangelical scholars reject this approach and prioritize propositional literary forms over narrative. Gordon Fee, a Pentecostal, argues against the use of narrative and historical precedent in establishing doctrine.[22] Stronstad has presented a persuasive argument supporting the place of narrative in a Pentecostal approach to establishing doctrine.[23] He builds his case by arguing that Acts 15 shows historical precedent to be prior to and superior to the proof from Scripture. Stronstad may take too extreme a position here but he does establish that historical precedent was sufficient

---

19. As Krister Stendahl observes, at this level Pentecostal and agnostic are equally capable. Stendahl, "Biblical Theology," 1:422. It is at the level of meaning that the believer and agnostic part company.

20. Stronstad, "Pentecostal Hermeneutics," 215–22. Stronstad points out that Pentecostals use narrative, especially the historical narrative of Acts in a particular manner.

21. Anderson, "Pentecostal Hermeneutics: Part 1," 2.

22. Fee, *Gospel and Spirit*, 100–104.

23. Stronstad, "Pentecostal Hermeneutics," 215–22. Stronstad makes a strong case that Luke, in the Gospel and Acts, intended to teach theology.

Twenty-first Century Pentecostal Hermeneutic Method

to establish a norm on at least one occasion. J. Ramsey Michaels writes, "There is nothing wrong in principle with deriving normative beliefs and practices from narratives."[24] Much more recently Joel B. Green has argued that Luke's Gospel as narrative is perhaps more subtle than didactic material but no less theological. Green argues Luke is deliberately teaching theology.[25] There seems to be adequate reason to accept Stonstad's contention that Pentecostals legitimately use narrative in their development of theology and practice; therefore, narrative criticism is both a legitimate and necessary method.

The purpose of this book is not to debate Pentecostal theology but to identify a legitimate and distinct hermeneutical approach. The intent is to present a distinct twenty-first century hermeneutic by which Pentecostals may continue their work of theology and speak effectively to the larger Christian body. Narrative is a major biblical genre and while scholarly consensus is lacking there is sufficient scholarly support to argue that narrative has a legitimate place in theological and doctrinal discussion. To those who claim otherwise we can ask, "by what authority should it be accepted that the narrative literature is in some way inferior for building doctrine?"[26] Subsequently we assert that narrative criticism is a method legitimately embraced in the twenty-first century by Pentecostals. The volume of narrative content in Scripture indicates it is an essential method.

For Pentecostals the narratives are true accounts. As such they are in Anderson's words, "the first step in the empirical-deductive process of establishing truth."[27] Pentecostals see God acting throughout church history as he did in Acts. If Scripture records God acting in a certain way Pentecostals conclude God acts in this way. This is part of the Pentecostal ethos, or as Archer puts it, part of the Pentecostal story which frames Pentecostalism's "Central Narrative Convictions."[28] Pentecostals will use narrative criticism deliberately acknowledging their biases, presuppositions, and theological positions. By doing so Pentecostals intentionally allow the text to challenge and or change them.

---

24. Michaels, "Evidences of the Spirit," 203.
25. Green, "Learning Theological Interpretation," 55–78.
26. Anderson, "Pentecostal Hermeneutics: Part 2," 16.
27. Ibid., 17.
28. Archer, *A Pentecostal Hermeneutic*, 96.

A Distinct Twenty-first Century Pentecostal Hermeneutic

For Archer, narrative criticism is "the method" for a Pentecostal hermeneutic[29] but the proposal here is that narrative criticism is only one component. Narrative criticism provides the tools to enable the hermeneut to navigate her way through various types of narrative and understand them. It is an important method since narrative comprises a large portion of biblical text. Narrative criticism focuses on the story-world of the text and is a text-centered approach. This resonates well with the Pentecostal understanding of Scripture and approach to interpretation. It allows Scripture to retain its primary position and gives room for interpretive imagination.

Reader-response is also part of the proposed methodology because postmodern communication theory recognizes a role for reader/hearer in the formation of meaning. The reader/hearer is significantly involved in the formation of meaningfulness or significance of a communication. Some proponents of reader-response present a position where a *radical reader* determines the meaning.[30] Pentecostalism's high view of Scripture cannot embrace such an extreme position yet we cannot ignore the place the reader plays in the formation of meaning and significance. In light of this, Vanhoozer's "Reader-Respect" approach seems more appropriate for in this approach the text limits the possible interpretations the reader might supply.[31]

In a distinct Pentecostal hermeneutic the text must be allowed to dominate the interpretive process. Only when the text holds the priority position can it inform, transform, and challenge the reader. A reader-dominated approach violates Pentecostalism's high view of Scripture among other essential Pentecostal beliefs. It is also true that the Pentecostal hermeneut will deliberately "incorporate . . . personal experiences, theological biases and other elements in their hermeneutic,"[32] since intentionality aids in preventing them from controlling the meaning found in the text. Bringing personal experience to the interpretive task enables the text's meaning to have significance. Twenty-first century Pentecostal hermeneuts will purposefully use a *conservative* reader-response criticism to acknowledge and give voice to the interpreter's role in making meaning and identifying meaningfulness.[33]

---

29. Ibid., 166ff.
30. Vanhoozer, "The Reader," 306.
31. Ibid., 305–12.
32. Anderson, "Pentecostal Hermeneutics: Part 1," 1.
33. Archer, *A Pentecostal Hermeneutic*, 171–82. Archer provides a healthy discussion

Twenty-first Century Pentecostal Hermeneutic Method

Archer, because of his focus on biblical narrative, completely ignores rhetorical criticism. However, rhetorical criticism has great value in aiding interpretation of the epistles especially. Although Pentecostals view Scripture through a Lukan lens they are very interested in the epistles. The "occasional" nature of the epistles makes them very helpful for Pentecostals who want to know how to live out apostolic Christianity in the twenty-first century. Rhetorical criticism aids the Pentecostal hermeneut as she or he seeks to interpret the epistles.

Language is made up of words and words are symbols not signs. Smoke is a sign that a fire exists, but the word dog has no direct relationship to a four-legged animal that barks; therefore, it is a symbol not a sign. Communication involves the placing together of these symbols in order to convey meaning. Foss states that we practice rhetorical criticism as "we engage in a process of thinking about symbols, discovering how they work, and trying to figure out why they affect us."[34]

In relation to literary communication rhetorical criticism investigates how the linguistic symbols work together to present a specific message. Theoretical principles of how specific types of communication operate help us both identify the type of literature (genre) we are dealing with and how that type of literature normally operates as communication. A legal document is written differently than a personal letter. Interpreting a last will and testament as though it were a personal letter could lead to some disastrous outcomes. Rhetorical criticism helps us identify literary genre and interpret them appropriately, therefore, it is a legitimate hermeneutical method in the Pentecostal context.

Canonical Criticism

Added to the Pentecostal interpretive arsenal of historical-grammatical method and literary critical methods is canonical criticism. Neither Archer

---

of how a conservative reader-response approach serves a Pentecostal hermeneutic. The critical issue is that a proper interaction between text and reader be maintained as meaning is negotiated by the interpreter. At times Archer seems to be more open to a freedom for the reader than I am comfortable with. I contend the text has meaning that must be understood and honored. There is real meaning in the text or it would not have been written. Inspiration suggests this meaning is relevant to all people in all contexts. This cannot be violated. The text may have underdeterminate meaning but it has meaning.

34. Foss, *Rhetorical Criticism*, 3. Foss' book provides good information on how to practice rhetorical criticism effectively.

A Distinct Twenty-first Century Pentecostal Hermeneutic

nor Lowenburg discusses canonical criticism; however, they broach the concept by noting that Pentecostals approach interpretation with a Lukan lens. Max Turner has observed, "it is the pronounced intertextuality of wording and themes between Luke and Acts that affords the reader the keenest interpretive insight into both texts."[35] It is generally accepted that Luke–Acts is a two-volume work by one author. As such they can be read together with great benefit. However, canonically the Gospel of John separates Luke and Acts and this canonical reality holds promise for Pentecostal interpretation and theology.

Pentecostal pneumatology is distinct in their view that the baptism in the Spirit is separate from and subsequent to salvation. They also contend (at least *classical* Pentecostals) that speaking in tongues is the initial evidence of baptism in the Spirit. There has been a strong debate between James D. G. Dunn and Pentecostal scholars Roger Stronstad and Robert Menzies on this issue. The debate has largely focused on the matter of subsequence. Canonical criticism assists Pentecostals in their theological position of subsequence for the baptism in the Spirit.

R. W. Wall claims that Acts provides a better sequel to the Gospel of John than Luke. Wall writes, "the importance of retaining the final shape of the NT rather than combining Luke and Acts as a single narrative is indicated by the significant roles performed by Peter and the Holy Spirit in Acts where Jesus is absent—roles for which Luke's Gospel does not adequately prepare the reader of Acts."[36] Wall's statement draws attention to the value of canonical criticism in that it allows the interpreter to approach Acts from a different angle than if Luke–Acts is read as a single document. Canonical criticism allows the interpreter to read Acts as continuing the story of Jesus in the four Gospels.

Joel Green, referring to the Dunn–Stronstad–Menzies debate, points out the significance of canonical criticism in that debate.[37] John chapters 14–16 contain Jesus' teaching on the Holy Spirit's post-ascension role. The Holy Spirit will continue the ministry of Jesus through his church. In John 20:19–23 Jesus appears to the disciples and breathes on them (New Testament conversion). The breath of God made man a living soul (Gen 2:7). The penalty for disobedience would be death (Gen 2:17). Jesus' breathing

---

35. Turner, "Luke and the Spirit," 282.

36. Wall, "The Acts of the Apostles," 29. Agreement with Wall's position here is not the critical issue.

37. Green, "Interpretation, Reflection, Formation," 440 ff.

Twenty-first Century Pentecostal Hermeneutic Method

on the disciples can be understood as restoration of the breath of God lost as consequence of the fall (conversion). This understanding of John 20:19–23 provides canonical support for Pentecostalism's understanding of subsequence. John 21:15–17 records Peter's restoration. This is preparation for Peter's leading role in the early section of Acts. This suggests that canonical criticism offers important aid for Pentecostals in their theological development of pneumatology. Brueggemann writes, "The recent recovery of canon as an interpretive reality has gone far to legitimate in a fresh way the theological intentionality of the text, and intentionality celebrated in a number of faith communities both Jewish and Christian."[38] Canonical criticism is a legitimate interpretive method and promises to offer twenty-first century Pentecostal a fresh place to do Pentecostal theological investigation, especially in the area of distinctives.

The Early Bible Reading Method

Both Archer and Noel call for the reengagement of the Bible Reading method in a twenty-first century Pentecostal hermeneutic. This book contends that canonical criticism is a more appropriate method to accomplish the task they intend. However the Bible Reading method was critical in the development of the early Pentecostal theology of baptism in the Spirit and provided the biblical grounding for their worldview. Though the method should not be reappropriated in the twenty-first century examining it brings insight into some essential aspects of Pentecostal interpretive strategy.

In the beginning Pentecostals followed the Holiness movement's Bible Reading method. However, Pentecostals employed this method in a unique way. They used the Bible Reading method from a Pentecostal perspective. That is, the Pentecostal story and the Latter Rain motif informed the way they understood the Scriptures and applied the Bible Reading method. It was the Bible Reading method that enabled Pentecostals to develop their doctrine of baptism in the Spirit.[39] Some would call the Pentecostal doctrine of baptism in the Spirit with the evidence of tongues an "extreme"[40]

---

38. Brueggemann, *The Book That Breathes*, ix.
39. Archer, *A Pentecostal Hermeneutic*, 124.
40. Eco, *Interpretation and Overinterpretation*, 110. The oneness doctrine expressed by Haywood is another "extreme" doctrine that arose from exercising the Bible Reading method. Haywood claimed that a clear reading of John 14:9 resulted in the conclusion that Jesus is the Father as well as the Son. Haywood, *The Victim of the Flaming Sword*,

A Distinct Twenty-first Century Pentecostal Hermeneutic

interpretation. To Pentecostals it is a self-evident truth. Their use of the Bible Reading method from a Pentecostal perspective enabled such interpretations.

Archer argues that the Bible Reading method was concerned with capturing the *inner texture of the text*.[41] Vernon Robbins identifies inner textual analysis as a means to examine and understand how words, word patterns, voices, etc. work together to produce meanings and meaning-effects.[42] The concern is preventing the potential misunderstanding of a text that might occur. Inner texture analysis enables the hermeneut to identify the intention of the text and the text's cues to its meaning. Rhetorical criticism and semiotics are tools adequate for this task. As already argued these are essential methods in the distinct twenty-first century Pentecostal hermeneutic hence there is no need to resurrect the Bible Reading method for this purpose.

The Bible Reading method is a form of proof texting and some today reject proof texting as a legitimate hermeneutical method; however, Bernard Ramm argued that there is a proper place for proof texting in hermeneutics.[43] He argued that it is an appropriate task for the Protestant interpreter to systematically collect and catalogue all the biblical facts on a subject. He qualifies this by arguing that historical-grammatical methodology must be applied to insure that all the texts gathered into the system are properly applicable to that subject. The final stage of the Bible Reading method was harmonization as the means to "effective doctrinal synthesis."[44] Archer argues that harmonization is part of a Pentecostal hermeneutical strategy and is necessary for one to have a "canonically informed biblical

---

17. This became a major dispute among Pentecostals and resulted in a division among their ranks. Interestingly, it was Pentecostals adherence to orthodox Christianity (what the Wesleyan Quadrilateral would call tradition) that resulted in the majority of them rejecting this interpretation.

41. Archer, *A Pentecostal Hermeneutic*, 163. Archer does not explain or illustrate how the Bible Reading method did this. It is not clear that it is necessary to use the Bible Reading method to capture the inner texture of the text. Consequently, Archer's position here is not adequately supported by evidence.

42. Robbins, *Exploring the Texture of Texts*, 7 ff.

43. Ramm, *Protestant Biblical Interpretation*, 172–78. See also, Klein et.al., *Introduction*, 160 for a similar position.

44. Archer, *A Pentecostal Hermeneutic*, 75. Harmonization assumes a world behind the text from which the texts being harmonized are drawn from. Harmonization then operates on assumptions shared with higher criticism methodology.

Twenty-first Century Pentecostal Hermeneutic Method

and systematic theology."[45] Twenty-first century Pentecostals must engage in serious doctrinal discussion and Archer proposes using the Bible Reading method without its "philosophical context" for this task.[46] How one empties the Bible Reading method of its philosophical context is uncertain, if indeed it is possible. A preferred approach is to apply canonical criticism along with other effective methodologies to the important task of ongoing theological investigation.

Pentecostals in the twenty-first century, like the early Pentecostals, primarily look to the Scriptures not to discover some proposition or historical event but to discover truth for today's life situation. Though twenty-first century Pentecostals will move beyond the hermeneutical practices of early Pentecostals they retain the core aspects of Pentecostalism's ethos and ideology. As a result their hermeneutic will use historical-grammatical, postmodern literary methods along with canonical criticism. Doing so respects the text's inherent meaning and limitation on possible meanings an interpreter might discern and/or impose. This eclectic approach to methodology also allows the interpreter's involvement in creating meaning and meaningfulness.

Conclusion

We are not attempting to create a new, novel or unique method since Pentecostals use the same methods as other interpreters. The historical-grammatical method aids in exegesis and various postmodern methodologies aid the Pentecostal hermeneut by allowing him to navigate between the twin towers of text-centered and reader-centered approaches. The twenty-first century Pentecostal hermeneut recognizes that interpretation looks for both meaning and meaningfulness and uses methods that enable both.

Pentecostal interpreters deliberately bring their community narrative, ideology and ethos to the task of interpretation. They do not allow these to dominate the text but are deliberate about bringing them to the interpretive process so they might avoid eisegesis. Pentecostals, because of their high view of Scripture, maintain openness for the text to correct, challenge, and re-form their beliefs and practices; therefore, methods, strategy, community ethos, presuppositions, and bias are subject to scriptural interrogation.

45. Ibid., 75.
46. Ibid., 161.

A Distinct Twenty-first Century Pentecostal Hermeneutic

The discussion, in chapter 3, of a biblical foundation for our proposed hermeneutic identified an interpretive strategy as well as necessary methodologies. The strategy identified suggested that the proposed hermeneutic strategy consist of the interaction of Scripture, Spirit, community, and trained leader. This strategy is worked out in the next chapter.

CHAPTER 6

TWENTY-FIRST CENTURY PENTECOSTAL HERMENEUTIC STRATEGY

Introduction

IN CHAPTER 5 THE discussion dealt with methodologies that are legitimately practiced by the Pentecostal hermeneut in the twenty-first century. Along with methodology there are several elements that interact in the process of interpretation. Archer and others identify Scripture, Holy Spirit, and community as the three elements interacting in the hermeneutical process. Our review of Acts 2 and 15 suggests four elements (Scripture, Holy Spirit, trained leader, and community) are involved in the interpretive process. In this book these four elements are presented as part of the strategy for a distinct Pentecostal hermeneutic for the twenty-first century. The term "strategy" is used here only to distinguish these four elements from hermeneutical methods.

The Holy Spirit

The discussion begins with the role of the Holy Spirit in a distinct twenty-first century Pentecostal hermeneutic.

Although Pentecostals prioritize Scripture in their interpretive strategy we begin the discussion with the Holy Spirit's place in the interpretive process. There are two primary reasons for doing so. First, it is perhaps the

A Distinct Twenty-first Century Pentecostal Hermeneutic

area of greatest contention and confusion between Pentecostals and non-Pentecostals. Second, there are aspects of the Holy Spirit's role and place that are best considered before discussing the other elements. For these reasons we begin our discussion with the role and place of the Holy Spirit in the interpretive process.

Every traditional, Christian method of interpretation acknowledges a place for the Holy Spirit in the interpretive process. The biblical model seen in Acts 2 and 15 identifies the Holy Spirit as active in the interpretive process, and the writer of the Pastoral Epistles claims a role for the Holy Spirit (1 Tim 3:16). Contemporary hermeneutic theories also argue for a legitimate place for the Holy Spirit and most, if not all, scholars accept some degree of pneumatic dimension to biblical hermeneutics. Pentecostals clearly assume a critical role for the Holy Spirit in their hermeneutic. The challenge is to accurately and adequately articulate how the Holy Spirit is engaged in the Pentecostal hermeneutic and how, if at all, that engagement differs from other approaches.

Most would agree that the Holy Spirit is active in three areas. First, the Spirit *via* inspiration is engaged in the production of the written text (1 Tim 2:15; Heb 1:1–2). Second, the Holy Spirit was engaged in the transmission of the text. As a consequence we can argue the locus of inspiration and authority is in the received text not some elusive *original manuscript*.[1] Third, the Holy Spirit is engaged in the interpretive process. The Holy Spirit's voice is not limited to an ancient text but continues to be heard in the present. He is speaking in the Pentecostal community, world, events, etc. that initiate the search for biblical answers to life's situations. The Spirit is also active in the interpreter, lay or trained, guiding them and granting insight into the text's meaning. As Archer acknowledges, "The role of the Holy Spirit in the hermeneutical process is to lead and guide the community in understanding the present meaningfulness of Scripture."[2]

A distinct Pentecostal hermeneutic does not, however, claim special insight available to the Pentecostal interpreter as a result of Spirit Baptism.[3] The Pentecostal experience of Baptism in the Spirit does not provide the Pentecostal hermeneut with a Spirit provided, *deeper insight*

---

1. Wooden, "The Role of 'the Septuagint,'" 144.

2. Archer, *A Pentecostal Hermeneutic for the Twenty-first Century*, 182.

3. F. L. Arrington and Howard Ervin are exceptions. Arrington and Ervin each argue for a special insight for Pentecostals because of their pneumatic experience. See Arrington, "Hermeneutics, Historical Perspective," 382; Ervin, "Hermeneutics," 16–23. These are elitist positions not shared by this author and most Pentecostals.

Twenty-first Century Pentecostal Hermeneutic Strategy

into Scripture's meaning.[4] Such claims do not represent a genuine Pentecostal hermeneutic. The Pentecostal experience impacts interpretation by creating specific presuppositions. These presuppositions are deliberately engaged by the Pentecostal hermeneut. However, contra Arlington and Ervin, Pentecostals do not possess some spiritual insight that is unavailable to non-Pentecostals.

The Holy Spirit illuminates the understanding of the interpreter. Paul addresses this issue in 1 Corinthians 2:10–14. Among evangelicals and Pentecostals there are two opinions concerning what this means. One school of thought argues that the human mind, unaided by the Holy Spirit, cannot grasp the revelation of Scripture. A second school of thought argues the problem in understanding Scripture is not intellect but will. Debating this issue is beyond the limits of this book, but what matters here is that Pentecostals do not differ from their evangelical brothers and sisters in how they understand 1 Corinthians 2:10–14.

Thomas points out that Scripture is normative for Pentecostals and they seek to live life in light of its teaching.[5] Knowing and doing God's will is the Pentecostal's primary motivation for reading and interpreting Scripture. All Pentecostals (academic, trained leader, and individual lay person) expect the Holy Spirit to speak through Scripture. They expect the Holy Spirit to reveal meaning in the text. Acts 2 and 15 provide biblical background and support for this expectation. The New Testament's use of the Old Testament also lends support for the Pentecostal understanding of the Spirit's role in interpretation. What a genuine, distinct twenty-first century Pentecostal hermeneutic does not do is claim special insight into Scripture's deeper meaning that is unavailable to non-Pentecostals. Pentecostal pneumatology and experience and their accompanying presuppositions may, however, result in Pentecostals identifying unique meaningfulness in a text.

Pentecostal pneumatology increases the danger of mistaking an inner voice of psychological need for the voice of the Spirit. Giving the Bible a proper place of authority is an aid to overcoming this danger. If God's word is encountered in the Scriptures then it is reasonable to assume that a too subjective interpretation of Scripture is improper. If God communicates to us through the words of the Bible then it "is hard to imagine God speaking a

---

4. The proposed Pentecostal hermeneutic enables spiritual insight beyond the historical-grammatical method; however, such insight and meaning does not derive from the Pentecostal experience of Spirit Baptism.

5. Thomas, "Reading the Bible," 118.

message through the words of Scripture that is unrelated to those words."[6] Thus the text of the Bible serves as a boundary around possible subjective meanings and applications that might arise from an inappropriate emphasis on the Spirit's role in hermeneutics. The Holy Spirit does not speak in the present in ways that contradict what he has spoken in Scripture.

Achtemeier recognizes the role of the Holy Spirit at work in aiding the writers of Scripture to communicate God's word to their audience. He argues that, only as we are "faithful to the impulse of the Holy Spirit" can we effectively communicate God's will and purpose for our time.[7] This suggests the Holy Spirit is actively engaged in aiding the interpreter (ancient or modern) to effectively re-present Scripture within a new context to express God's will and purpose for that context. We see this in the Gospel of Luke. Thiselton says, "Luke's very way of re-presenting the events of the gospel, and of interweaving them with the overarching frame of the Old Testament and other intertextual material, portrays Luke himself as a model interpreter of theological truth."[8] Though the Spirit does not contradict Scripture he is actively engaged in aiding the interpreter to re-present Scripture so that God's will in a current context is revealed.

In this role the Holy Spirit engages with the interpreter, Scripture, and community. The activity is beyond objective observation, consequently any attempt to describe the Spirit's involvement in a Pentecostal hermeneutic is limited. In John chapters 13–17 Jesus makes it clear that the Holy Spirit will continue his ministry through the life of his disciples. Fowl states, "The Spirit's intervention and interpretive work is crucial if the followers of Jesus are faithfully to carry on the mission Jesus gives them."[9] We can conclude that the outcome of the Spirit's involvement in the interpretive process is the enabling of disciples to continue Jesus' ministry. For Pentecostals the role of the Spirit is twofold: first, the Spirit guides and empowers the church to fulfill its missionary task; second, the Spirit enables the church to understand Scripture and reality to enable living obediently as the people of God in the world.

---

6. Ferguson, *Biblical Hermeneutics*, 125.

7. Achtemeier, *Inspiration and Authority*, 138. Achtemeier is arguing that the Holy Spirit was active as the writers of Scripture were shaping the traditions to communicate God's will to their audience; however, he would recognize that the Holy Spirit is also engaged in our retelling of those traditions to our community.

8. Thiselton, "The Hermenetical Dynamics," 22.

9. Fowl, *Engaging Scripture*, 98.

Twenty-first Century Pentecostal Hermeneutic Strategy

A critical point for a Pentecostal hermeneutic to answer is how this operates and how one can determine what is and is not the activity of the Spirit. As Arrington suggests the starting point is for the Pentecostal hermeneut to approach Scripture prayerfully and with their mind open to the witness of the Spirit.[10] The current context of the community draws attention to what the Spirit is currently speaking. The operation of charismata (1 Cor 12:3–12, 28; Rom 12:6–8), visions, experience, and testimonies are also means by which the Spirit speaks to the community. However as the Wesleyan Quadrilateral, the Pentecostal high view of Scripture and Paul's admonition would each suggest, Scripture must be held above, and allowed to sit in judgment on, these other means of speaking. Scripture, trained leaders and the community interacting assist the hermeneut in discerning the voice of the Spirit.

The Holy Spirit manifests his presence within the community of faith (1 Cor 12:7). Charismatic gifts, preaching, teaching, ministry, prayer, etc. are ways the Holy Spirit may speak and manifest his presence. As Thomas notes, and the personal experience of this writer affirms, the community participates in assessing the validity of these various manifestations and determining if they are genuinely the voice of the Spirit.[11] Acceptance or rejection may take place immediately or may occur over time as the community carefully considers the manifestation. This is where trained leaders perform a critical role. The Pauline Epistles and the tasking of Timothy and Titus all point to the critical role of trained leaders in aiding the community to determine the validity of messages presented via supposed manifestation of the Spirit.

A further validating element is the response of those outside of the community. Believers of other traditions, even non-believers, can and do respond to Pentecostal interpretation. Pentecostals believe God is at work in his world. Though they embrace the "Full Gospel" they do not believe the Spirit works exclusively in them. Missionaries engage in mission fully convinced the Spirit has been active in these places long before they arrive. Pentecostals agree that the Spirit is at work among all Christians. Consequently as Archer notes, "Pentecostals will discern what the Spirit is saying to them from outside their community."[12] The "tradition" quadrant of the Wesleyan Quadrilateral enables the Spirit to speak using the voice of the

---

10. Arrington, "The Use of the Bible," 105.
11. Thomas, "Reading the Bible," 119.
12. Archer, *A Pentecostal Hermeneutic*, 184.

broader church. In this way the Holy Spirit may provide a corrective and/or validating word to the Pentecostal community.

First Corinthians 2:10–14

Speaking of the Holy Spirit's activity in the interpretive process requires us to discuss the *pneumatic person*.[13] First Corinthians 2:10–14 is helpful here. Paul clearly states that unbelievers do not *accept* the things of the Spirit. He does not say they do not intellectually grasp what the Scriptures say. The issue is belief. If a person does not believe in miracles then Jesus' walking on the water is foolishness to them. Consequently unbelievers understand but reject what Scripture says. Believers, on the other hand, understand and embrace the claims of Scripture. What differs for the pneumatic person is that the Holy Spirit has changed their will not their intellectual capacity.

Anderson notes a second important point here: There is a difference between meaning and meaningfulness or significance.[14] Meaningfulness or significance has to do with the emotional impact of a word, phrase, sentence, or account on a person. It is necessary to distinguish between understanding what something means and its meaningfulness or significance. The word "meaning" is often used when "significance" is intended. Let me provide a personal illustration. On November 9, 2008 there was an obituary in the *Guardian*. The obituary was for Donna Dianne Purdy. Many people read the obituary and understood what it meant but it had no emotional impact on them. Some read it, understood what it meant, and experienced an emotional response, because they had some level of relationship with Donna and her obituary had meaningfulness. I read it and filled the page with tears, experiencing a deep emotional trauma, because Donna Dianne Purdy was my wife. The Holy Spirit brings meaningfulness and significance to Scripture for the pneumatic person. This is what Paul means in 1 Corinthians 2:10–14.

---

13. I use the term pneumatic person to refer to believers. In 1 Cor 2:10–14 Paul is speaking about the difference between those who have the Spirit and those who do not. He is distinguishing between believers and non-believers. The term pneumatic person is used to acknowledge that disciples of Christ have the Spirit of God. As such they are pneumatic persons.

14. Anderson, "Pentecostal Hermeneutics: Part 2," 15.

Twenty-first Century Pentecostal Hermeneutic Strategy

Arden Autry correctly recognizes that an authentic Pentecostal hermeneutic must recognize both the *correct* and *creative* reading of Scripture.[15] The baptism in the Spirit adds a significant dimension for Pentecostals as pneumatic persons. They believe the Spirit will give understanding of a text to the reader. The difference is that Pentecostals as pneumatic persons may give added weight to an interpretation if it is believed to be revealed by the Holy Spirit.[16] There is the danger of an elitist attitude subtly at work in the thinking of some Pentecostal hermeneuts.[17] This could lead to a tendency to give more credence to the creative reading than at times is legitimate.[18]

Historical-grammatical method provides one level of understanding leading the interpreter to what the text meant in its original setting. What it

---

15. Autry, "Dimensions Of Hermeneutics," 31. The "correct" reading is understood to be the reading as attained through the exercise of historical-grammatical exegesis. The "creative" reading is that reading which engages the intuitive and imaginative activity of the reader.

16. Mark McLean has accurately, in my view, levelled the accusation that Pentecostals are open to the criticism that they actually abandon the canon as authoritative and allow fresh revelations from the Holy Spirit to be authoritative. McLean, "Toward A Pentecostal Hermeneutic," 35. Though I would agree with McLean in the statement I would disagree with a blanket application to Pentecostals in general. Most Pentecostals would not disregard Scripture if some fresh revelation were to contradict, or not be in accord, with biblical teaching. Some expressions of Pentecostalism clearly set Scripture aside in favor of fresh revelation (those holding to the "*rhema* word" view are one example). However, the great majority of Pentecostals continue to hold a high view of Scripture and its authority.

17. Anderson, "Pentecostal Hermeneutics: Part 2," 13–22. Anderson claims the text has a fixed, objective meaning, and identifies the view that Spirit baptism enables the interpreter to discover a deeper meaning as elitist. Although I disagree with Anderson's limiting the Holy Spirit to a fixed, objective meaning I agree that an elitist attitude is a serious danger. In fact, elitism exists among Pentecostals and must be addressed.

18. It is at this point that I would differentiate between a "devotional reading" and "hermeneutical reading" of Scripture. By devotional reading I mean those times when the believer reads the word of God in order to hear from God at a personal level. There is an interpersonal interaction between the human spirit and the Divine Spirit that edifies, strengthens, corrects, convicts, and encourages the believer as they hear God speaking through his word. I believe this to be a personal encounter with the Divine that refreshes the human spirit. The *truth* heard there is not for general consumption but is individual and personal. (Lest I be misunderstood, I am not suggesting that doctrine, practice, belief or truth in the sense of history or proposition is intended here. What I am referring to is more in the line of communion, fellowship and reassurance of love and acceptance that one receives as they commune with God in the practice of spiritual disciplines.) By hermeneutical reading I mean the more technical task of reading Scripture for the purpose of preaching, teaching and understanding what the text says, means, and how it should be interpreted and applied for the community of faith.

A Distinct Twenty-first Century Pentecostal Hermeneutic

cannot do is provide the contemporary meaning and or meaningfulness.[19] A Pentecostal hermeneutical axiom is: "Scripture given by the Holy Spirit must be mediated interpretively by the Holy Spirit."[20] The distance between biblical text and interpreter has always been a hermeneutical problem. Numerous methodologies help overcome that distance. The Holy Spirit overcomes the distance by "serving as the common context and bridging the temporal and cultural distance between the original author and the modern interpreter."[21] Pentecostals strive under the illumination of the Spirit to go beyond the objective literal meaning of the text to arrive at a spiritual meaning that speaks to the real issues people face in their daily life.[22] However, the Holy Spirit's role in the interpretation of Scripture has never been explained nor its specifics spelled out—it is a mystery. As the role of the Spirit in the inscripturating process is beyond investigation, so it is in the interpreting process.[23] What we can observe and measure is the interpretations offered as the Spirit's activity. In the interpretive dimension a distinct Pentecostal hermeneutic is open to novel interpretations as long as they are validated through appropriate criteria, Scripture, and community assessment. The challenge is to identify means by which we may legitimately

---

19. Arrington, "The Use of the Bible," 103. Thiselton reminds us, "historical enquiry alone is not enough for genuine *understanding* (*Verstehen*) of the text in the fullest sense" (Thiselton, "The Hermenetical Dynamics," 17). Thiselton claims this is the view of scholars involved in the Scripture and Hermeneutics project.

20. Arrington, "The Use of the Bible," 104.

21. Ibid., 104. Arrington goes on to say that through the Holy Spirit the word of God becomes alive and speaks to our present situation with new possibilities for personal and social transformation. In some ways this is close to a Barthian understanding of the Bible becoming the word of God. Pentecostals would not see Scripture as less word of God if there were no "encounter."

It is important to point out here that the illumination of the Holy Spirit is available to every believer—Spirit baptized or not. The difference here is that Pentecostals assume experiential encounter is part of the interpretive activity while many evangelicals understand the illuminating work of the Spirit to occur under the surface in the exercise of historical-grammatical methodology.

Lowenburg writes, "The Holy Spirit communicates through Scripture as He open's spiritual eyes to understand the written revelation" ("A Twenty-first Century Pentecostal Hermeneutic," 24).

22. A real difficulty is that there is no way to measure this subjective aspect of meaning. There is no way to objectively differentiate between illumination and creative imagination. Perhaps, there is no difference! The real issue is that a distinctive twenty-first century Pentecostal hermeneutic will give space to such interpretations as authoritative.

23. French Arrington offers four guidelines to aid the interpreter to rely on the illumination of the Holy Spirit. See Arrington, "The Use of the Bible by Pentecostals," 105.

Twenty-first Century Pentecostal Hermeneutic Strategy

differentiate between genuine Holy Spirit illumination and other impulses posing as such.

Sensus Plenoir

Deeper meaning, multiple meanings, etc. are subjects of great interest in hermeneutics in the postmodern debates of communication and interpretation.[24] Pentecostal pneumatology can lead to vulnerability in this area. Consequently, it is important to discuss the concept of deeper meaning in Scripture. The choice to place this discussion under the role and place of the Holy Spirit rather than Scripture is because in Pentecostal circles deeper meaning is most often attributed to the work of the Spirit.

Pentecostals such as Arrington and Ervin claim the Spirit gives *deeper* meanings to Pentecostals because of their experience of baptism in the Spirit. This is elitist. Pentecostals do not have a mystical connection with the "other" that is not available to all believers. But the question still remains, "Is there the possibility of a deeper meaning in the text?" If so, how is the deeper meaning accessed? What is the role of the Spirit in revealing deeper meaning?

The role of the Spirit in the hermeneutical process is to lead and guide the community and hermeneut into the present significance of Scripture. Archer and Lowenburg contend that the Spirit speaks and has more to say than just Scripture, but that the Spirit does not contradict Scripture.[25] Although most, if not all, Pentecostals would maintain that the Spirit can and does speak *extra-biblia*, they will claim he does not speak *contra-biblia*. Consequently, the Scriptures remain the priority and authority. The Holy Spirit does lead and guide so that Scripture's meaningfulness and significance are understood. However, what he speaks is closely connected to Scripture and will not contradict it.

Matthew 1:23 is a biblical example of deeper meaning. Matthew's interpretation of Isaiah 7:14 is only possible if one accepts a deeper meaning in the Isaiah text. Some refer to Matthew's use of Isaiah 7:14 as an example

---

24. Bartholomew et. al., *Reading Luke*, 55–149. This volume, these pages particularly, illustrate the scholarly interest in these areas.

25. Archer, *A Pentecostal Hermeneutic*, 182ff. Lowenburg, "A Twenty-first Century Pentecostal Hermeneutic," 25. Lowenburg seems to follow Arrington and is open to the same criticisms. Lowenburg's statement that the Spirit can speak *tabula rasa* goes undefined and leaves the door open to any kind of imaginative interpretation.

A Distinct Twenty-first Century Pentecostal Hermeneutic

of a text having a double meaning. Anderson argues that, as in the case of Isaiah 7:14, a deeper meaning is inherent in a text only when the deeper meaning is given later in Scripture.[26] In the case of Isaiah 7:14 the deeper meaning is given later in Matthew 1:23. We may ask if a deeper meaning might be inherent in a text whether or not a later Scripture provides that deeper meaning? What in Isaiah 7:14 helps us know it has an inherent deeper meaning other than Matthew's interpretation? Lowenburg argues on the basis of 1 Corinthians 2:14 that the Spirit aids understanding and discernment thereby revealing deeper meaning in the text.[27] Unrestrained, this method becomes an allegorizing of the Bible. Matthew 1:23 and scriptures like it establish that, in some cases, a text has a deeper meaning, but it does not yet seem possible to establish a legitimate exercise that distinguishes texts that have deeper meaning from those that do not; therefore, the best approach seems to be limiting deeper meaning to that which arises from the fuller revelation of the whole of Scripture.[28]

Anderson points to Galatians 4:24–31 and 2 Corinthians 3:6–18 as examples of *sensus plenior* found in Scripture itself.[29] In these instances Paul clearly expands the interpretation beyond authorial intent. Paul's interpretation is without question beyond that which the author could have imagined or intended. Anderson's governing principle of allowing deeper meaning only when that meaning is provided by a later text is certainly safe but may be too restrictive. Oss' position that allows for deeper meaning as long as that meaning is canonically consonant is less restrictive and perhaps more amenable to Pentecostal theology and hermeneutics.[30]

Pentecostals believe Scripture contains predictive prophecy. In those cases the author could not have known the full meaning of what they wrote.

---

26. Anderson, "Pentecostal Hermeneutics: Part 1," 9.

27. Lowenburg, "A Twenty-first Century Pentecostal Hermeneutic," 25–26. Lowenburg believes that the work of the Holy Spirit goes beyond providing meaningfulness and significance. He also conjectures that the more one is filled with the Spirit the greater one's ability to understand the mind of God. This is clearly elitist and leads to unrestrained creative interpretation. Lowenburg's position also suggests the more "spiritual" the interpreter the greater is their capacity to receive deeper meaning from the Spirit. The potential for pandemonium latent in this understanding is extreme. A legitimate, distinct twenty-first century Pentecostal hermeneutic does not follow Lowenburg into this potential quagmire.

28. Oss, "Canon as Context," 105–7. Oss is a Pentecostal scholar who argues for a canonical control of *sensus plenior*.

29. Anderson, "Pentecostal Hermeneutics: Part 1," 9.

30. Oss, "Canon as Context," 105–7.

Twenty-first Century Pentecostal Hermeneutic Strategy

The intended audience could not have known the full meaning of what was spoken or written. In some instances the Bible provides understanding. Sometimes history reveals the meaning. In some instances the full meaning is yet to be revealed. A legitimate, distinct twenty-first century Pentecostal hermeneutic makes room for a deeper understanding of prophecy to emerge. However, it is not open to the uncensored, judgment-free, critique-resistant flights into imagination sometimes witnessed in these days.

Clearly a case can be made for a legitimate place for *sensus plenior*. Scholars will widely vary on how *sensus plenior* fits into a hermeneutic strategy. Although, the Holy Spirit leads the church to continue the ministry of Christ until his return, his function is not to entertain disciples with ever widening, fanciful interpretations of Scripture. His purpose is to promote Christ not elevate hermeneuts. A legitimate, distinct twenty-first century Pentecostal hermeneutic will take a conservative approach to *sensus plenior*. When neither history nor Scripture clearly identify the deeper meaning of a prophecy, a Pentecostal hermeneut must use caution and speak in possibilities. Where the fuller light of Scripture seems to bring deeper meaning to light, the Pentecostal hermeneut will articulate the idea. However, a legitimate, distinct twenty-first century Pentecostal hermeneutic will not lead someone to fall into the labyrinth of unrestricted allegorizing that is so attractive to some.

The role of the Spirit in the interpretive process is widely acknowledged but very difficult to describe. Chuck Kraft's statement is worth hearing: "No receiver of a message ever understands exactly what the communicator intends . . . the Holy Spirit . . . assists in interpreting His Word."[31] As evidenced in Acts 2 and 15 the Spirit may use current events to bring Scripture, trained leader, and community into dialogue to discover what God is saying to the church. As a result of conversion, the Holy Spirit indwells the believer and by changing their will enables them to understand Scripture (1 Cor 2:10–14). In the Pentecostal context the operation of the charismata, dreams, visions, etc. are also means by which the Holy Spirit speaks. These may provide insight into meaning and meaningfulness of Scripture, but interpretations arising from the mystical activity of the Spirit are always subject to the scrutiny of Scripture itself. In a distinct Pentecostal hermeneutic the weight given the Spirit's activity in interpretation may surpass that granted within other communions, but it is never allowed to supersede Scripture. Scripture is always given the place of priority and

---

31. Kraft, "Interpreting in Cultural Context," 248–49.

A Distinct Twenty-first Century Pentecostal Hermeneutic

ultimate authority, and our attention must now turn to consider Scripture's role in a distinct twenty-first century Pentecostal hermeneutic.

Scripture

As in the case of the Wesleyan Quadrilateral, Scripture is authoritative and holds the primary position for Pentecostals. Scripture is interpreted to establish doctrine, train disciples in righteousness, and provide biblical answers to life's circumstances. Pentecostal statements of faith identify inerrancy and verbal-plenary inspiration as residing in original manuscripts and they approach the received text as inspired—though not necessarily without error. Pentecostalism's high view of Scripture leads to prioritizing Scripture in the distinct twenty-first century hermeneutical strategy.

Consequently, personal and community experience are subject to scriptural scrutiny. Interpretations attributed to the work of the Holy Spirit are subject to scriptural review and evaluation. Interpretations proposed by trained leaders (scholar, pastor, or layperson) also submit to the assessment of Scripture. Pentecostal bibliology requires that its hermeneutic respect Scripture's priority position. Methodology, strategy, interpretive elements, presuppositions, etc. in a legitimate, distinct twenty-first century Pentecostal hermeneutic each work in submission to Scripture's primacy and analysis.

The current hermeneutical discussion within Pentecostalism is somewhat chaotic. Scholarly opinion relative to the *locus of meaning* is varied. Some contend meaning resides solely in the text. Others take extreme reader-response positions where meaning is the creation of the interpreter. Even a desultory examination of preaching reveals that pastoral interpretive method is extremely chaotic. Most Pentecostal pastors, even in the Majority World, have some level of training from Bible colleges that teach the historical-grammatical method of exegesis. However, far too often in their preaching pastors abandon good hermeneutical method for "fanciful interpretation."[32] This is only possible if Scripture is allowed to slip from its place of primacy. A hermeneutical strategy that prioritizes Scripture promises to bring appropriate order to what is now a somewhat chaotic state.

---

32. Anderson, "Pentecostal Hermeneutics: Part 1," 5. Anderson goes on to say, "these methods and conclusions are not taught at Pentecostal colleges and seminaries, and they do not represent a legitimate Pentecostal hermeneutic."

Twenty-first Century Pentecostal Hermeneutic Strategy
Pentecostal Bibliology

Pentecostals generally take a literalist[33] approach to understanding the Bible. This enables them to "interplay Scripture with contemporary life and present the text as a reflection of common experience."[34] They welcome and expect divine intervention in daily life in a manner that resonates with the biblical accounts, especially the Gospels and Acts. They find in Scripture correspondence with contemporary life. They relate the divine actions in the life of biblical characters as reason to expect the same today. Their testimonies emphasize the miraculous and unusual happenings in their community and focus on divine intervention in real life situations.[35] Mesters speaks of Pentecostals as ordinary people interpreting the Bible using the tools of "their own lives, experiences, and struggles."[36] In the language of Joel B. Green, Scripture *projects* a "world" *into* which readers are drawn to enter, and within which they are addressed and re-formed.[37] For Pentecostals Scripture is a world the Holy Spirit uses to address, inform, re-form, and creatively engage their current world. Standing above experience, belief and practice Scripture calls them into alignment with Jesus' teaching.

Pentecostals often move from experience to Scripture in the hermeneutical process. The use of testimonies aids the practice of relating the Bible to contemporary experiences of perceived divine intervention.[38] As has been shown, there is solid biblical foundation for moving from experience to Scripture (Acts 2 and 15 and the Epistles). Scripture is sought in an effort to understand world events, personal circumstances, and a wide range of current events. A legitimate, distinct twenty-first century Pentecostal hermeneutic enables interpretation to move from experience to Scripture, but Scripture always stands over experience.[39]

---

33. For early Pentecostals literal would have meant historically accurate.

34. Anderson, *An Introduction To Pentecostalism*, 226. Literalist here means historical and truthful.

35. Archer, "Pentecostal Hermeneutics," 64.

36. Mesters, "The Use of the Bible," 9.

37. Green, *The Theology of the Gospel of Luke*, 4–6.

38. Often within the testimony the speaker will interject Scripture. Scripture is used to validate what is being said, illustrate the truth being proclaimed, interpret the event being described, and to provide a biblical foundation for the claims being made.

39. Here is where the historical-grammatical method with its focus on what the text meant is helpful. Anderson, "Pentecostal Hermeneutics: Part 2," 13. Anderson writes, "I contend that at this basic level of exegetical method (discovering what the text meant), all

A Distinct Twenty-first Century Pentecostal Hermeneutic

Accepting the historicity of Scripture leads Pentecostals to exegete the world and life from a supernaturalistic stance. Pentecostals are committed to the belief that the Bible holds the answers to life's problems such as poverty, injustice, disease, oppression, unemployment, hunger, loneliness, anxiety, etc. This is especially true in Africa and Majority World contexts where these issues are extreme. Scripture provides a limitless supply of answers—miraculous and otherwise—to these problems. Trusting Scripture's historical reliability empowers Pentecostals to speak authoritatively about life's problems and their solutions, since they believe God can do now what he has done in the past.

From the beginning Pentecostals read the Bible with "a thoroughly popularistic, pre-critical, text-centered approach."[40] They hold to what Anderson calls "plenary relevance,"[41] that is, all Scripture is relevant and holds the answers to the totality of life situations. All one must do is read, believe, and obey Scripture. In the twenty-first century Pentecostal hermeneutic, as in the Wesleyan Quadrilateral, Scripture is prioritized and offers solutions, hope, guidance, and divine intervention if the individual submits and obeys.[42] Scripture, "as the illumined mind . . . blends Spirit and text, and acknowledges revelations that are subjective and objective, past and present,"[43] speaks prophetically to today's disciple.

Pentecostals view Scripture as the inspired word of God that came into existence as an act of God's self-revelation. Scripture reveals God to the reader and she is exposed to the penetrating light of God. The text examines the reader as she exegetes the text. The text is to be taken seriously and handled faithfully. To unpack meaning the starting point is the historical-grammatical approach that enables the exegete to identify what the text says and what the original author intended to communicate to his audience.[44]

This author departs from Fee and those who restrict interpretation to deducing from the text such general, timeless principles as may be

---

interpreters take the same approach when they do their work correctly."

40. Wacker, *Early Pentecostals*, 71. See also, Archer, "Early Pentecostal Biblical Interpretation," 68.

41. Anderson, *Introduction To Pentecostalism*, 225.

42. Strauss, *How to Read the Bible*, 42. Strauss emphasizes the need to prioritize Scripture if we are to avoid the slippery slope of unrestrained spiritualization in our interpretations.

43. Lowenburg, "A Twenty-first Century Pentecostal Hermeneutic," 28.

44. Anderson, "Pentecostal Hermeneutics: Part 2," 13.

Twenty-first Century Pentecostal Hermeneutic Strategy

applied to similar contemporary situations.[45] We agree with Archer who identifies this approach as far too restrictive.[46] Pentecostals hold that God speaks *through* Scripture; therefore, hearing Scripture is hearing God. They interpret Scripture to understand God's message to them. Scripture may not have been written *to* us but it was written *for* us. Literary critical approaches to interpretation allow for interaction between text and reader in the creation of meaning enabling the interpreter to *hear* God's voice. This resonates far better with the African interpreter and Scripture itself than a rigid "text only" approach to meaning.

Pentecostals, like evangelicals, recognize that Scripture conveys God's word *via* an anthology of literature. The diversity of biblical genres points to God's preferred method of communication as being imprecise rather than as universal, timeless propositional statements. Since a full range of genres is found in Scripture, Archer's choice of narrative criticism as *the* authentic Pentecostal method is also too restrictive and limiting. Since God speaks using diverse literary genres, a legitimate, distinct twenty-first century Pentecostal hermeneutic must apply various literary critical methodologies. This allows Scripture to speak, the interpreter to actively hear, and meaning to emerge in accordance with Scripture's nature as a literary anthology.

This is the kind of interaction we see when we look at Acts 2 and 15. Whether we look at Joel 2 or Amos 9, it is obvious that Peter and James are interpreting those texts subjectively. Jude is clearly interpreting 1 Enoch from a christological and theological stance rather than its authorially intended meaning.[47] The use of Scripture in the New Testament points to a less precise understanding of meaning than the modern scientific methodologies allow.[48] Literary critical methodology is amenable to interpretation that balances between objectively and subjectively determined meanings and resonates with a Pentecostal view of Scripture. These are important methodological approaches in a legitimate, distinct twenty-first century Pentecostal hermeneutic.

---

45. Ibid., 14.

46. Archer, *A Pentecostal Hermeneutic*, 148–54.

47. Bauckham, *2 Peter, Jude*, 94.

48. Pinnock, *The Scripture Principle*, 218–19. Pinnock says, "The idea that a text has only one meaning is a modern, scientific prejudice that does not correspond either to the Bible's own view of itself or to the Christian experience of using Scripture."

A Distinct Twenty-first Century Pentecostal Hermeneutic

Pentecostals hold the view that most Scripture came about by revelation[49] and is the record of God's self-revelation. Although many theologians have struggled to divest revelation of any historical foundation or connection, they have been unsuccessful. Niebuhr concludes, "It remains true that Christian faith cannot escape from partnership with history."[50] God's self-revelation in Scripture is undeniably connected to history.[51] Christianity, unlike many other religions, understands revelation to be centered in certain historical events, with the life, death, burial and resurrection of Christ as chief among them. (e.g., 1 Cor 15:3–4) There is also a subjective aspect to revelation, and Protestant theology has struggled to determine how objective history and subjective experience work together in the process of revelation and interpretation.[52] The essence of one's relationship with God through Christ Jesus is subjective and personal, but the reliability of certain historical facts is essential to the validity of Christianity. The real Jesus who lived in Palestine is at the center of God's revelatory activity (Heb 1:1–4).

Some portions of Scripture, like genealogies, arise from natural knowledge and the process of research (e.g., Kings and Chronicles). Such materials, though inspired, are not necessarily revelation though they may contain revelatory material. Opinions would vary on the amount of biblical material falling into the category of non-revelatory but Pentecostals take a conservative position on this issue. It could also be argued that not all "revelation" made it into Scripture (John 21:25). Paul's argument in Romans 1 and Jude's reference to Enoch (Jude 14–15) point to extrabiblical revelation of both a general and specific nature. How much revelation remains outside the biblical record is beyond our knowing. Why some revelation did not find its way into the biblical record remains unknowable. All we can contend, is that, at least from a Pentecostal perspective, most of the Bible consists of revelation and any extrabiblical revelation, ancient and/or contemporary, must be subject to Scripture.

---

49. Archer, *A Pentecostal Hermeneutic*, 157. He writes, "the Pentecostal community recognizes the Bible as sacred revelation—the inspired, authoritative word of God." Revelatory, as used here, refers to what Brueggemann calls the "theological intentionality" of Scripture. Brueggemann, *The Book That Breathes*, ix. Scripture is revelatory in that it gives us what we could not discover ourselves—a knowledge of God and how one lives life in relationship with him.

50. Niebuhr, *The Meaning of Revelation*, 59.

51. Enns, "Preliminary Observations," 219.

52. Ibid., 219–20.

Twenty-first Century Pentecostal Hermeneutic Strategy

Recognizing the biblical material as primarily revelatory relates to authority and hermeneutical methodology. If the hermeneut is dealing with revelatory material then the hermeneutical task must be conducted with diligence and care. If the text is revelatory, then its originally intended meaning is significant. The interpreter is constrained to give attention to this meaning. Extrabiblical revelation such as that supposedly operating in the charismata must also submit to scriptural examination. Prioritizing Scripture protects against the potential dangers of unrestrained creative imagination and extrabiblical revelation.

Brueggemann's presentation of the revelatory nature of Scripture aligns with Pentecostalism's overall approach to Scripture. Brueggemann relates the revelatory nature of Scripture with its presentation of a "world."[53] The text of Scripture creates a story-world that the reader encounters.[54] This world contends with all other worlds that call for the reader's attention. The rhetoric of Scripture creates a reality that confronts both the reader's reality and all other realities that call for the reader's acceptance. Scripture is revelatory since we could know of its world in no other way. This understanding of revelation resonates with Pentecostalism's high view of Scripture and openness to Scripture's confronting beliefs and practices. For Pentecostals, Scripture reveals God's preferred world and invites us to allow our reality to be transformed. Scripture can only fulfill this critical function when it is given a prioritized and authoritative role.

Within charismatic Pentecostalism there is a trend toward abandoning Scripture for direct, fresh revelation given directly to the worshipper.[55] McLean notes that this abandonment of the canon is subtle at first. Perhaps one of the more insane forms of this understanding of revelation is seen in the concept of "soul marriage."[56] Dislodging Scripture from its place

---

53. Brueggemann, *The Book That Breathes*, vii.

54. Thiselton, "The Hermeneutical Dynamics," 7. Thiselton understands Scripture as creating a story-world that invites the reader to enter. This story-world seeks to re-form the reader's reality.

55. McLean, "Toward a Pentecostal Hermeneutic," 35. McLean draws attention to this trend as early as 1984 in a paper delivered at the annual meeting of the Society for Pentecostal Studies.

56. Soul marriage is the identification of one's sexual desires with the promptings of the Holy Spirit. I observed the devastating effect of this in the early 1990s. Close friends of mine became sexually involved believing they were being led by the Spirit as soul mates. They left their spouses and children and were married. The man was a pastor of an independent Pentecostal church that had gone the direction of direct revelation. Some time later he had an affair with another married woman in the fellowship. He

A Distinct Twenty-first Century Pentecostal Hermeneutic

of primacy as the supreme revelation creates vulnerability to all forms of spiritual insanity and abuse. A legitimate, distinct Pentecostal hermeneutic recognizes the revelatory nature of Scripture and contends that Scripture stands over everything that presents itself as revelation.

The words of Robert Guelich are worth hearing here: "Yet one of the cardinal teachings of the Evangelical Christian community about the Scriptures has maintained that Scripture is our ultimate authority for faith and practice. This authority is based on what the Scriptures 'said' as written by writers inspired by the Holy Spirit and not what the Scriptures 'mean to me.'"[57] Like Guelich, Pentecostals hold to an inherent authority for Scripture that arises from its revelatory nature.

Thiselton argues that the authority of the Bible "derives from the operative statutory or institutional validity of transforming speech-acts in Scripture."[58] Pentecostals take the position that Scripture is authoritative because it is the word of God. Interpretation enables the reading community to advance toward the eschaton—that point of final judgment when God's promises will be fully realized in time. The reading community embracing scriptural authority, through its interpreters, engages in an ongoing process of correcting, testing, reevaluating, and restating the meaning of the biblical texts for belief and practice.

Closely related to the concept of Scripture as revelation is the issue of inspiration.[59] God the Holy Spirit brought Scripture into being through the process called *inspiration*. The question is: *How did God cause the final product of written Scriptures to come into being?* The answer to this question

---

rationalized his infidelity as the leading of the Spirit.

57. Guelich, *Mark 1–8:26*, xxxv.

58. Thiselton, *Authority and Hermeneutics*, 137.

59. John R. Levinson's thesis that the Breath of God (Gen 2:7) during the creation of Adam produces a holy spirit holds interesting possibilities concerning our understanding of inspiration. Levinson, *Filled with the Spirit*. Levinson's thesis builds on several Old Testament texts (Gen 2:7; 6:17; 7:22; 41:38; Job 12:7–10; 33:4; 34:14–15, and Micah 3:8). These texts together seem to link the breath of God and the Spirit of God. Levinson argues that the breath of God given mankind at creation is a holy spirit. Levinson's thesis has interesting implications for hermeneutics and our understanding of inspiration. However there are a number of issues that need addressing. First, what is the relationship between "holy spirit" and the divine "Spirit"? What is the impact of the fall? How do we understand evil, demonic spirits and the potential for demonization of humans in relationship to Levinson's thesis. These and many other questions must yet be answered by Levinson and/or others. Because of the embryonic nature of Levinson's thesis its implications are not dealt with here. Levinson's thesis does present interesting considerations that a distinct Pentecostal hermeneutic must give attention to in the future.

Twenty-first Century Pentecostal Hermeneutic Strategy

might be called one's view of inspiration. Kantzer identifies the problem we face in answering this question: "The mechanics of inspiration are left unexplained."[60] What we are left with are theoretical possibilities. Every theory struggles with two dimensions: 1) the divine component; 2) the human element. Various positions could be summarized into one of the following six theories: Dictation,[61] Providential,[62] Ecstatic,[63] Illumination,[64] Existential Encounter,[65] and Verbal Plenary.[66] The majority of Pentecostals officially hold to some form of Verbal Plenary inspiration that is less restrictive than a Dictation model.

The statement of faith for the larger Pentecostal denominations such as, PAOC, AOG, etc., expresses a verbal plenary view of inspiration that also attributes inerrancy to the original documents. The PAOC statement says: "The whole Bible in the original is, therefore, without error and, as such, is infallible, absolutely supreme and sufficient in authority in all matters of

---

60. Kantzer and Gundry, *Perspectives on Evangelical Theology*, 116.

61. Claims that the Holy Spirit dictated the text word for word.

62. This theory is based on God's providential care over creation as expressed in Rom 8:28 (God works everything together for good—even the sinful acts of men). This view argues that God providentially oversaw the creative activities of individuals so that his word was written. That God could have acted in such a way cannot be denied. However, we are still left with the question "How did God *providentially* oversee the project?"

63. The belief that the writers of Scripture were like mystics overcome with ecstasy. They found themselves in a trance; therefore, their writing bypassed their rational faculties. This view can be found in Hellenistic Judaism and some early church fathers (Athenagoras, Tertullian). It never received a wide support because it is so slanted toward the divine.

64. The authors of Scripture were inspired much like the author of any literary work. We speak of music, novels, etc. being inspired or inspiring. By that we mean the manifestation of talent or insight. This view of inspiration sees the scripture as the expression of human religious thinking. This view almost eliminates a divine involvement in the process.

65. This view holds that inspiration is not so much a quality of the Scriptures themselves but occurs at a moment of personal encounter with the word. The Scriptures become the word of God to us when we encounter God in and through them. This view was popularized by Karl Barth but developed by nineteenth-century thinkers such as Schliermacher.

66. This view holds that God the Holy Spirit moved upon individuals and caused them to write down God's divine revelation. The individual personality, culture, vocabulary, and character of the writer were not bypassed or eliminated in this process. However, the Holy Spirit so superintended the writing of scripture that the very words are inspired and not merely the ideas or concepts. In their original, the Scriptures were recorded without error.

A Distinct Twenty-first Century Pentecostal Hermeneutic

faith and practice."[67] In Galatians 3:16, Paul builds a theological point on the grammatical number of a single word ("offspring" vs. "offsprings"). If inspiration only relates to concepts and ideas, such an argument is impossible. We cannot absolutely affirm a verbal plenary inspiration model from Galatians 3:16 but can conclude from its argument that inspiration extends to more than concepts or ideas.

The Greek of 2 Timothy 3:16 also supports the view that inspiration applies to the text and not merely to the ideas and thoughts of the writers. First, it is important to note 2 Timothy 3:16 says "all (*pasa*) scripture (*graphé*)" is God-breathed. This means that the "God-breathed" quality, whatever it is, must be applied to *all* Scripture not merely its concepts. Second, 2 Timothy is referring to the Hebrew Scriptures, not the New Testament in its original intent. However, the church has historically applied 2 Timothy 3:16 to the New Testament also. Thus the doctrine of verbal plenary inspiration rests on "tradition" as well as Scripture.

Verbal plenary views of inspiration are challenged by our knowledge and understanding of the true nature of Scripture. The development of the Septuagint also challenges verbal plenary views of inspiration.[68] The Septuagint, Dead Sea Scrolls, and manuscript evidence clearly reveal more than one version of some Scripture portions circulating at the same time. Each of these copies was treated as inspired and authoritative. Glenn Wooden reminds us that we ought to take seriously the development of the Hebrew Bible and the extensive use of the LXX by Paul, Matthew, Luke, and others.[69] For nearly two millennia the church has used translations without too much concern for *original* texts. Wooden goes on to state:

> What this implies is that in practice, for the church, the locus of inspiration is not in the text as originally produced, but in the text as received and used in the church at various times and in various languages. Such inspiration must, therefore, be attributed to the continuing work of God, not to an infusion of power into original texts that are no longer accessible to us and of which we have only faulty copies and uncertain reconstructions.[70]

---

67. General Constitution and By-Laws (2010), The Pentecostal Assemblies of Canada, 2450 Milltower Court, Mississauga, Canada, 2.

68. Wooden, "The Role of 'the Septuagint,'" 139.

69. Ibid., 144.

70. Ibid.

Twenty-first Century Pentecostal Hermeneutic Strategy

Pentecostals officially hold to verbal plenary inspiration of the original manuscripts,[71] but in practice treat the received text as fully inspired. A twenty-first century Pentecostal hermeneutic continues to engage the received text as inspired and authoritative. Original languages, text critical issues, culture, historical context, etc. are consulted to aid in understanding the received text, but it is the received text that is interpreted and given the place of priority and authority.

The nature of Scripture as revelation and inspired supports Pentecostalism's prioritizing Scripture in the interpretive process. Experience and tradition are secondary to Scripture and must submit to its scrutiny. The charismatic element of Pentecostal worship and life is subject to the examination of Scripture. Scripture's primacy and supervision of the interpreter's creative imagination is a critical aspect of a distinct twenty-first century Pentecostal hermeneutic.

Inspired Scripture as revelation comes to us as communication through language; therefore, language is an important part of hermeneutics. It is perhaps the hottest of all the hermeneutical issues debated today.[72] Postmodernism has questioned almost every *a priori* pertaining to language that would have been in place fifty years ago. Structuralism, deconstructionism, and many other -isms have expressed and assessed how its proponents believe language works from every angle imaginable. The admonition of Achtemeier is appropriate: "Modern scholars must therefore exercise the greatest care in their study of literary forms so that they can recognize what that form would communicate to its hearers."[73] It is critical that the twenty-first century Pentecostal interpreter be informed of how language forms and genre used in Scripture communicated to their audiences. Historical-grammatical methodology, rhetorical criticism, narrative criticism, etc. help the Pentecostal hermeneut understand and interpret the received text from a linguistic perspective.

The interaction between reader and text receives much attention in current discussions on hermeneutics as it relates to language and

---

71. There is a need for a serious scholarly debate on this issue. However, this book is neither the place to begin nor to engage in that debate.

72. Archer, *A Pentecostal* Hermeneutic, 157 ff. See also, Brueggemann, *The Book That*, and Foss, *Rhetorical Criticism*.

73. Achtemeier, *Inspiration and Authority*, 137. Achtemeier points out the significance of a prophetic oracle taking on a legal form to indicate the prophet intends to draw attention to the rupture of God's law; that certain elements were essential to reporting a miracle in the Hellenistic world, etc.

A Distinct Twenty-first Century Pentecostal Hermeneutic

meaning.[74] Every theory of hermeneutics must address this issue. Some, like Fee, argue for the absolute control of the text and authorial intent over meaning. Others hold a position for completely unrestricted ability for the text to produce meaning or significance for the reader or congregation in that given moment.[75] A legitimate, distinct twenty-first century Pentecostal hermeneutic must stand between these two extremes. Scripture must have some inherent meaning or it has no authority, but it is also widely accepted that the interpreter (via the influence of the Spirit) also contributes to the creation of meaning.

Daniel Block identifies the importance of literary genre and recognizing the role of both text and interpreter in hermeneutics. Commenting on the book of Ruth he says, "This composition bears several different meanings. But to say this is not to free the reader to make any sense of the text whatever. As in the reading of any document, ancient or modern, we must pay careful attention to the literary conventions employed by an author to get the points across."[76] Block's statement lends credence to the importance of literary criticism in the interpretive process. As argued in this book literary criticism embraces a realistic recognition that Scripture expresses God's word through literature recognizing the role of both text and interpreter without surrendering Scriptures dominant position.

As an anthology of literature the Bible contains everything from apocalyptic to historical narrative. Each literary form (historical narrative, narrative, law, poetry, parable, prophecy, theodicy, epistle, etc.) differs from the others. The interpreter must be aware of the literary genre and apply specialized tools in interpreting that particular form. The Pentecostal hermeneut must prepare to capably handle each literary form. Only with such preparation can the Pentecostal (or any) hermeneut effectively deal with all biblical literature. For this reason, we propose that a legitimate, distinct twenty-first century Pentecostal hermeneutic will employ the full range of literary critical methods.

Early Pentecostals agreed with modernists that historicity was required for truth to be present. This meant the biblical stories must have actually happened or they were not true since the genre of biblical story

---

74. See Archer, *A Pentecostal Hermeneutic*, 158–64. See also Bartholomew et al., *Reading Luke*, and Brueggemann, *The Book That Breathes*. These monographs are a very small sampling of materials that deal with the issue of language. There are also a myriad of articles dealing with the subject of language and meaning formation.

75. Autry, "Dimensions of Hermeneutics," 37.

76. Block, *Judges and Ruth*.

Twenty-first Century Pentecostal Hermeneutic Strategy

was equated with a modernistic understanding of historiography. No credible twenty-first century Pentecostal scholar would hold to such a view and our twenty-first century hermeneutic cannot operate from that viewpoint. Contemporary Pentecostal scholars, like others, recognize biblical literature to be an anthology of genres conveying truth via story, parable, epic, epistle, and a host of other literary genres as well as propositions. This requires a hermeneutical strategy that employs methods that enable Scripture's various genres to convey "truth" without always having to meet the standard of historiography that modernity would demand. The book of Jonah conveys its truth just as powerfully if it is a parable as if it is an historical event. Allowing that truth is conveyed through various literary forms, requires the use of various interpretive methods but does not dislodge Scripture from its position of supremacy.

Authorial Intent

Recognizing Scripture as literature raises the issue of author and authorial intent in the interpretive process. Scripture without inherent meaning cannot hold a superintending position over Spirit, community, and trained leader. Inherent meaning flows from authorial or original intent. A legitimate Pentecostal hermeneutic recognizes a place for authorial intent.[77] Pentecostal groups that ignore authorial intent in favor of immediate spiritualized meaning are in reality practicing an extreme reader-response hermeneutic and ignore Pentecostalism's high view of Scripture. Although this is passed off as an operation of the Holy Spirit, it is unrestrained imagination masquerading as revelation. A legitimate Pentecostal hermeneutic that holds to the supremacy of Scripture cannot go in this direction.

Authorial intent is one means of fencing the text against unlimited interpretation. Without some hedging of meaning a text can be made to mean almost anything the preacher desires. Potential meaning is limited only by the interpreter's imagination and the inherent danger here is obvious. However, without some freedom from authorial intent, valuable meaning will be lost. Authorial intent must be held in creative combination

---

77. During my research I have not found a Pentecostal scholar calling for a full reader-response interpretive method. Archer recognizes that narrative criticism is a form of reader-response. Archer, following Vanhoozer, calls for a "Reader-Respect" approach. He says, "the conservative reader affirms both the openness of the text as well as the constraints of the text" (Archer, *A Pentecostal Hermeneutic*, 173). See also Vanhoozer, "The Reader," 309.

A Distinct Twenty-first Century Pentecostal Hermeneutic

with reader-provided signification, if Scripture is to communicate in all its richness to the twenty-first century Pentecostal community.

There is debate over how well we in the twenty-first century can identify authorial intent. This writer acknowledges that we are likely unable to identify with absolute certainty the originally intended meaning. We cannot fully put ourselves in the place of writer and audience; therefore, we cannot absolutely claim to know what the author's intention or the audience's reception was. However, we agree with Autry that we can usually achieve an "adequate" knowledge of the author's intention from the literary, historical, and social context of the text.[78] An adequate knowledge, though partial, is not necessarily false, useless, or irrelevant.[79] People write to be understood and to the extent we are able to put ourselves in the place of the original audience we can hear as they would have heard. Current knowledge of the history, culture, language, and mindset of the biblical audiences is not perfect but can enable us to hear the text adequately. The hermeneutic strategy proposed in this book assumes we can access an adequate knowledge of authorial intent.

A legitimate, distinct, twenty-first century Pentecostal hermeneutic understands the text to contain inherent meaning rooted in authorial intent. The text constrains reader-produced, imaginative interpretations. A text without meaning cannot inform, challenge, or transform the reader.[80] Without inherent meaning Scripture cannot stand over Spirit, interpreter, and community. Scripture is stripped of authority and significance and becomes nothing more than a prop, if it contains no inherent meaning.

We should also pay attention to the New Testament's use of the Old Testament in this regard. Obviously New Testament writers did not bind themselves to authorial intent when using the Old Testament. Isaiah 7:14 is a case in point. Had Matthew adhered strictly to authorial intent he would not have used this text in relation to the birth of Jesus. Matthew deliberately chooses to quote from the LXX rather than the MT to offer his interpretation of Jesus' birth as the promised Messiah. Isaiah is likely referring to the birth of Hezekiah and has no messianic intention. The Holy Spirit, on the other hand, could be said to have inspired Isaiah, LXX translators, and Matthew. The Holy Spirit's intent, or perhaps more accurately the Holy Spirit's later interpretation, may be beyond authorial intent. Therefore, giving

---

78. Autry, "Dimensions of Hermeneutics," 35.
79. Carson, "Hermeneutics," 15.
80. Vanhoozer, "The Reader," 317.

absolute control to authorial intent may rob the contemporary church of vital truth and light[81] and may silence the voice of the Spirit.

Therefore, this is a place where this writer would want to engage the Holy Spirit. The Pentecostal view of Scripture is that the ultimate author is the Holy Spirit. This being the case, approaching Scripture to hear its message should be done prayerfully and with an expectation that the Holy Spirit will aid in the process of understanding.[82] We must wrestle with the question: "Did the Holy Spirit intend a meaning beyond the authorial intent?" The ultimate intention of Scripture is knowledge of God. To accomplish this, Scripture records revelatory events and experiences. Thus the world of the text is of vital concern to the interpreter.[83] Authorial intent exists and can be adequately accessed via exegesis and it is ignored in the interpretive process to the peril of everyone. Authorial intent is one of the elements that both the Spirit and Scripture bring to bear upon the interpreter and interpreting community. This prevents meaning and meaningfulness degenerating into self-serving, manipulative interpretations or worse.

Allegory and Typology

Some Pentecostals use allegory and typology extensively. This is especially true within African Pentecostalism. The danger of allegorization is that it allows the interpreter to give a text any meaning she wishes. Allegorization can be a reader-response approach gone out of control but allegory is a genre found in Scripture. As evidenced in Galatians 4:21–31 allegory is also an interpretive method used in Scripture. Pentecostalism's high view of Scripture, acknowledgement of authorial intent, and recognition of meaning in the text allows for a very limited, controlled use of allegorization in interpretation.

---

81. Hawk, *Every Promise Fulfilled*, 19 ff. In discussing narrative Hawk draws attention to the necessary role of the reader to complete the negotiation of meaning.

82. Archer, *A Pentecostal Hermeneutic*, 173–74.

83. Ricoeur, *Essays on Biblical Interpretation*, 100. Ricoeur says, "what is finally to be understood in a text is not the author or his presumed intention . . . but the sort of world beyond the text as its reference." This approach, intentionally or unintentionally, would open the text to meaning produced by whatever direction of thought the text stimulates. This is too open ended. There are limits to the meaning a text might have and a distinct twenty-first century Pentecostal hermeneutic must find the balance between overly restricted and overly liberated interpretation.

A Distinct Twenty-first Century Pentecostal Hermeneutic

Allegory finds meaning in a text different from its literal or surface meaning. The allegorical method assumes the literal sense conceals the spiritual or eternal truth. Rabbinic Judaism makes much use of allegorical method especially in the Pentateuch. Paul also uses this approach (1 Cor 9:8–12; Gal 4:21–26). Hebrews 7:2–10 is a New Testament use of allegory. Until the third century the early church fathers made regular use of this method.[84] This spiritualizing approach has a place, albeit, in my opinion, a very limited place, in the hermeneutical process. Pentecostals are perhaps more at risk of abusing this method than others because of their specific pneumatology. This tool should be limited to those portions of Scripture that are clearly allegorical in nature or where, coupled with other approaches, it aids to provide clarity.

Michael Kyomya speaks to his African colleagues on this subject. He embraces the historical-grammatical method as an important corrective to the wholly subjective interpretation allegorization leads to.[85] Kyomya acknowledges that words have a range of meaning but within a text the range of meaning is restricted. The text provides boundaries that control the possible meaning of individual words resulting in a limitation to possible meaning within the text itself. Kyomya also recognizes the literary aspect of Scripture pointing to the use of literary critical methodology that allows Scripture to speak and be interpreted according to its proper genre. Kyomya's position lays a good foundation for the hermeneutic proposed in this book.[86] Bringing historical-grammatical method alongside the new literary methodologies enables the Pentecostal hermeneut to navigate between the cliffs of restrictive objectivism and uncontrolled creative subjectivism. As a biblical genre and interpretive method allegorization has a legitimate, though very limited, place in a twenty-first century Pentecostal hermeneutic.

One complication of allegorization is the lack of any criteria that controls interpretation. For example, the five stones of 1 Samuel 17:40 have been used to represent the five wounds of Jesus, the five letters in the name JESUS, the fivefold gifts of Ephesians 4:11, etc. by various African pastors. In Africa the more creative the interpretation the more spiritual the preacher

---

84. Anderson refers to allegorization as the Alexandrian style of interpretation. Anderson, "Pentecostal Hermeneutics: Part 1," 9.

85. Kyomya, *A Guide To Interpreting Scripture*, 17–63.

86. Ibid., 17 Kyomya states that human and divine authors "never contradict each other, although sometimes the divine author intends a referent that is grander and deeper than the human author realized."

Twenty-first Century Pentecostal Hermeneutic Strategy

is perceived to be. Creative allegory and charismatic delivery draws large crowds, therefore it is very attractive in the African context. Authorial intent, revelation, and inspiration oppose the unrestrained meaning that can result from allegorical interpretation. Literary critical methodology combined with historical-grammatical method helps the hermeneut establish boundaries that limit and define the acceptable use of allegory.

Typology also has a legitimate place since many Old Testament figures, cultic elements and events can be viewed as types of Christ. The Pauline Epistles are one example of how Scripture itself makes use of such typology. The person and work of Christ are illuminated in a number of helpful ways through such types. Again, typological interpretation must be controlled. It cannot be allowed to function unrestrained. A genuine connection between type and antitype must be established before a typological interpretation is accepted.

Typology, or the establishing of connections between two persons, events or objects, occurs within Scripture and generally occurs between Old and New Testament material. Paul finds connections between Jesus and Adam, Moses, and Abraham. The book of Hebrews finds connections between Jesus and several Old Testament signators. Behind typology lies the premise that God controls history and causes earlier individuals or events to embody characteristics that reappear at a later time.[87] The earlier may be used to aid understanding of the later. This tool of interpretation must be used with caution and safeguards in place. Where Scripture identifies a typological relationship the interpreter is safe in following this interpretive method. Typological connections not identified in Scripture may be legitimate but caution is advised. Applying the interpretive methods identified in chapter 4 will assist the interpreter to determine if a genuine typological relationship exists.

Perhaps the most common forum in which hermeneutics occurs is that of the preacher. The preacher has the difficult task of bringing the Bible's message to bear upon contemporary life issues. Translating the principles, proclamations, insights, and propositions of Scripture into language understandable and applicable in the modern world is not easy. The biblical material rises out of an agrarian, pre-scientific world.[88] Bringing

---

87. Ferguson, *Biblical Hermeneutics*, 86.

88. It must be noted that in the Pauline literature we see a Greco-Roman, urban world. Many of Paul's illustrations are drawn from this context. However, much of the Bible has an agrarian, pre-scientific background.

A Distinct Twenty-first Century Pentecostal Hermeneutic

its message, without distortion, to our postmodern, technological, globalized audience is complicated. This is the challenge facing the Pentecostal hermeneut. The temptation to bow to the domineering power of relevance is intense. Allegory and typology can offer an easier road to relevance than the labor of applying proper methodology and careful interpretation. This temptation must be resisted. A legitimate, distinct twenty-first century Pentecostal hermeneutic practiced by scholar and pastor must follow proper methodology and respect Scripture's supervisory place.

The Old Testament in Pentecostal Interpretation

Pentecostals understand themselves as New Testament disciples of Jesus but are not Marcionite in their position toward the Old Testament. The Old Testament retains a legitimate place in the canon and functions as Scripture. A distinct twenty-first century Pentecostal hermeneutic interprets the Old Testament christologically through a Lukan lens and in light of New Testament revelation.

The primary Pentecostal distinctive is their belief that there is "a continuity of the ways in which God works in the world from the time of the Resurrection to the Second Coming."[89] They believe in a baptism in the Spirit that empowers for service as in the early church. They believe God does miracles today and that the Holy Spirit is the agent in the believer's life through whom these miracles occur. A Pentecostal interpretation of the Old Testament is informed by Pentecostal theology.

Pentecostals are not dispensationalists although they frequently use dispensational language and have adopted the eschatology of dispensationalism[90] Formal dispensationalism teaches that the kingdom of God is not now present on earth.[91] Pentecostals reject this view. For Pentecostals the kingdom is not fully come but is very present during the period between Jesus' resurrection and second coming.[92] The abundance of teaching on

---

89. Anderson, "Pentecostal Hermeneutics: Part 2," 21.

90. Ibid.

91. Ibid. Formal dispensationalism teaches that the kingdom was offered to the Jews who rejected it. Jesus took it back to heaven with the plan of revealing it after the second coming at the end of the church age. During the church age the kingdom is not present.

92. It is true that Pentecostals disagree on the extent of the Kingdom's presence. Some, a small minority, are of the kingdom now group. Most see the kingdom as present but believe the kingdom will only be fully present in the millennium.

Twenty-first Century Pentecostal Hermeneutic Strategy

the nature of the kingdom in the Gospels makes little sense if Jesus takes the kingdom back to heaven in the ascension. A Pentecostal interpretation of the Old Testament is filtered through this theological position.

Anderson suggests this distinctive provides Pentecostal hermeneutics with its primary significance and ability to contribute to Christian interpretation.[93] It is also important to how Pentecostals interpret the Old Testament, because it records God's activity in history. Reading these accounts informs us of God's nature, character, and activity. Pentecostal theology results in their belief that we can expect God to act in the present as he has acted in the past. The Old Testament accounts of God intervening supernaturally offers hope that he will do so in the present. These supernatural occurrences also confirm Pentecostal presuppositions and "continually informs our theology"[94] because the God of the Old Testament is not different from the God of the New Testament. A distinct twenty-first century Pentecostal hermeneutic embraces the Old Testament as an important part of Scripture and interprets it through a Lukan lens, Pentecostal theology, and in light of later New Testament revelation.

Community

The Holy Spirit initiates and aids interpretation to equip and motivate the community to fulfill its mission. Scripture, because of its nature and role, is object and superintendent of the interpretive process enabling the community of faith to live as the people of God in the world. We now turn our attention to community, the third element in the Pentecostal hermeneutic proposed in this book.

According to Anderson, Pentecostalism and charismatic Christianity in all its diversity is the fastest expanding religious movement in the world today.[95] The largest Christian congregation in the world, Yoido Full Gospel Church, Seoul, South Korea, is a Pentecostal congregation.[96] Anderson's description of five Pentecostal churches (the five largest churches in the world) clearly illustrates both the commonality and diversity within Pentecostalism.[97] Roebeck captures Pentecostalism's diversity by referring

---

93. Anderson, "Pentecostal Hermeneutics: Part 2," 21–22.
94. Ibid., 22.
95. Anderson, *Introduction To Pentecostalism*, 1.
96. Ibid.
97. Ibid., 1–9.

A Distinct Twenty-first Century Pentecostal Hermeneutic

to a "range of Pentecostalisms."[98] Within this wide diversity there is also a distinct Pentecostal story with a shared worldview, pneumatology, and missional purpose. As shown in chapter 2 there is sufficient commonality to legitimately refer to a worldwide Pentecostal community of faith. Since the role of community has become an important part of the debate in hermeneutics[99] and we can legitimately speak of a Pentecostal community of faith, we can consider the place of that community in a twenty-first century hermeneutic.

Biblical hermeneutics is generally practiced from within a particular faith community. Pentecostals are part of the larger Christian community and have much in common with it. However, they are more particularly a distinct Pentecostal Christian community and it is their Pentecostal identity that most impacts their hermeneutics. It is their distinctiveness that underlies the need for a particular hermeneutic.

Autry points out that this reality produces two consequences. First, private interpretation must be open to being informed by the understanding of the community. Second, biblical interpretation is a community task.[100] Harry Stout demonstrates the significance of community within the religious framework.[101] He argues convincingly that how we explain past religious history is tied to the community to which we belong. One's hermeneutical strategy, therefore, is closely allied, if not intrinsically linked, to community affiliation. Consequently, discussing a specific hermeneutical strategy must occur within the context of a clear, comprehensive, and accurate understanding of the community in which the discussion occurs. The idea of the objective observer, long since rejected as possible, cannot be part of our hermeneutic strategy.[102]

---

98. Roebeck, "Making Sense," 18.

99. Brueggemann, *The Book That Breathes*, vi. Brueggemann states, "the status of interpreter (or interpreting community) is now an important one."

100. Autry, "Dimensions of Hermeneutics," 45. I would also add that private interpretation should be open to critique from others outside the Pentecostal faith community. This idea is likely implied in Autry's use of "informed" but I believe there is value in clearly pointing out that private interpretation should expose itself to wide ranging critique. See also Higgenbotham and Patton, "Body Ethics," 2–7.

101. Stout, "Theological Commitment," 44–59.

102. Anderson, "Pentecostal Hermeneutics: Part 2," 18–22. Anderson points out that a Pentecostal hermeneut *deliberately* brings personal experience, historical experience and ideology to the interpretive task. This is what makes a Pentecostal hermeneutic distinct. What cannot happen in a Pentecostal hermeneutic is subjugating the text to these Pentecostal presuppositions.

Twenty-first Century Pentecostal Hermeneutic Strategy

Stout notes that our community connection results in a point of view from which we cannot escape. The story of our community colors our worldview by placing "an imperceptible, thin veil over our perceiving."[103] There is an inescapable coloring of all reality that is so ingrained that we could not totally remove it even if we could accurately identify it. Chapter 2 defined Pentecostalism and its early hermeneutics to establish the community identity and perspective that operates as part of the proposed hermeneutical strategy. It was shown that Pentecostals globally belong to a distinct, if variegated, community with a similar history and a common ethos. They embrace the apostolic Christianity described in Acts as prescriptive for the twenty-first century church and interpret Scripture through a Lukan lens. Perhaps the strongest bond among them is their belief that they are engaged in the final harvest before the parousia. The community's history, ethos, story, and missional purpose inform the interpreter and interpretation.

It is almost universally recognized that the objective observer does not exist. Everyone approaches a text from a specific community stance. One's cultural location and theological positioning influences how they approach interpretation.[104] Although early Pentecostals used the Bible Reading method, as did the Holiness camp, they did so out of a different community context. The Pentecostal doctrine of tongues as evidence of baptism in the Spirit resulted from their unique use of the Bible Reading method. The Pentecostal community is noncessationist, nondispensationalist, restorationist, praxis focused, eschatologically oriented, and missionally driven. It embraces the broader Christian metanarrative but, as Archer points out, as a restorational movement Pentecostals understand themselves as the true representation of Christianity in the world.[105]

The work of Stout and others points to the influence of one's community context on the practice of hermeneutics. Our community context informs our metanarrative and provides a narrative tradition that in turn influences how we determine meaning.[106] Alasdair MacIntyre claims that one's narrative tradition provides the context from which interpretive

---

103. Stout, "Theological Commitment," 47.

104. Harry Stout argues that the community to which one belongs influences how one explains past religious history and Scripture. Ibid., 44–59.

105. Archer, "A Pentecostal Hermeneutic," 98.

106. Ibid., 96–99.

A Distinct Twenty-first Century Pentecostal Hermeneutic

practices can be understood.[107] Pentecostals, like all interpreters, read and interpret Scripture using presuppositions that are community based.

For the Pentecostal community, Scripture is read primarily to discover how one ought to live life as the people of God. As restorationist nondispensationalists the Pentecostal community does not recognize a clear line of distinction between the world of the text and their contemporary world. In their reading of Scripture these two worlds are often merged and Scripture is read with the expectation that the Holy Spirit will do again what he has done in the past.

One of MacIntyre's central theses is important here. He argues that we must understand what stories we find ourselves a part of before we can determine what we are to do.[108] Since reading Scripture, for Pentecostals, is praxis driven, the story they see themselves as part of critically informs the meaning(s) they find in the text. Consequently, the better the hermeneut understands their story the better equipped they are to practice hermeneutics. They are also better able to filter out the ways in which that story *distorts* the interpretation.

Dan Hawk in discussing the concept of narrative tradition refers to the role of plot.[109] He argues that the narrative tradition results in a plot that is operational in the reading process resulting in the reader making connections between the world of the text and the reader's context. This "plot" results in a dynamic process between text and reader that affects interpretation.[110] Since Pentecostals read Scripture for the purpose of discovering how to live life or, as Archer calls it, developing a "'praxis' theology,"[111] the dynamic of internal plot merges the "then" and "now," and biblical stories are read so as to complement the community narrative. Stanley Fish identifies a danger here by pointing out that this may result in the interpretive community exercising a final authority over the text and ultimately deciding what the text means and controlling the hermeneutical operation.[112]

Since Pentecostals lend authority to both experience and Scripture there is a real danger that the community role in the interpretive process

---

107. MacIntyre, *After Virtue*, 214 ff. See also MacIntyre, *Whose Justice? Which Rationality?*.

108. MacIntyre, *After Virtue*, 216 ff.

109. Hawk, *Every Promise Fulfilled*, 18–29.

110. Ibid., 27.

111. Archer, *A Pentecostal Theology*, 31.

112. Fish, *Is There A Text*, 293. See also, Vanhoozer, "The Reader," 306.

Twenty-first Century Pentecostal Hermeneutic Strategy

could minimize Scripture's role.[113] The appropriate corrective is found in Pentecostalism's bibliology and a distinct hermeneutic that shares the Wesleyan Quadrilateral's view that Scripture holds the primary place in the interpretive strategy. The community role never supersedes that of Scripture. This is in accord with Pentecostal theology and hermeneutical intention and places scriptural authority above experience and community. Such a position is in line with Pentecostalism's core ethos for Pentecostals have historically allowed Scripture to critique their praxis and theology; in fact, they approach Scripture seeking its critique. Allowing the broader Christian community to speak through our shared "tradition" also provides some check and balance. A distinct Pentecostal hermeneutic for the twenty-first century embraces Scripture's authority over community and recognizes the place of "tradition" in interpretation above individual novelty.[114] Through "tradition" and ongoing dialogue the broader church speaks to (critiques) the Pentecostal community.

The Latter Rain motif[115] is a significant aspect of Pentecostalism's community identity. Pentecostals read Scripture, including the Old Testament, through a Lukan lens with an emphasis on Acts.[116] Acts 2 is especially important for it is the scriptural foundation for Pentecostals' restorationist self-understanding and seeing themselves as the people of the Latter Rain. Pentecostals believe God, via the Pentecostal revivals of the nineteenth and twentieth centuries, was restoring the charismata of apostolic Christianity

---

113. There will be varying degrees of how this operates within particular subgroups of Pentecostals. Some will emphasize text over experience. Others will emphasize experience over text. Yet others will hold them in a dynamic tension sometimes leaning to one side and at other times leaning to the other. There was an extreme movement in the 1980s and '90s that began recording all prophetic words and tongues and interpretation with the view that they were of equal authority as Scripture. To what extent this continues I cannot accurately say but I suspect it is practiced at least in some places.

114. D. Wesley Myland would argue for this position. His lectures on hermeneutics at Stone Church, Chicago, May through June 1909, became important documents guiding early Pentecostals in their approach to interpreting Scripture. Myland, who supported the Pentecostal view that one comes to comprehend through one's experience with the Holy Spirit also argued that Scripture must validate one's "experiential redemptive knowledge" (Myland, *The Latter Rain Covenant*, 107).

115. The Latter Rain concept did not originate with Pentecostals. It was present among the Holiness groups from which Pentecostalism emerged. The Holiness groups believed that the Latter Rain would bring in the end time harvest. A. B. Simpson, founder of the Christian and Missionary Alliance, was a leading figure who held this view. For an overview of Simpson's "Latter Rain" views see: Nienkrichen, *A. B. Simpson*, 65–68.

116. Archer, *A Pentecostal Hermeneutic*, 114.

A Distinct Twenty-first Century Pentecostal Hermeneutic

to the church and pouring out the Latter Rain promised in Joel. The purpose of this restoration and the Latter Rain was to bring in the final harvest prior to the return of Christ. Accordingly Pentecostals see themselves participating in God's redemptive activity that is channelled through Christ and manifested in the community by the Holy Spirit.

Pentecostals adopted the Latter Rain of Joel referenced in Acts 2 as the explanation for the Pentecostal revival at the turn of the twentieth century.[117] Myland states this early Pentecostal view well: "the first Pentecost started the church, the second Pentecost unites and perfects the church unto the coming of the Lord."[118] This motif filtered and informed everything, giving meaning to the Pentecostal experience and aiding the interpretation of Scripture. The Latter Rain motif enabled Pentecostals to interpret Old and New Testament from a promise-fulfillment strategy.[119] As such, they saw themselves as participants in the fulfilment of these promises.

Pentecostals continue to see themselves as the Latter Rain people of God. The passage of a century has diminished *urgency* for some but it has not removed the Latter Rain understanding and anticipation of the return of Christ. Pentecostals continue to hold to an imminent return of Jesus and the need to evangelize the world before that occurs. They continue to view the baptism in the Holy Spirit as an empowerment for bringing in the harvest and complete Jesus' mission. They retain the eschatological pneumatology

---

117. The Latter Rain motif allowed early Pentecostals to see themselves as the prophetically promised Latter Rain people. This meant that apostolic faith, power, authority and practice had been fully recovered. Faupel, *The Everlasting Gospel*, 39. The signs and wonders (especially healing and tongues) that accompanied their worship were evidence or proof that this belief was true. These early Pentecostals used dispensational terminology as part of their Latter Rain theology. However, they did not engage the dispensational rules used by Fundamentalists. Lawrence, *The Apostolic Faith Restored*, 15. Dispensationalists argued that the charismata ended with the apostles according to God's plan. Pentecostals argued that corruption in the church and lack of faith lie behind the loss of the charismata. They also argued that there had always been a remnant in the church among whom these gifts operated. They held that *"these signs shall follow them that believe"* was part of the New Covenant and was now being fully restored through the Pentecostal movement.

118. Myland, *The Latter Rain Covenant*, 84–85. Myland, like most early Pentecostals, was premillennial and pre-tribulation in his theology. Contemporary Pentecostalism would be predominantly premillennial but not necessarily pre-tribulation. The Pentecostal Assemblies of Canada amended their General Constitution in the 1990s to a "pre wrath" rapture position rather than a pre-tribulation position exclusively. This is further evidence that Pentecostals remain open to altering their theology and praxis as a result of hermeneutics and or pragmatism.

119. Archer, *A Pentecostal Hermeneutic*, 100.

Twenty-first Century Pentecostal Hermeneutic Strategy

of early Pentecostalism. Perhaps as a result of their impoverished circumstances, African Pentecostals (perhaps all Majority World Pentecostals) are expressing a higher level of expectancy and urgency than many Western Pentecostals. As the African influence increases the twenty-first century may witness another heightened wave of Pentecostal missions. The Latter Rain motif continues to inform the Pentecostal worldview and ethos and is, therefore, a significant contributor to the community's metanarrative.[120]

As an element in a distinct Pentecostal hermeneutic "community" generally operates at the level of presuppositions, bias, and *a priori*.[121] This means that community is often operating without our being aware but understanding and an awareness of how community might impact interpretation is essential. The hermeneut, as far as possible, should move the community's influence from the realm of background into the foreground of awareness. In this way preconceptions are not allowed to subjugate the text and allow the interpreter's presuppositions to inform interpretation and meaning but do not force meaning upon the text (eisegesis).

Culture and community are inseparably linked; in fact, one might argue that it is cultural uniqueness that distinguishes one community from another. Connected to community cultural elements are involved in the hermeneutical process.[122] They create specific predispositions and bias is partly related to cultural issues. By recognizing the cultural elements of the Pentecostal community the Pentecostal hermeneut can approach interpretation deliberately as an informed Pentecostal offering a distinct interpretation of Scripture empowering the community to do life as the Latter Rain people of God. This distinct interpretation may also be offered to the broader church for its consideration and critique.

Pentecostals are restorationists and see themselves as bringing something vital back to the church that was lost, or nearly lost.[123] This restora-

---

120. Ibid., 114 ff. Archer holds that the Latter Rain motif is the central element in the Pentecostal metanarrative.

121. Anderson, "Pentecostal Hermeneutic: Part 2," 13–22. Anderson suggests that part of Pentecostalism's distinctive hermeneutic is their "deliberate" recognition and employment of their biases, presuppositions, ideology and etc. (ibid., 10–11).

122. Thiselton, *New Horizons*, 9 Thiselton points out that culture is at work in the text as well as in the mind of the interpreter. See also Archer, *A Pentecostal Hermeneutic*, 95 ff. Archer effectively argues that current hermeneutic theory recognizes the important role community culture has for the interpretive process. Archer also clearly identifies sufficient evidence to support the claim that Pentecostals are a distinct community with a distinguishing culture/worldview.

123. Most Pentecostals believe the baptism of the Holy Spirit with initial evidence

tionist self-perception is an important cultural marker in the Pentecostal community. As the largest Protestant expression of Christianity in the world Pentecostalism's restorationism takes on new meaning and significance. One could argue that Pentecost has been restored and the current need is to ensure it is not lost again. This reality indicates that cultural elements within a community are not stagnant but experience change over time and such changes may impact interpretation. In the twenty-first century Pentecostals continue to operate from a Latter Rain, restorationist perspective as they interpret Scripture but will do so taking into account cultural transitions taking place within Pentecostalism.

Pentecostals are also part of the broader Christian community and they share important elements of their community metanarrative with all Christians. These elements, like the distinctive elements, will impact hermeneutics. The broader Christian church includes martyrs, heretics, missionaries, hermits, clergy, laity, educated, uneducated, etc. Cultures, historical context, geographical settings, theological emphasis, and numerous other factors vary over generations. It is this historical community that has given us the traditions that define orthodox Christianity and these traditions impact us in various ways as we engage Scripture in the hermeneutical process.

The broader community may at times apply restraining pressure and at other times offer a directional pressure on the Pentecostal community. In this vein the Wesleyan Quadrilateral offers help and direction for a twenty-first century Pentecostal hermeneutic since "tradition" is one of the quadrilateral's elements. The way/s in which the church historically has understood a text (tradition) may dissuade Pentecostals from the pursuit of new horizons as was the case for the majority of Pentecostals in relation to the oneness doctrine.[124] Sometimes the historical community offers fresh (to the contemporary exegete) insights by looking at the text through

---

of speaking in tongues can be traced through church history. In fact, some Pentecostal writers go to great lengths to prove this point. Henry Aline's wrestling with the Spirit through the night would, by many Pentecostals be construed as a baptism in the Holy Spirit experience with the assumed accompanying glossolalia. The argument in support of these historical proofs is always circular and generally not clear in the text at hand.

124. Exercising the Bible Reading method from a Pentecostal perspective led to the oneness doctrine yet the majority of Pentecostals rejected this position on the basis of tradition. Although Scripture did not use the term "Trinity" the majority of Pentecostals saw the patristic Church's development of Trinitarians as biblically sound. This is a good example of how tradition can assist Pentecostals as they engage in hermeneutics. See Archer, *A Pentecostal Hermeneutic*, 82–93.

Twenty-first Century Pentecostal Hermeneutic Strategy

lenses unfamiliar to us. Old perspectives can be enlightening and fresh to our contemporary setting; therefore, the historical community can, and will, engage us to look at texts in new and interesting ways. The Pentecostal community in a distinct twenty-first century hermeneutical strategy should remain open to the voice of the broader church inviting its critique and insights as aids in the interpretive process.

Lowenburg argues that Acts 2 and 15 reveal *mission* as an underlying interest of interpretation.[125] In Acts 15 James calls attention to the Spirit's agenda of bringing multitudes of Gentiles into the church. In Acts 1 Jesus restricts the activity of the disciples to wait in Jerusalem until receiving the Holy Spirit who will empower them for mission. In Acts 2 it is the baptism in the Spirit that results in 3000 conversions and the activity of the Spirit throughout Acts is to expand the borders of the church. Miracles, signs, wonders, sermons, and the Holy Spirit's guidance of the church all serve the purpose of mission—bringing the gospel to the ends of the earth. Pentecostal ethos, metanarrative and self-understanding as a restorationist, Latter Rain people of God are encapsulated in this missionary purpose.

Much has changed within the Pentecostal community over the past century. The doctrine of tongues as initial evidence is no longer universally held and a singular view regarding the rapture no longer exists. Views concerning end times are varied and divergent but agreement does exist concerning the importance of mission. All would agree that the church's mission is to bring the gospel to all people and make disciples of all ethnic-linguistic groups before Jesus returns. All other activities of the church, important as they might be, are secondary to this primary mission. A robust Pentecostal hermeneutic will empower and mobilize the church to reach the unreached and enable Pentecostals to engage in a vigorous discussion around Pentecostal doctrine.

The community offers a corrective to individual voices and interpretation as a subordinate partner, with Scripture.[126] The community administrates historical and traditional perspectives and is the arbiter of community held beliefs, norms, practices, and doctrines. Community is guardian of the metanarrative that creates identity and as such protects against inappropriate individual interpretations. The community provides the individual with traditional perspectives that can "moderate extremism,

---

125. Lowenburg, "A Twenty-first Century Pentecostal Hermeneutic," 24.
126. Archer, *A Pentecostal Hermeneutic*, 96.

A Distinct Twenty-first Century Pentecostal Hermeneutic

radical individualism, and impractical abstractions."[127] In the North American context the moderating influence of the community is an important correction to a strong individualism. In Africa the challenge is for the community to allow, even encourage, individual leaders to emerge and offer their trained critique. The African Pentecostal community must encourage youth, women, and capable servant leaders to develop and use their hermeneutical skills.

In the twenty-first century the Pentecostal community looks vastly different from what Archer describes. The majority of twenty-first century Pentecostals, seemingly ignored by Archer, live in the Majority World, sometimes called Emerging, or Third World. Africa forms a significant part of the contemporary Pentecostal community. Africans tend to have a more intuitive grasp of the cultural dynamics in the biblical text and a greater appreciation for the supernatural powers referenced in Scripture than Western Pentecostals. Accordingly their interpretation sometimes differs significantly from their Western fellows. Recognizing the value, significant numbers, and increasing academic power of the African Pentecostal church, a legitimate, distinct twenty-first century Pentecostal hermeneutic must enable and encourage their voices.

The Pentecostal community interacts with Scripture, Spirit, and trained leader in the task of interpreting Scripture. Led and empowered by the Spirit, subordinate to Scripture, and interfacing with trained leaders, the community brings the special aids of metanarrative, ethos, experience, and ideology to the interpretive task. Although trained leaders stand apart to speak to the community they are part of the people to whom they present their interpretation/s of Scripture. Comprised of other trained leaders, persons highly qualified in fields other than theology, individuals from every walk of life, social strata, ethnic background, etc., the community receives or rejects the offered interpretation. *Under the governance of Scripture and influence of the Spirit community and trained leader engage each other in a delicate dance of challenge and counter-challenge in the critical task of interpreting Scripture.* Having considered the role of the community we must now turn our attention to the role of the trained leader.

---

127. Lowenburg, "A Twenty-first Century Pentecostal Hermeneutic," 29.

Twenty-first Century Pentecostal Hermeneutic Strategy

The Trained Leader

Ephesians 4:11 lists leadership gifts, one of which is "teacher," that Christ gives to his church. The Pastoral Epistles (Timothy and Titus) identify an *ability* to teach as a criterion for serving as elders in the church. In the Gospels, Jesus chose twelve men to be with him in the rabbinical style of discipling followers and it seems clear that Christ intended trained, equipped leaders to teach the larger community. Within the Pentecostal community there are scholars and pastors who serve the community as trained leaders. Generally pastors have the more direct connection with the community; therefore, the *interpretation* of Scripture heard within the community comes primarily from pastors. Occasionally laity exercising spiritual gifts (especially tongues, interpretation, and prophecy) provide interpretation to the community. A distinct twenty-first century Pentecostal hermeneutic must identify the role of trained leader and identify their relationship to Scripture, Spirit, and community in the interpretive process.

The individual as a member of the faith community is an essential aspect of hermeneutics, yet Archer gives no attention to this essential feature of the hermeneutical process.[128] Pastors, teachers, and academics who are members of the Pentecostal community serve important roles within the community as they study the text, interpret it, and present those interpretations to the community. They offer those interpretations to the community as arbiters of life so the community is equipped to effectively fulfill its mission.

In Acts 15 Peter offers a *testimony* (witness) pointing to Gentile inclusion without circumcision. Barnabas and Paul add their testimony of the *charismata* (immediacy of God's presence) occurring among the Gentiles. James eventually stands and gives a biblical interpretation in support of the decision to reject the Pharisaical position and include Gentiles without circumcision. Clearly Paul was highly trained and qualified as a capable interpreter of Scripture. Peter, as one of the twelve, is arguably trained as a result of his time with Jesus. Barnabas as a companion of Paul might be viewed as a leader who had some level of training. James clearly is knowledgeable of Scripture and speaks from an authoritative platform as a recognized

---

128. Some of Archer's discussion of community is more relevant to individual interpreters than to a group as the term community would suggest. Archer seems to treat scholar, pastor, and congregation together under the category of community. It is true they are part of the community; however, the trained leader serves from a place of authority in the interpretive activity.

A Distinct Twenty-first Century Pentecostal Hermeneutic

leader in the Jerusalem church. These individuals were obviously accountable to their community but spoke as trained and qualified leaders within that community which they called to move beyond tradition and accepted cultural norms to a new way of understanding the people of God based on the interpretation of Scripture.

The Pastoral Epistles clearly point to the importance of trained leaders. Timothy and Titus, as disciples of Paul, qualify for this designation. In 2 Timothy 3:10 Paul tells Timothy, "You, however, know all about my teaching." To Titus he writes, "You must teach what is in accord with sound doctrine" (Titus 2:1). These statements imply Paul trained Timothy and Titus to equip them for the teaching task. They are sent on a mission of setting the assemblies in Ephesus and Crete in order. Here we see the importance placed on trained leaders in the first-century church. The letters to both Timothy and Titus call for the appointment of qualified persons in leadership over congregations with one of the requirements being "qualified to teach" (Titus 1:9; 1 Tim 3:2).

Trained individuals are essential spokespersons in the community of faith. They interpret Scripture to equip the community for mission and, as in Acts 15, the interpretation may call the community into a new path for the future. In Acts 2 Peter interpreted Joel 2:28–32 to explain and make sense of the current event being experienced by the church and witnessed by the crowd. Peter's interpretation served the church and world. In Acts 15 James interpreted Amos and gave the church missional direction for future outreach and resolved a major ecclesiastical crisis. Although part of the community, trained leaders sometimes stand apart from the community to present a "reformational and transformational message."[129]

Scripture can only perform its task of challenging, calling, transforming, and reforming the church as trained leaders, prophet-like, stand apart from the community and speak to it. Faith, doctrine, and practice are only challenged as inspired (prophetic) voices speak. For Pentecostals, the authoritative challenge to faith, practice, and doctrine must come from Scripture. Consequently there is an important place for individuals trained and equipped to adequately interpret Scripture and offer the necessary critique of current faith, experience, practice, and doctrine. It is these individuals who must be fully equipped to employ appropriate hermeneutical methodologies to interpret Scripture; therefore, our Bible colleges must train and equip potential leaders to effectively employ the eclectic methodologies

---

129. Lowenburg, "A Twenty-first Century Pentecostal Hermeneutic," 29.

Twenty-first Century Pentecostal Hermeneutic Strategy

identified in chapter 4 from a Pentecostal stance. It also requires that the trained leader operate within the framework of the quadratic interaction among Scripture, Spirit, community and trained leader.

The trained leader is required to interpret Scripture in order to teach sound doctrine, provide scriptural explanation for current events, and provide biblical responses to real life issues. Peter's use of Joel 2:28–32 is an example of a qualified leader interpreting Scripture to explain a current event and give meaning to a spiritual experience. He took an inspired Old Testament text, manipulated its words and aspects of its meaning, and brought it into a new context, thereby creatively delivering a "new, contextual meaning and message to his Jerusalem audience."[130] Peter created new meaning going far beyond what Fee, Oleka, and others would allow, but it cannot be argued from this that the contemporary Pentecostal hermeneut, under the guidance of the Holy Spirit, can manipulate any text in whatever way he wishes.[131] From Peter's use of Joel we can argue that there is a legitimate place for the interpreter (led by the Spirit, supervised by Scripture, and growing out of/taught within and accountable to the community) in the creation of meaning. Peter's hermeneutic is more like that of Straus and Duval and Hays than that of Fee and Oleka.[132] His method resonates more with postmodern literary methodology than with the historical-grammatical method. A distinct twenty-first century hermeneutic will employ a Petrine-like interpretive freedom of postmodern literary methodologies that allow a place for the interpreter in the creation of meaning. Textual limiters and historical-grammatical investigation fence creative interpretation but do not eliminate it. In the end the Pentecostal hermeneut using literary critical and historical-grammatical methodology brings a Pentecostal interpretation to the community and possibly to the church at large.

In the early years of Pentecostalism the general practitioners of hermeneutics were pastors of local assemblies. Speaking of Pentecostalism in Canada Douglas Rudd writes: "Pioneer Pentecostal preachers came from all walks of life: trained clergy, fisherman, farmers, tradesman, business people, and professionals."[133] Many of the early leaders, male and female,

130. Ibid., 5.

131. Peter's position, the book of Acts being itself Scripture, and a unique operation of the Spirit through inspiration are distinct attributes of the text in Acts 2. The contemporary Pentecostal interpreter does not share these attributes; therefore, cannot assume authorization to manipulate Scripture.

132. Lowenburg, "A Twenty-first Century Pentecostal Hermeneutic," 4–5.

133. Rudd, *When the Spirit Came Upon Them*, 31. This would be true of the United

were uneducated and their approach to Scripture was often devotional in nature. How one "got the message for Sunday"[134] seems to me to form an important aspect of the early Pentecostal hermeneutic. Getting Sunday's message often involved seasons of prayer and "waiting on the Spirit" with Bible in hand until some text or idea came to mind. They prayed, read and waited until they perceived they had heard from the Spirit.[135] This prayerful approach to interpretation is not unique to Pentecostals and, as mentioned earlier, is an important aspect of acknowledging the Spirit's role in the interpretive process. Accordingly the trained leader is encouraged to embrace a prayerful approach to interpretation as a deliberate attempt to engage the Spirit's contribution.

Like the community to which they belong, the Pentecostal hermeneut brings *personal* and *historic* experience to the interpretive task.[136] Lowenburg's position that the "Spirit can speak *tabula rasa*"[137] is, in my view, unsustainable. Anderson points out that experience can assist the interpretive process for similarity of experience to the biblical material enhances interpretation.[138] Due to the experience of being baptized in the Spirit, and other charismatic experiences Pentecostals have a greater experiential affinity to some portions of Scripture than non-Pentecostals. Stronstad points out that the Pentecostal's experience of salvation (common to all Christians) and charismatic experience (including baptism in the Spirit) informs their hermeneutic.[139] What is distinct for Pentecostals is the kind of experience they bring to the hermeneutical task. Pentecostals deliberately engage their personal experience in the hermeneutical process but experience is never

---

States also.

134. This phrase was common language among the early Pentecostal pastors. There was a belief that one must hear direct from God for the message to be delivered in the Sunday services. A great deal of time and intercession was invested in "getting the message from the Lord."

135. This has been reported to me by numerous first and second generation Pentecostal leaders. How one knew they had heard from God varied from person to person. After 'getting the message' most would then study the text and prepare the sermon.

136. Anderson, "Pentecostal Hermeneutics: Part 2," 18–20.

137. Lowenburg, "A Twenty-first Century Pentecostal Hermeneutic," 25.

138. Anderson, "Pentecostal Hermeneutics: Part 2," 18.

139. Stronstad, "Pentecostal Experience and Hermeneutics," 25. Pentecostals are not unique in this. Stronstad effectively argues that all interpreters bring personal experience to the interpretive task.

Twenty-first Century Pentecostal Hermeneutic Strategy

properly elevated above Scripture and is always open to the critique of Scripture and community.

Trained leaders in the Pentecostal tradition include historical experience in their hermeneutic as an aid to interpretation. Pentecostal ecclesiology supports the use of historical experience for it sees God functioning in the world until the parousia in the same way he did in Acts. In John 9 the Pharisees rejected a miracle performed in front of them because they had no theological categories for it. "Historical experience," says Anderson, "has a significant impact on hermeneutics."[140] He points to the Pentecostal understanding of healing and the role of women in ministry as examples of historical experience's influence on interpretation. Historical experience enables us to appreciate the transcendent God's activity that gives rise to something new in reality.[141] In connection with this Anderson points out that Pentecostals read Acts with "a sense of familiarity, empathy and understanding that can only come from having experienced what the text describes."[142] Pentecostals "use real life experience with an awareness and admission of the fact and the belief that it is an appropriate step in a legitimate hermeneutic."[143]

Stronstad argues that experience be placed at the beginning of the hermeneutical process as a presupposition and at the end of the process as verification while William Menzies places experience at the end as verification. Anderson points to strict cessationists and fanatical charismatics as evidence against placing experience at the beginning of the process,[144] however, this would seem to fly in the face of what we observe in Acts 2 and 15. Eliminating experience as a bias or presupposition seems an impossible task, so perhaps the better approach is to critically examine and evaluate the experience being brought into the interpretive process, and at what stage it is being used. The place for, and use of, experience in the interpretive process is, and will continue to be, controversial; but sufficient for now is to acknowledge that the trained leader using a distinct twenty-first century Pentecostal hermeneutic will embrace experience as part of the interpretive process.

140. Anderson, "Pentecostal Hermeneutics: Part 2," 20.

141. Ibid., 20.

142. Ibid., 19.

143. Ibid. Anderson claims this is a clear difference between Pentecostal hermeneuts and others.

144. Ibid., 20.

A Distinct Twenty-first Century Pentecostal Hermeneutic

The trained leader, like everyone else, comes to the text, or any aspect of life for that matter, with a set of assumptions and attitudes that act as a filter through which we interpret the text or event. We may attempt, with varied success, to limit their impact but we cannot eliminate them; therefore, wisdom admonishes the interpreter to be aware of them. Ferguson identifies the existence of four types of pre-understandings: informational, attitudinal, ideological, and methodological.[145] These act as filters as the trained leader works to interpret Scripture.

Ferguson speaks of faith as a pre-understanding essential to hermeneutics[146] in a way that is informative to a Pentecostal hermeneutic, since Pentecostals understand themselves to be in relationship with God the Holy Spirit in a very specific way. The attitudinal aspect of faith, as Ferguson calls it, is relevant here because Pentecostals understand their relationship with God in terms congruent with their pneumatology and this will impact their interpretation. The hermeneut, in a Pentecostal context, is a person of faith holding to Pentecostal theology and experience. The biblical text, the medium through which God's self-revelation in Christ occurs, is interpreted and understood from the perspective of this specific experiential stance. Ferguson reminds us that faith is formed within a community[147] and, as a result, our understanding of God and interpretation of Scripture attesting to God's self-revelation in Christ will reflect this community culture. Community interacts with the individual in the interpretive process by providing them with a worldview and pre-understandings that function as interpretive filters.

Essential to the hermeneutical task is an effort to diligently work against the inevitable distortions produced by pre-understanding, yet the trained leader's pre-understanding must contain sufficient assumptions and attitudes to enable an accurate knowledge of the text. Ferguson says, "It has been suggested that certain qualities in the interpreter are necessary for a sound interpretation. For example, it is necessary to have empathy and rapport with the author . . . . one must be open and listening . . . one must have a living relation to the message of the text . . . and one should be aware that the task of hermeneutics is larger than explaining the text,

---

145. Ferguson, *Biblical Interpretation*, 13.

146. Ibid., 18–22. Faith here is understood to refer to a belief in and acceptance of the gospel.

147. Ibid., 21.

Twenty-first Century Pentecostal Hermeneutic Strategy

but is a quest for the understanding of new modes of being."[148] Faith then is an essential pre-understanding requisite for the Pentecostal hermeneut since: "The person of faith has a certain amount of ideological affinity with the authors of biblical records, sharing with them a common belief in the subject matter about which they write."[149]

The trained Pentecostal leader interprets Scripture with a hermeneutical strategy in which Scripture stands over the interpreter. Pentecostal theology and bibliology require the trained leader to submit to Scripture's superintendence in her interpretation and her involvement in the creation of meaning for the text. Since the Bible is God's self-revelation and as such is the product of revelation, the word of God and inspired Scripture are authoritative for belief and practice. As a trained leader, the Pentecostal hermeneut subjects pre-dispositions, ideology, biases, etc. to the supremacy of Scripture. She comes to Scripture prepared to alter any aspect of belief or practice that Scripture might show to be contrary to the will of God. A distinct twenty-first century Pentecostal hermeneutic requires the interpreter to interact with Scripture from this position.

Critical to keeping the trained leader on track is the clear awareness of the preacher's task to proclaim the timeless message of the Bible. She is entrusted with the responsibility of managing and dispensing the mysteries of God, she is not commissioned to imagine great, edifying words and then look for a biblical text that seems to support them. The message does not originate with the preacher, it originates with God and is communicated through the Bible. Ferguson speaks of the use of Scripture in the teaching ministry of the church:

> The use of the Bible in the educational ministry of the church carries with it all the risks of the undisciplined and uninformed use of the Bible in preaching. It can be made to say nearly anything which the teacher would like it to say and can even be a destructive force in the hands of a manipulative person. To ensure the proper usage of the Bible in the teaching ministry of the church, it is as necessary as it was in the case of preaching and worship that the teacher preserve the delicate balance between being faithful to the intent of Scripture and allowing at the same time the Scripture to give perspective and guidance on current issues and problems.[150]

---

148. Ibid., 181.
149. Ibid.
150. Ibid., 121–22.

A Distinct Twenty-first Century Pentecostal Hermeneutic

The trained leader, as preacher and teacher, is commissioned to proclaim God's word to God's people enabling them to carry out God's mission in their time, context and culture.

Scripture, as the inspired word of God, is eternal and authoritative but is also the product of human beings, inspired by God, who write in their own style, vocabulary, and personality within a particular context. Consequently Scripture has, as Gordon Fee states, "locked into it a degree of ambiguity, accommodation and diversity."[151] Since God's means of communicating with humankind contains these elements of eternality and ambiguity it is important that a distinct twenty-first century Pentecostal hermeneutic recognize these realities. In so doing the trained leader employing a distinct twenty-first century Pentecostal hermeneutic strives to capture God's word and convey his truth in contemporary language with relevance. The "eternal" nature of Scripture as God's word cautions against unrestrained imaginative interpretation, while its being a human product opens the door to some level of interpretive freedom for the interpreter.

The role of the trained leader within the Pentecostal community is especially important for Africa since 63 percent of adults and 47 million youths (ages 15–24) are illiterate.[152] African poverty, limited access to education, and other social issues mitigate against these statistics changing rapidly in the future. Consequently the African Pentecostal community is more dependent than Westerners on trained persons if they are to *hear* God's word. The importance that Pentecostal leaders be properly trained in a distinct Pentecostal hermeneutic is also amplified by this reality.

A further issue that immediately confronts the hermeneut and requires careful attention during the course of exegesis and hermeneutics is the cultural conditioning of the Scriptures themselves. The Pentecostal practitioner must seek to identify the cultural elements that are in play in the world of the text. Effective hermeneutics results in Scripture, a text generally from a foreign culture, to engage the readers within their familiar culture. Once identified, the interpreter must determine if the cultural aspects of the text are immediately transferable or if they must be interpreted. In *Gospel and Spirit*, Fee states, "our own cultural predispositions determine how we decide if a text is culturally 'first century' or is culturally

---

151. Fee, *Gospel and Spirit*, 35.
152. UNESCO Institute for Statistics, "Adult and Youth Literacy."

Twenty-first Century Pentecostal Hermeneutic Strategy

relevant."[153] Fee provides some guidelines that will be helpful to the Pentecostal hermeneut in the twenty-first century.

a. Determine the central core of the message of the Bible and distinguish between that central core and what is dependent upon and/or peripheral to it.

b. Note whether the matter in hand is inherently moral or non-moral, theological or non-theological.

c. Note when the NT has a uniform witness on a given point and when there are differences within the NT itself.

d. Distinguish between principle and specific application. NT writers sometimes support absolute principle with an application that is not absolute. First Corinthians 11:12–16: *if culture is not relative then the culture in which the biblical text was given becomes normative.*

e. Keep alert to cultural differences between the first century and the twenty-first century that are not immediately obvious. First-century women were not normally educated.

f. Exercise Christian charity on *this point*—differences exist—so be gracious.

Two principles of translating from the first century to the contemporary context:

1. In "translating" from the first century context to another, the two contexts must be genuinely comparable.

2. Usually the "extended application" is seen to be legitimate because it is otherwise true; that is, it is clearly spelled out in other passages where it is the intent.[154]

Awareness of and proper attention to the cultural conditioning of the Bible enables the preacher to proclaim Scripture as a "witness to God's will and to his purposes for his people."[155] Whether through poetry or parable, the biblical witness is recorded by individuals who were culturally and historically located; therefore, the text they created contains cultural elements.

---

153. Fee, *Gospel and Spirit*, 12.

154. Ibid., 13–16. The Pentecostal interpreter in the twenty-first century can benefit from these guidelines and their application should be carefully communicated to pastors and laypersons alike.

155. Achtemeier, *Inspiration and Authority*, 135.

A Distinct Twenty-first Century Pentecostal Hermeneutic

Achtemeier says, "Because world views and situations change, traditions must be interpreted anew and the witness given anew."[156] Historical-grammatical methodology can illuminate the cultural elements that operate in the world of the text and aid today's Pentecostal interpreter in bringing the biblical witness to God's revelation faithfully to their audience. In this way the Pentecostal hermeneut effectively witnesses to the will and purposes of God from Scripture to her twenty-first century audience.

The African Pentecostal reader of Scripture approaches the text as fully inspired and authoritative, engaging what Stein would call "semantic autonomy."[157] They approach the Scripture as though it came direct from God to them, what some would call a radical literalism. For African readers the human author is somewhat irrelevant since the real author is God who communicates directly to them in their situation through the biblical text. This perspective can result in total disregard for the cultural elements imbedded in the text and their natural connection to the agrarian lifestyle of Scripture might exacerbate this problem. A distinct twenty-first century Pentecostal hermeneutic will move the African interpreter to give more attention to the human agency of Scripture while challenging the western interpreter to give more room to the Spirit and the interpreter in determining meaning.

Pentecostalism emphasizes an ongoing personal relationship with the Holy Spirit flowing out of the Baptism in the Spirit that should mature into a lifestyle of walking in the Spirit and empowering one for witness and mission. The person baptized in the Spirit should function with charismatic gifts to edify the body of Christ and bring the transforming power of God's kingdom into the contemporary context (1 Cor 12–14). African Pentecostalism is especially challenged in the area of social reform and transformation; therefore, Pentecostal hermeneutics must enable the African church to serve their context well. As Lowenburg points out the African Pentecostal church must address "tribalism, biblically guided political engagement, gender equality, a balanced ministry of evangelism and compassion, Pentecostal servant leadership, and a biblical assessment of

---

156. Ibid., 135.

157. Stein, *A Basic Guide*, 18–19. African readers of Scripture often interpret the text as fully inspired and authoritative but also as though it came directly to them from God. Lowenburg says of African readers, "There is no concern for or even awareness of human authorship or historical context. The text has meaning independent of what the human author intended to convey" (Lowenburg, "A Twenty-first Century Pentecostal Hermeneutic," 8). It is this approach that is called "semantic autonomy."

Twenty-first Century Pentecostal Hermeneutic Strategy

African religions and traditional cultural practices."[158] The challenge is real and intense. Fortunately a lively Pentecostal hermeneutic that embraces historical-grammatical and literary critical methodologies and embraces the interpretive interaction among Scripture, Spirit, community, and trained leader will enable the Pentecostal interpreter to negotiate between static and creative meaning in the text.

Conclusion

A distinct twenty-first century Pentecostal hermeneutic engages an eclectic methodology and I have here argued for a quadradic interaction among Scripture, Spirit, community, and trained leader. The four interact creatively in the interpretive event, but Scripture always holds the primary position. Its nature as inspired word of God, Pentecostal theology, and bibliology require that a distinct twenty-first Pentecostal hermeneutic recognize the primacy of Scripture. From this vantage point Scripture challenges, encourages, re-forms, and enlightens interpreter and community in order that they might fulfill their mission of taking the gospel to the whole world.

The community, via its influence on the interpreter, brings specific ideological predispositions into the interpretive action. After Scripture, community also serves to arbitrate the acceptability or truthfulness of interpretations offered by the hermeneut. The community's metanarrative, theological stance, traditions, experience, and current context incite and inform the interpretive process.

The Holy Spirit continues to speak to and lead God's people through Scripture, charismata, experience, etc. The Spirit's role in our hermeneutic is impossible to quantify and describe but he is active in enabling community and individual interpreter to understand Scripture meaning and meaningfulness. The activity of the Spirit, whatever form it takes, is always intended to move the church toward fulfilling its mandated mission. The distinct Pentecostal hermeneutic does not see a place for the Spirit different than for non-Pentecostal interpreters. Pentecostal pneumatology is distinct and informs interpretation but this does not mean a Pentecostal interpretation is more spiritual.

The interpreter (trained leader) approaches Scripture as a member of the Pentecostal worldwide community. Her primary concern is to faithfully communicate the message of Scripture to her contemporary audience. She

158. Stein, *A Basic Guide*, 23.

A Distinct Twenty-first Century Pentecostal Hermeneutic

approaches her task humbly; prayerfully seeking the aid of the Spirit in the interpretive process, open to Scripture's scrutiny, and submitted to its primacy. The interpreter offers her interpretation to the community and willingly listens to the community's response, so that together they can determine if God's voice has been heard.

A distinct twenty-first century Pentecostal hermeneutic is not a novel methodology strategy. It is the use of common methods from a distinct Pentecostal perspective and the creative interaction among Scripture, Spirit, community, and trained leader. Scripture stands above, and the Spirit moves among community and trained leader, leading to a Pentecostal understanding of the text.

CONCLUSION

As the largest and fastest growing Protestant expression of Christianity, Pentecostalism must address the current state of affairs regarding its hermeneutics. Chapter 1 offered several indicators, such as the call from academics, the distinctive nature of Pentecostalism, theoretical developments in communication theory and hermeneutics, and the changed nature of the twenty-first century world in support of the conclusion that a distinct hermeneutic is legitimate and necessary for Pentecostals. Failure to develop an appropriate, distinct hermeneutic leaves Pentecostals voiceless to a church that should, and desires to, hear that voice. The intent of this book to offer such a hermeneutic is shown to be legitimate and needed.

Pentecostalism's distinctive nature arises from its historical roots and its early years of development as presented in chapter 2. Pentecostalism's Holiness, revivalist background provided its theological foundation and impetus. A particular energy and worship style informs Pentecostalism's core ethos and nature worldwide. The Lukan lens and Latter Rain motif were shown to direct Pentecostals to employ the Bible Reading method in a distinct manner. Myland's lectures on biblical interpretation (latter published as a monograph) became the leading influence in early Pentecostal hermeneutics, embedding within Pentecostalism an interpretive mindset that is open to meaning beyond authorial intent. Pentecostalism's pneumatology, bibliology, and experiential orientation easily embrace, perhaps even require, a more open approach to interpretation than strict adherence to authorial intent. Therefore, the approach proposed in this book openly adopts methods and strategy that are open to meaning arising from an interaction between text and reader.

A Distinct Twenty-first Century Pentecostal Hermeneutic

Pentecostals are conservative in their bibliology, holding to a verbal plenary understanding of inspiration. The Pentecostal community will reject an interpretive approach that does not honour Pentecostal theology, and have a foundation in Scripture. Such a hermeneutic would be viewed as being unfaithful to Pentecostalism's essential nature. Therefore, chapter 3 investigated Acts 2 and 15 along with Matthew 1:23 and Jude 14–15 for the purpose of identifying a biblical foundation for a distinct Pentecostal hermeneutic. This exercise concluded that the scriptural evidence supported an interpretive method and strategy that was open to meaning beyond authorial intent, but was not open-ended and without restraints on imaginative interpretation. It further identified four elements: Scripture, Spirit, community, and trained leader, interacting in the process of interpretation. This pointed to the need to develop a hermeneutic with methodologies that would enable such an interaction and a strategy as to how Scripture, Spirit, community, and trained leader would collaborate during interpretation.

Chapter 4 laid out a starting point by proposing a proper role for hermeneutics and examining early Pentecostal interpretation along with Myland's dual meaning concept. We argued that the underlying reason for proposing a hermeneutic, distinct or otherwise, is so Scripture can be interpreted and its meaning shared with the community of faith. The discussion also offered insight into some of Pentecostalism's core values and ethos that must form part of any interpretive strategy that proposes to be Pentecostal.

Interpretation requires, among other things, methodology; therefore, chapter 5 argued for appropriate methods for the hermeneutic proposed in this book. What is clear is that the methods Pentecostals use are common to all faith communities, establishing that methodology is not what is distinctive about Pentecostal hermeneutics. The methods offered as appropriate in this book move beyond those proposed by Fee and Archer. We also resist Archer's and Noel's claim that Pentecostals return to the Bible Reading method, even if it is modified in some unspecified way. Unlike Archer who rejects any real place for the historical-grammatical method we suggest it has a helpful, but limited place. The methodology proposed here is eclectic, embracing a limited and defined use of historical-grammatical method in concert with the various literary critical methods of more recent communication and hermeneutic theory. This eclectic methodology is open to the cooperation between text and reader in the creation of meaning while restricting the reader from freelance interpretation.

Conclusion

The final chapter offered a description of how Scripture, Spirit, community, and trained leader interact as these methods are employed to identify the meaning and meaningfulness of a biblical text. The nature of Scripture as inspired revelation, Pentecostal theology and bibliology, and theoretical arguments led to a conclusion that Scripture's role is primary and that it stands over Spirit, community, and trained leader in a distinct Pentecostal hermeneutic. Though difficult to describe and impossible to observe the Spirit is acknowledged to be active at several levels in the interpretive process, and is able by various means to assist the hermeneut to discover both meaning and significance in the Scripture. The community, although often in the shadows, was shown to significantly impact interpretation by supplying a metanarrative, presuppositions, and ideology for the interpreter. Following an offered interpretation the community's role is to discern if the understanding being offered is legitimate. Therefore, the community's role first predisposes the interpreter in certain ways, and then evaluates proposed interpretations. The trained leader, the final element, is critical to the process for they are both *trained* and the *interpreter*. They serve as the focal point in the strategy by giving voice to Scripture, receiving the Spirit's input, and bringing the Scripture's re-formational message to the community as well as investigate Scripture in response to the community's need. This interpreter must be well trained in the methods used and both informed of and committed to the strategy implemented. Deviation from the strategy that gives Scripture primacy while being open to the Spirit's enlightenment, and unfaithfulness to the community's core nature and role may result in an interpretation but it will not be a "Pentecostal" interpretation.

The discussion of hermeneutics among Pentecostals is likely to continue for some time to come. The hermeneutic offered in this book does not answer all the questions and has not addressed all the issues but it has offered a methodology and strategy that is faithful to Pentecostalism's essential nature, recognizes an appropriate place for both text and interpreter, and can legitimately be considered a distinct twenty-first century Pentecostal hermeneutic. This proposal is submitted in an effort to further the current debate and offer a hermeneutic that can actually be implemented.

APPENDIX A

Explanation

APPENDIX A IS AN outline for a bachelor degree advanced level course that instructs students and equips them to begin using a twenty-first-century distinctive Pentecostal hermeneutic. The purpose of the course is to provide a starting point for professors choosing to use this monograph as the foundation for a course in Pentecostal hermeneutics.

We begin with the syllabus for the Pentecostal Bible College of Malawi where I serve as president. Since this is an advanced course, admission requires the student to have passed specific prerequisite courses. The course requirements and methods of evaluation are identified along with the expected outcomes. The course is included in the college calendar with the description found in the syllabus to enable students to decide whether or not they wish to enrol. (Student feedback following the first few times the course is taught will provide helpful information on how it may be improved)

Following the syllabus is the course description that is a summary outline of the thirteen weeks of study. As a bachelor level course it is set up as thirteen weeks with three hours per week of classwork. Each week, except week 3 which is a three-hour seminar setting, classwork is divided between a ninety minute lecture and ninety minute lab. The lectures are designed to present the material that is contained in the thesis as may be seen from the titles and summary. The lab is designed to give the students opportunity to work independently and as a group while practicing the theory presented in the lecture. The purpose of the lab is to encourage the

Appendix A

students to begin the task of mastering the interpretive skills and strategy offered in this thesis.

Pentecostal Bible College of Malawi

A Twenty-first Century Pentecostal Hermeneutic

PR3211

Syllabus

Credit Hours: 3

Instructor:

Course Description:

This course builds on the general hermeneutical principles presented in the course 'Introduction to Hermeneutics.' The focus of this course is introducing the student to background and foundational elements underlying an authentic twenty-first century Pentecostal hermeneutic. The background that informs Pentecostalism's ethos and community narrative is explored. The relationship of Pentecostal ethos and community narrative to a Pentecostal hermeneutic is considered. A biblical foundation for a distinctive Pentecostal hermeneutic is established with particular attention given to Acts 2 and 15.

    The course is divided into two 90 minute sessions per week. The lectures provide the theoretical information. The course also includes a lab. The lab is designed to provide the students with the opportunity to practice the various aspects of a twenty-first century Pentecostal hermeneutic. The students will be divided into groups of five to eight for the lab work. Once the work group is formed it will remain constant. This will allow the

Appendix A

students to form a *community*. Further details of the lab work appears in the assignment section.

PREREQUISITES:

CH1201—Pentecostal History

BS2101—Introduction to the Bible

PR2203—Pentecostal Distinctives

PR3101—Introduction to Hermeneutics

Required Texts:

Harlyn Graydon Purdy. *A Distinct Twenty-first Century Pentecostal Hermeneutic*. Eugene, OR: Wipf & Stock, 2015.

Optional Texts:

Gordon Fee. *New Testament Exegesis: A Handbook for Students and Pastors*. 3rd edition Louisville: Westminster John Knox Press, 2002.

Kenneth J. Archer. *A Pentecostal Hermeneutic for the Twenty-First Century: Spirit, Scripture and Community*. London: T. & T. Clark International, 2004.

Hermeneutics Reader. This is a collection of 12 articles dealing with issues related to the material covered in this course.

Recommended Reading:

Robert Alter. *The Art of Biblical Narrative*. New York: Basic Books, 1981.

Robert Alter. *The Art of Biblical Poetry*. New York: Basic Books, 1985.

Craig G. Bartholomew, Joel B. Green, and Anthony C. Thiselton, eds. *Reading Luke*. Grand Rapids: Zondervan, 2005.

Appendix A

Course Objectives:
At the end of the course students will:

- The student will be able to write a coherent argument for the necessity for a distinct Pentecostal hermeneutic.
- The student will be able to write an brief essay identifying Pentecostalism's roots and their relationship to Pentecostal hermeneutics.
- The student will be able to demonstrate early Pentecostal hermeneutics (Bible Reading Method & Myland's method) by demonstrating its use with three textual examples.
- The student will be able to explain the Pentecostal ethos and its relationship to Pentecostal hermeneutics via a written essay.
- The student will be able to demonstrate Pentecostalism's Lukan lens and how it relates to Pentecostal hermeneutics by demonstrating it using at least three biblical texts.
- The student will be introduced to various theories of meaning and interpretation as they relate to a Pentecostal hermeneutic and demonstrate their application to biblical texts and illustrate examples of each with at least one textual example.
- The student will gain an understanding of the biblical foundation for a Pentecostal hermeneutic and be able to describe this in writing.
- The student will gain an understanding of how Scripture, Spirit, Trained Leader and Community interface in a twenty-first century Pentecostal Hermeneutic and be able to demonstrate this with at least three textual examples.
- The student will gain an understanding of the Pentecostal application of various contemporary interpretive methodologies and be able to demonstrate their use with at least one textual example.

Course Requirements:

Class Participation (20%)

Class participation includes involvement in class discussion, in class assignments that might arise and faithfulness in background reading for the course.

Appendix A

Each student is expected to read the text. The articles in the reader should be read prior to the class in which the material it relates to is covered.

Lab (50%)

For the lab work each student will be assigned to a working group of not less than five and not more than eight. Once assigned to a group the student will remain part of that group for the duration of the course..

The student may be required to complete independent preparatory work for the group work. When this is the case the student will be required to submit a copy of their independent work to the instructor at the beginning of the lab.

Each lab is designed to provide the students with an opportunity to practice the material being covered in the lectures. Students will practice a twenty-first century Pentecostal hermeneutic. Labs are designed to provide students with a forum to put into practice the material covered in the lectures. Labs also allow students to investigate, review and/or discover principles in practice that relate to a Pentecostal hermeneutic. Students also gain experience in how each of the four quadrants of the Pentecostal hermeneutic (Scripture, Spirit, trained Leader and Community) are engaged and interrelated in a twenty-first century Pentecostal hermeneutic.

For each lab students will select a secretary who will keep a record of a) the discussion; b) ideas and concepts discussed; c) outcomes; d) questions that arise in the discussion and e) three or four main conclusions reached by the group. A copy of these records will be submitted to the instructor for marking purposes. Groups may also be asked to make a class presentation that will be graded.

Appendix A
Final Exam (30%)

Academic Integrity:

Academic integrity is expected of all students at Faith School of Theology. Since cheating or plagiarism compromise academic integrity, such practices will result in disciplinary action.

Cheating

Though not limited to the following, cheating includes the copying or use of unauthorized aids in any academic assignment. Students found guilty of cheating may receive a failing grade in the assignment or exam or face other disciplinary action.

Plagiarism

When completing assignments, students must acknowledge their use of resource material. (All research papers at Faith School of Theology must adhere to the MLA Handbook.) Students are guilty of plagiarism if they present the ideas of someone else as their own or if they submit work for which they have already received previous credit. To prevent this from occurring, students should ensure that all original material is acknowledged by referring to the original author, using footnotes or, when applicable, by using quotation marks. Plagiarism will normally result in the student receiving no mark for the assignment / exam in which it occurred.

Course Description

The course covers twelve weeks. There are 3 hours of lecture each week. The course also includes a three hour lab. The lab is designed to offer the students a framework for putting their Pentecostal hermeneutic into practice. The following is a brief overview of the course.

Week 1. Why a distinct Pentecostal hermeneutic?

Lecture:

A natural question for a contemporary Pentecostal to ask is, 'Do not all Christians practice hermeneutics in the same way?' Why do we need a *distinct* Pentecostal hermeneutic? This lecture argues that a distinct twenty-first century Pentecostal hermeneutic is legitimate and necessary. The lecture presents a brief review of various distinctive hermeneutic approaches currently practiced (i.e. feminist, liberation, etc.). The community to which the interpreter belongs powerfully impacts interpretation. This and many other theoretical arguments support the concept of a distinctive hermeneutic. Current theory clearly shows that interpretation is related to community identity. Evidence is presented showing Pentecostalism as a distinct community. A distinct twenty-first century Pentecostal hermeneutic is legitimate and necessary since Pentecostalism is a distinct community. The lecture offers evidentiary support for understanding Pentecostals as a distinct representation of the broader Christian community. There is a discussion of what Pentecostalism shares in common with the broader Christian community. There is also a discussion of Pentecostalism's distinctive characteristics. The ultimate goal of the lecture is to establish that a distinct twenty-first century Pentecostal hermeneutic is essential.

Appendix A
Lecture Outline:

Community narrative and interpretation

Interpretation always occurs within a context. The interpreter brings her or his self to the interpretive process. In a twenty-first-century Pentecostal hermeneutic the interpreter brings their Pentecostalism into the process.

Examples of distinctive hermeneutics

In the twenty-first century there are numerous distinct approaches to interpretation within biblical hermeneutics. Only a few of the many approaches are identified: Marxist, Feminist, Liberation and Economist hermeneutics. The interpretation of some of Jesus' parables offered by these different perspectives are presented as evidence of how one's distinctive community context shapes interpretation.

Pentecostalism: a distinct expression of Christianity

From its beginning Pentecostalism has been viewed from without and within as a distinct expression of Christianity. First, the response of the Church to the early Pentecostal movement identifies them as distinct. Second, their own self-understanding, world-view and experience identifies them as distinct.

Pentecostalism's pneumatology as interpretive filter

Pentecostalism's pneumatology means they understand reality and normalcy differently than non-Pentecostals. This impacts their interpretation of Scripture and current events.

Pentecostalism's world-view as interpretive filter

Pentecostals see the world differently than non-Pentecostals. This world-view also impacts their interpretive activity.

Appendix A

Lab:

In preparation for this week's lab the students will read: Douglas Jacobsen, 'Pentecostal Hermeneutics in Comparative Perspective,' a paper presented to the Annual Meeting of the Society for Pentecostal Studies, 13–15 March, 1997 (Oakland, California). This paper is a helpful discussion of 'Foundational Narrative Convictions' and their relationship to hermeneutics. It also aids in understanding how community relates to interpretation.

The student is expected to come to the group meeting having a working knowledge of the information contained in this paper. The student will prepare a summary of the main points in the article in preparation for the group lab.

The group will discuss the issues covered in the paper.

Week 2. Pentecostalism's Interpretive Lens

Lecture

Pentecostalism's Holiness background influences the Pentecostal interpretive lens. Some of the early Pentecostal leaders were trained pastors in the Holiness tradition. Consequently the Wesleyan Quadrilateral likely has some influence in Pentecostal interpretive process. The lecture provides a brief overview of the Wesleyan Quadrilateral. Restorationism, Latter Rain motif and revivalism also form part of the Pentecostal interpretive lens. There will be a discussion of how these elements impact Pentecostal interpretation. Pentecostals also approach Scripture through a Lukan lens. We will explore how this Lukan lens informs the interpretation of a text.

Matthew's quotation of Isaiah 7:14 is a clear biblical example of an interpretive lens at work. Matthew has a Christocentric lens. The author is convinced Jesus of Nazareth is the promised Messiah. Matthew then interprets the Old Testament in light of his Christocentric perspective. Isaiah 7:14 did not refer to the birth of Jesus in its original context. However, Matthew interprets the text as though it were referring to Jesus. Matthew 1:23 and 2:18 are used as case studies. The case studies provide an understanding of how an interpretive lens functions.

Appendix A
Lecture Outline:

Wesleyan Quadrilateral

The Wesleyan Quadrilateral is briefly identified and explained. It is argued that the early Pentecostals brought with them an interpretive influence rooted in the Wesleyan Quadrilateral. It is also argued that the Wesleyan Quadrilateral offers help for controlling against unrestrained imagination in a twenty-first century Pentecostal hermeneutic. Its relationship with early Pentecostalism's roots enables it to operate as somewhat of an insider.

Restorationism

Early Pentecostals believed the Holy Spirit was restoring Apostolic Christianity to the Church through the Pentecostal revival. They did not see themselves as a new expression of Christian faith. Rather they saw themselves as the Church as it was intended to be from the beginning. The concept of restorationism and its implications are discussed.

Latter Rain Motif

The Latter Rain motif is a biblical concept that links God's promise to Israel (Deuteronomy 11:10–15) with Joel 2: . This lecture is a brief introduction as to how this concept shaped early Pentecostal self-understanding. Because of its importance it will be discussed in greater detail in a later lecture.

The Lukan Lens

The Book of Acts took a central role in Pentecostal interpretation. All Scripture was read through the Luke-Acts pneumatology. For Pentecostals the Luke-Acts pneumatology differed from Paul's. Luke's pneumatology saw Baptism in the Spirit as subsequent to salvation and for the purpose of power for ministry. Acts presented the normative life for the Church. This is the Pentecostal interpretive lens.

Appendix A

Lab

D. Wesley Myland figures prominently in Pentecostal hermeneutics. His hermeneutical lecture series delivered in 1909 at Stone Church, Chicago was printed in the book *The Latter Rain Covenant and Pentecostal Power: With Testimony of Healings and Baptism*. Myland was a trained Methodist minister and his book lays a firm foundation for Pentecostal interpretation. The student's will read this book in preparation for the lab. While reading the student will take special note of hermeneutical principles evident in Myland's presentation. In the lab they will discuss their findings and as a group identify how the Latter Rain motif and Lukan Lens serve in the formation of a twenty-first century Pentecostal hermeneutic.

Week 3. Approaches to Biblical Interpretation

This week the lecture and lab periods will be brought together in a seminar setting. The seminar brings lecturer and students together in discussion. In preparation for the seminar students will read, Anthony C. Thiselton, 'The Hermeneutical Dynamics of "Reading Luke" as Interpretation, Reflection and Formation,' in Craig G. Bartholomew, Joel B. Green and Anthony C. Thiselton, eds. *Reading Luke*. Grand Rapids, MI.: Zondervan, 2005. This chapter provides brief summaries of a variety of interpretive approaches and methodologies. It also speaks about interpretive lenses. The material will provide stimulus for discussion relating to the various aspects of interpretation that are relevant to a distinctive twenty-first century Pentecostal hermeneutic.

Week 4. Biblical Foundations

Lecture

The primary Biblical foundation for a twenty-first century Pentecostal hermeneutic is found in Acts 2 and 15. Peter's Pentecostal sermon includes an interpretation of Joel 2:28–32. James, in Acts 15, uses Amos 5:9 to provide Scriptural support for the Jerusalem council's decision. Both passages are clearly in a Pentecostal context. As such they provide an interpretive model for Pentecostal interpretation. The analysis of these passages identifies an interpretive process that involves the interaction of four elements. There

Appendix A

is a clear place for Scripture, Holy Spirit, Trained Leader and Community in the interpretive process. Other relevant Scriptures are discussed in the lecture (i.e., 1 & 2 Timothy, Titus, etc.) A twenty-first century Pentecostal hermeneutic will incorporate these four elements.

Lab

This lab will require each student to accomplish a pre group assignment. The purpose of the lab is to allow students to bring the four elements of the Pentecostal hermeneutic together in an interpretive task. In preparation for the group lab each student will individually interpret 1 Cor. 11: .

The student will follow a prescribed process for their independent study of the text. The student will read the text through at least twice in a single sitting. After reading the text they will spend fifteen minutes in prayer inviting the Holy Spirit to aid their interpretation. After the time in prayer they will read the text again and then write out the meaning of the text as they understand it. The interpretation of the text must be within the context of their current worshipping community. The purpose of this exercise is to allow the student to bring Scripture, Holy Spirit and Trained Leader together in the interpretive process.

The students will each bring their individual interpretations to the group gathering. The group will discuss and evaluate the individual interpretations. This brings the community element of the Pentecostal hermeneutic into the process. It allows the community of peers to assess, critique and evaluate the interpretations. The group then will arrive at an interpretation of the text.

Week 5. Scripture—its place

Lecture

This lecture deals with the 'place' of Scripture in the twenty-first century Pentecostal hermeneutic. Pentecostals have a very high view of Scripture. They hold to a verbal plenary view of inspiration. Consequently, the words of Scripture are important. The text holds a place of priority over experience, personal interpretation and / or any other revelation. The Pentecostal posture is one of surrender to the authority of the text. This means that

Appendix A

Pentecostals will alter belief or practice if it becomes clear that the Scriptures teach something different.

Lab

The students will discuss and prepare a group presentation in this lab. The presentation will describe what prioritizing Scripture in the interpretive process looks like in practice. The students will re-enact a scenario that I personally experienced. A guest minister comes to the Church. He presented himself as a prophet. He claimed to operate in the gifts of the Spirit. In this particular instance he told a story in preparation to offering to pray for people.

The story he told dealt with his mother. She was working at a hotel and was hoping for a promotion. A new manager was appointed and he did not like the preacher's mother. She called and asked him to pray for her situation. He asked, 'What do you want? Do you want him to die?' Her response was in the affirmative. He then told her to deposit $20,000.00 in his account and he would pray that her boss would die. She deposited the money the next day and he prayed that her boss would die. He claimed that the next day his mother's boss was airlifted home to die.

Discuss: The students will discuss how various individuals and groups should respond if Scripture is prioritized. What should the pastor do? What is expected of elders? What should other Church leaders do? What ought to be the response of the congregation?

Continue: After telling the story the preacher then invited the people to come up and place 1000.00 MKW on the altar, touch the pulpit and whatever obstacle was standing in their way would be removed. Many in the congregation came, paid their money and touched the pulpit.

Discuss: Why could this happen in a Pentecostal Church? Is Scripture being given the place of priority in this instance?

Continue: The next day the minister was arrested and 750,000.00 MWK confiscated by the police. The story was in the Tuesday newspaper. The Church was also named.

Discuss: What kind of testimony is this? What would this scenario look like if Scripture had been prioritized in this congregation?

Appendix A

Week 6. Scripture—its role

Lecture

For Pentecostals Scripture reveals the mind and will of God. Scripture is the record of God's self-revelation and the story of God's saving activity. Scripture also, as David Moessner points out, has a formative role. Scripture invites the reader/s in as participants. This invitation to participate intends to offer us r*eformation* into the person / people of God. A critical role of Scripture is to lead the Christ follower from where they are to where they ought to be.

Scripture is not the only source of revelation but it is the primary source. Scripture confirms, validates or critique's all other forms of revelation. Scripture does not deal directly with everything that is presented to us as a revelation. However, it does provide many principles that aid our assessment of these revelations. There is general revelation and here Scripture clarifies and specifies general revelation. For Pentecostals, revelation also occurs via the charismata, dreams, visions, etc. Scripture provides Pentecostals with a concrete means of evaluating these other forms of revelation.

Lab

This lab is a case study. Each group will be given a different case. For this project we are assuming three groups. The first group will be given a case study of a pastor who presented a vision for the church claiming it came as a revelation from God. The church is told that they must sell all their material possessions, including the church facilities, etc. They are then to give the funds to support widows and orphans in the third world. Each family can retain enough resources to sustain themselves for twelve months. They are told they will not need more than that since the Lord revealed to the pastor that He would return before the twelve months were finished.

The second group will look at an instance of an individual giving a prophetic word in the public worship service. After quoting Jeremiah 29:11 an individual stands and gives an exhortation (word of prophecy in Pentecostal terminology). The prophecy affirms that the Lord knows the congregations current circumstances. He knows of their hardships and has seen their suffering. They are not forgotten nor deserted. The Lord is working out His plan for them. Soon they will begin to see this plan for their good and prosperity unfold. The night is nearly ended and the bright new day

Appendix A

about to dawn. It is an affirming and encouraging word. The group is asked to consider how Scripture might aid the congregation in how to respond to this ministry of the Spirit.

The third group will be given an instance of an individual coming to the pastor with a 'word from the Lord.' The word is one of correction. The individual tells the pastor the Lord has sent them to warn the pastor to repent from his lies or judgment will come. Again the group is asked to determine how Scripture ought to be properly applied here.

In each of these instances the group is asked to determine if the revelation should be considered genuine. They are asked to provide Scriptural support for their conclusions. Each group will present their findings to the class in a class presentation.

Week 7. The Holy Spirit

Lecture

In this lecture we explore the role of the Holy Spirit in relation to Scripture and interpretation. The Holy Spirit was and is active in the Scriptures. Pentecostals understand the text of Scripture to be inspired. They expect the Spirit to actively engage them in the interpretive process. The occasional nature of the epistles illustrates how the Spirit uses current circumstances, the interpretation of Scripture, the trained leader and the community to lead the Church into an understanding of God's purposes. An important aspect of the Spirit's involvement is the issue of layered meaning. The lecture develops and illustrates the issue of layered meaning as it relates to a twenty-first century Pentecostal hermeneutic.

Lecture Outline:

The Holy Spirit as author of Scripture.

The discussion considers the implications of holding the Pentecostal view of inspiration.

Appendix A

The Holy Spirit and deeper meaning

This part of the lecture considers the ideas such as allegorization, typology and spiritualizing interpretive approaches under the guise of revelation by the Holy Spirit. Matthew 1:20–25 is used as a biblical base to discuss the legitimate role of the Holy Spirit to expose deeper meaning in the text.

The Holy Spirit and pesharim

This portion of the lecture presents a brief discussion of *pesher* interpretation. Biblical, Qumran and Rabbinical examples of *pesher* interpretation are presented.

The Holy Spirit and extra biblical revelation

The lecture will touch on issues of charismata and their proper place. All extra biblical revelation is subject to Scriptural and Community investigation.

The Holy Spirit using events to guide the Church

A brief reference to Acts 2 and Acts 15 which show current events as the instigation for the Holy Spirit's guidance of the Church into a new and distinct future is brought to the students.

Lab

In this lab the students will review the early Pentecostal oneness doctrine controversy. Students will investigate the events surrounding the development of this doctrine. The students will investigate the interpretive method employed by Frank Ewart and G. T. Hayward in reference to the oneness doctrine. The oneness doctrine posed a threat to the doctrine of salvation as it added baptism in Jesus' Name and baptism in the Spirit with evidence of tongues as requisites for salvation. Students will read the rebuttals from Trinitarian Pentecostals. The students will discuss how the Holy Spirit used experience, tradition, Scripture, etc. to lead the majority of Pentecostals to reject the oneness doctrine. The purpose is to enable Students to recognize the ongoing work of the Spirit in the Church.

Appendix A

Week 8. The Holy Spirit

Lecture:

Revelation in early Pentecostal understanding

The place for experiential knowledge

Acts 15 is considered from the perspective of experience's role in the process of identifying God's will for the Church's future.

1. *revealed* by the Holy Spirit
2. *validated* by Scripture
3. *confirmed* by the community

Dispensational elements

Lab

First Corinthians chapter 11 offers a theology of the Eucharist. This chapter is written in response to the situation of division that existed in the Corinthian congregation. Students are asked to investigate 1 Corinthians to determine how the Holy Spirit is using the current experience at Corinth to lead the Church into a proper understanding of the Eucharist. Students will consider the current Pentecostal practice of observing communion in light of what they discover in 1 Corinthians. Students will offer a critique of the current Pentecostal practice and offer recommendations for change based on what they learn from 1 Corinthians.

Week 9. The Trained Leader

Lecture

There is substantial support in Scripture for the role of a trained leader in the interpretive process.

Appendix A

Lecture Outline:

First John 2:27 (John 16:13)

This text is obviously addressed to groups. This points to the activity of the Spirit within the believing community. The question is how this might manifest within the group. Glenn Wooden argues it most likely manifests in the group through teachers who are part of the group. This text, because of its ambiguity and obvious connection to the community of faith, is a good place to begin the discussion of trained leaders. Trained leaders speak from within and among the community not outside or above.

First Timothy 3:1–10

Timothy is commanded to put leaders in place at Ephesus. This lecturer assumes the titles given these leaders are not formal titles or offices such as develop later. A critical requirement for these leaders is their ability to teach. They must know and hold the 'deep truths.' This text helps lay a biblical foundation for the important role of trained leaders in the congregation. One of their tasks is to teach the assembly.

First Timothy 4:11–16

Here Timothy is commanded to teach specific things. He, as a trained leader, is commanded to teach the Scriptures. Teaching of necessity includes interpretation.

Lab

Students are asked to discuss the issue of training leaders within the Pentecostal context. They are presented with a case study of a new church plant. The church opens with a membership of 25 persons. They are provided with profiles of each of the founding members, including the founding pastor. Students are asked to identify the persons that should be called into leadership roles. They are then asked to identify ten critical issues that the pastor would need to include in a leadership training program to fully equip these persons for leadership in the church.

Appendix A

Week 10. The Trained Leader

Lecture

Second Timothy 2:15

The prime text dealing with the need to study Scripture. As a trained leader Timothy is instructed to continue learning.

Second Timothy 3:10–17

This passage clearly identifies Timothy as a trained leader. He is carefully instructed to teach Scripture which is useful to equip the congregation in godliness and faith.

Titus 1:5–9

Titus is tasked to set the assembly in Crete in order. This lecturer assumes the offices identified in Titus are not formal titles and or offices as they become later in the Church. However, these persons are being given positions of leadership among the congregation. The ability to teach the apostolic doctrine is a key qualification for these leaders. This text supports the biblical place for trained leaders in the interpretive process.

Titus 2:1–15

Titus, a disciple of Paul, may legitimately be identified as a trained leader. In this passage the word 'teach' occurs several times. Titus, a trained leader, is to teach and train the congregation.

Lab

This lab is also a case study. The students are given the catalogue for Master's College and Seminary (one of the leading Bible Colleges for the Pentecostal Assemblies of Canada). Students are asked to review the catalogue to identify those elements that actually train and equip potential leaders for the task of interpreting Scripture. Students are asked to identify elements in the training program that are too weak or missing. They are then asked to identify elements that should be added to strengthen the training program.

Week 11. The Community

Lecture

Current interpretive theory recognizes how community shapes the interpreter and in so doing impacts the interpretive process. The lecture looks in general at community's role in establishing bias, preconceptions, ideology, etc. that the interpreter carries with them into the interpretive process. The lecture looks specifically at the Pentecostal community to identify the specific contributions it might make to the interpreter's presupposition base in the interpretive project.

Lab

Students are presented with Leon Morris' interpretation of 1 Corinthians 12–14 in *Spirit of the Living God: The Bible's Teaching on the Holy Spirit*. London: Inter-Varisty Press, 1960. They will also look at William Barclay's commentary on the Lukan miracle of feeding the 5000 (Luke 9). Students are asked to identify what community understandings are informing the interpretive process for these authors. They will then look at these same texts through a Pentecostal community lens and identify the difference this makes.

Week 12. The Community

Lecture

Here the lecture looks at the contemporary context of the Pentecostal community. Special attention is given to the African Pentecostal community. The discussion considers African specific concerns and issues that form the contextual background for African Pentecostals. The lecture also considers how the African Pentecostals are approaching interpretation. The lecture attempts to project how some of those elements may reshape the broader Pentecostal community.

Appendix A

Lab

The students are given several scriptures: John 8:31–38; Matthew 8:5–13; 8:28–34; Romans 1:18–32. Students are asked to read the African Bible Commentary dealing with these passages (including Yusufu Turaki's comment re homosexuality, p. 1381). Students will discuss how the African interpreters see elements in the text directly related to African community. They will discuss how this might be different from a Western perspective. It is important for them to identify points on which there might be differences of opinion between African and Westerner. In light of the expansion of the Pentecostal Church in Africa students are asked to consider how this might impact the broader issue of Pentecostal hermeneutics.

Week 13. Methodological Issues related to a twenty-first century Pentecostal Hermeneutic

Lecture

The lecture presents a discussion of the eclectic use of methods presented in the thesis. Students are encouraged to embrace historical-grammatical and literary critical methods as their interpretive tools. The lecture points to the students to the places where they can continue to develop these skills following this course.

Lab

This lab is a group discussion. Prior to the group gathering the students will each read Max Turner, 'Luke and the Spirit: Renewing Theological Interpretation of Biblical Pneumatology,' in Bartholomew, Craig G., Joel B. Green and Anthony C. Thiselton, eds. *Reading Luke*. Grand Rapids, MI.: Zondervan, 2005 pp. 267—293. This chapter deals with issues of Lukan pneumatology. Turner points out that Luke is not concerned to show *how* Jesus experienced the Spirit. Is Luke 3:16 integral to all Christian discipleship? Turner suggests it is only with Acts that true light dawns. Acts canonical position following the gospel of John may also have significance for Pentecostal pneumatology. Students are asked to discuss in what ways Turner's understanding of Lukan pneumatology is similar to and differs from a Pentecostal pneumatology rooted in the Lukan material.

APPENDIX B
Definitions

Bible Reading Method—A synchronic common sense interpretive method that relied upon commonsense inductive and deductive reasoning. The method was used to trace key themes and topics throughout Scripture. These verses were understood to represent the full witness of Scripture on a subject. The verses were synthesized into a doctrine. This was the primary method early Pentecostals used to formulate their doctrines.

Cessationism—The belief that the charismatic events experienced by the Apostles ceased as part of normative Christianity after the death of the Apostles in the first century CE.

Evangelicalism—The contemporary North American usage of the term reflects the impact of the Evangelical/fundamentalist controversy of the early 20th century. Evangelicalism is the middle ground between the theological liberalism of the mainline denominations and the cultural separatism of Fundamentalism. Evangelicalism has therefore been described as "the third of the leading strands in American Protestantism, straddl[ing] the divide between fundamentalists and liberals" (Mead, "God's Country?"). Many would identify Pentecostalism as a sub-group of Evangelicalism. Though Pentecostalism shares much in common with Evangelicalism there is sufficient difference to view them as distinct movements.

Fundamentalism — Fundamentalism refers to a movement begun in the late 19th and early 20th century British and American Protestant denominations among evangelicals who reacted energetically against theological and cultural modernism. Fundamentalists felt certain doctrines, especially inerrancy, were being misinterpreted or rejected by many scholars. Fundamentalists view these doctrines as the fundamentals of Christian faith.

Appendix B

Fundamentalism holds to and promotes "the Fundamentals"—a ten-volume set of essays, apologetic and polemic written by conservative Protestant theologians to defend what they saw as Protestant orthodoxy.

Liberalism—Liberalism is an *experience* oriented approach to faith and truth. The style of hermeneutics practiced by liberal scholars is often characterized as non-propositional. The Bible is considered an anthology that documents the human authors' beliefs and feelings about God *at the time of its writing*—within a historical or cultural context. Thus, liberal Christian theologians do not claim to discover truth propositions but rather create religious models and concepts that reflect the contexts from which they emerge. Liberal Christianity looks upon the Bible as a collection of narratives that explain, epitomize, or symbolize the essence and significance of Christian understanding. Thus, most liberal Christians do not regard the Bible as inerrant, but believe Scripture to be "inspired" in the same way a poem is said to be "inspired" and passed down by humans. Liberalism is the theological framework embraced by most mainline denominations from the nineteenth century onward.

Mainline—Mainline Protestant churches are a group of churches that contrast in history and practice with evangelical, fundamentalist and/or charismatic Protestant denominations, though some mainline churches include evangelicals and charismatics. Mainline Protestants were a majority of all churchgoers (including non-Protestants) in the United States until the early 20th century, but now constitute a minority among Protestants. Mainline churches include the United Methodist Church (UMC), the Evangelical Lutheran Church in America (ELCA), the Presbyterian Church, the Episcopal Church, Congregationalist, etc.

Modernity—a nineteenth- and twentieth-century Western cultural worldview that was an intensive extension of Enlightenment beliefs. It is characterized by strong belief in human progress through scientific, rationalistic reasoning from the perspective that a person can be neutral and objective. Scientific and historical verification were the means of validating all truth claims.

Pentecostalism—A Christian restorational revivalist movement that emphasizes the continuing work of Jesus Christ through the personal agency of the Holy Spirit, proclaiming Jesus as Savior, Sanctifier, Spirit Baptizer, Healer and Soon Coming King. Pentecostals envision themselves as a restoration of New Testament (Apostolic) Christianity living in the "last days."

Definitions

Restorationism—a movement that perceives itself as restoring to the Church some belief or practice that had been lost in the process of Church history. The Reformation was a restorationist movement returning to the Church the concepts of *sola scriptura* and *salvation by faith alone.*

BIBLIOGRAPHY

Achtemeier, Paul J. *Inspiration and Authority: Nature and Function of Christian Scripture.* Peabody, MA: Hendrickson, 1999.
Adamo, David T. *Africa and the Africans in the Old Testament.* Eugene: Wipf & Stock, OR, 2001.
Adeyemo, Tokunboh, ed. *Africa Bible Commentary.* Nairobi: Word Alive, 2006.
Alter, Robert. *The World of Biblical Literature.* New York: Basic Books, 1978.
Anderson, Allan. *An Introduction To Pentecostalism.* Cambridge: Cambridge University Press, 2004.
Anderson, Gordon L. "Pentecostal Hermeneutics: Part 1." *Paraclete* 28/1 (1994) 1–11.
———. "Pentecostal Hermeneutics: Part 2." *Paraclete* 28/2 (1994) 12–22.
Anderson, Robert Mapes. *Vision of the Disinherited: The Making of American Pentecostalism.* Peabody, MA: Hendrickson, 1979.
Archer, Kenneth J. "Early Pentecostal Biblical Interpretation." *Journal of Pentecostal Theology* 18 (2001) 32–70.
———. *A Pentecostal Hermeneutic for the Twenty-first Century: Spirit, Scripture and Community.* New York: T. & T. Clark, 2004.
———. "Pentecostal Hermeneutics: Retrospect and Prospect." *Journal of Pentecostal Theology* 8 (1996) 63–81.
Arrington, French L. "The Use of the Bible by Pentecostals." *Pneuma* 16/1 (1994) 101–7.
Autry, Arden C. "Dimensions Of Hermeneutics In Pentecostal Focus." *Journal of Pentecostal Theology* 3 (1993) 29–50.
Bartholomew, Craig G., Joel B. Green, and Anthony C. Thiselton, eds. *Reading Luke.* Scripture and Hermeneutics 6. Grand Rapids: Zondervan, 2005.
Bartleman, Frank. *Azusa Street: The Roots of Modern Day Pentecost.* South Plainfield, NJ: Bridge, 1980.
Bauckham, Richard J. *2 Peter, Jude.* Word Biblical Commentary 50. Dallas: Word, 1998.
Block, Daniel I. *Judges and Ruth.* The New American Commentary 6. Nashville: Broadman & Holman, 1999.
Blumhofer, Edith. *Pentecost in my Soul: Exploration in the Meaning of Pentecostal Experience in the Assemblies of God.* Springfield, MO: Gospel, 1989.
———. *Restoring the Faith: The Assemblies of God, Pentecostalism, and American Culture.* Urbana: University of Illinois Press, 1999.
Braaten, Carl. *History and Hermeneutics.* Philadelphia: Fortress, 1966.

Bibliography

Bray, Gerald. *Biblical Interpretation: Past and Present.* Downers Grove, IL: InterVarsity, 1996.

Brueggemann, Walter. *The Book That Breathes New Life: Scriptural Authority and Biblical Theology.* Minneapolis: Fortress, 2005.

Bultmann, Rudolf. "A Reply to the Theses of J. Schniewind." In *Kerygma and Myth*, edited by Hans-Werner Bartsch. New York: Harper & Row, 1961.

Burgess, Stanley M., and Gary B. McGee, eds. *Dictionary of Pentecostal And Charismatic Movements.* Grand Rapids: Zondervan, 1988.

Cargal, Timothy B. "Beyond the Fundamentalist-Modernist Controversy: Pentecostals and Hermeneutics in a Postmodern Age." *Pneuma: The Journal of the Society for Pentecostal Studies* 15 (1993) 163–87.

Carson, D. A. "Hermeneutics: A Brief Assessment of Some Recent Trends." *Themelios* 5/2 (1980) 15–22.

Cerillo, Augustus, Jr. "Interpretative Approaches to the History of American Pentecostal Origins." *Pneuma* 19 (1997) 29–49.

Cox, Harvey. *Fire From Heaven: The Rise of Pentecostal Spirituality and the Reshaping of Religion in the Twenty-first Century.* Reading: Addison-Wesley, 1995.

Craig, James D. "'Out and Out For The Lord': James Eustace Purdie, An Early Anglican Pentecostal." MA thesis, Toronto School of Theology, 1995.

Croatto, Severino. *Biblical Hermeneutics.* Maryknoll, NY: Orbis, 1987.

Cullmann, Oscar. *Christ and Time.* London: SCM, 1951.

Dayton, Donald W. *Theological Roots of Pentecostalism.* Peabody, MA: Hendrickson, 1987.

Daneel, M. L. "Christian Mission and Earth-Care: An African Case Study." *International Bulletin of Missionary Research* 35 (2011) 135.

Davis, Ellen F., and Richard B. Hays, eds. *The Art of Reading Scripture.* Grand Rapids: Eerdmans, 2003.

Doriani, Daniel M. *Getting the Message: A Plan for Interpreting and Applying the Bible.* Phillipsburg, NJ: Presbyterian & Reformed, 1996.

Duvall, J. Scott, and J. Daniel Hays. *Journey into God's Word: Your Guide to Understanding and Applying the Bible.* Grand Rapids: Zondervan, 2008.

Eco, Umberto, Richard Rorty, Jonathan Culler, and Christine Brooke-Rose. *Interpretation and Overinterpretation.* Cambridge: Cambridge University Press, 1992.

Enns, Peter. "Preliminary Observations on an Incarnational Model of Scripture: Its Validity and Usefulness." *Calvin Theological Journal* 42 (2007) 219–36.

———. "Would Jesus Get Hired to Teach an Old Testament Seminary Course?" http://www.patheos.com/blogs/peterenns/2013/08/would-jesus-get-hired-to-teach-an-old-testament-seminary-course-today/.html.

Ervin, Howard M. "Hermeneutics: A Pentecostal Option." *Pneuma* 3 (1991) 11–25.

Ewart, Frank J. *The Phenomenon of Pentecost.* Rev. ed. Hazelwood, MO: Word Aflame, 1975.

Faupel, D. William. *The Everlasting Gospel: The Significance of Eschatology in the Development of Pentecostal Thought.* Sheffield, UK: Sheffield Academic Press, 1996.

Fee, Gordon. *Gospel and Spirit: Issues in New Testament Hermeneutics.* Peabody, MA: Hendrickson, 1991.

———. *New Testament Exegesis: A Handbook for Students and Pastors.* 3rd ed. Louisville: Westminster John Knox, 2002.

———. *To What Extent Exegesis? Essays Textual, Exegetical, and Theological.* Grand Rapids: Eerdmans, 2001.

Bibliography

Fee, Gordon, and Douglas Stewart. *How To Read The Bible For All Its Worth*. 3rd Ed. Grand Rapids: Zondervan, 2003.

Ferguson, Duncan S. *Biblical Hermeneutics: An Introduction*. Atlanta: John Knox, 1986.

Fish, Stanley. *Is There A Text In This Class? The Authority of Interpretive Communities*. Cambridge, MA: Harvard University Press, 1980.

Foss, Sonja. *Rhetorical Criticism: Exploration and Practice*. Long Grove, IL: Waveland, 2009.

Fowl, Stephen E. *Engaging Scripture: A Model for Theological Interpretation*. Malden, MA: Blackwell, 1998.

Funk, Robert W. "The Watershed of the American Biblical Tradition: The Chicago School, First Phase, 1892–1920." *Journal of Biblical Literature* 96 (1976) 4–22.

Green, Joel B. "Hermeneutical Approaches to the Tradition." In *Eerdmans Commentary on the Bible*, edited by James D. G. Dunn, 972–88. Grand Rapids: Eerdmans, 2003.

———. "Interpretation, Reflection, Formation: Unfinished Business." In *Reading Luke: Interpretation, Reflection, Formation*, edited by Craig Bartholomew et al., 437–51. Grand Rapids: Zondervan, 2005.

———. "Learning Theological Interpretation from Luke." In *Reading Luke: Interpretation, Reflection, Formation*, edited by Craig Bartholomew et al., 55–78. Grand Rapids: Zondervan, 2005.

———. *The Theology of the Gospel of Luke*. Cambridge: Cambridge University Press, 1995.

Guelich, Robert A. *Mark 1–8:26*. Word Biblical Commentary 34A. Dallas: Word, 1989.

Harrington, Hannah. "Pentecostal Hermeneutics and Postmodern Literary Theory." *Pneuma* 16/1 (1994) 109–14.

Hart, Trevor. *Faith Thinking: The Dynamics of Christian Theology*. London: SPCK, 1995.

Hawk, L. Daniel. *Every Promise Fulfilled: Contesting Plots in Joshua*. Louisville: Westminster/John Knox, 1991.

Higgenbotham, J., and P. Patton. "Body Ethics: 'Hermenetworks': Rank and File Hermeneutics." *Searching Together* 13/4 (1984) 2–7.

Jacobsen, Douglas. "Pentecostal Hermeneutics in Comparative Perspectives." Paper, Annual Meeting of the Society for Pentecostal Studies., Oakland, CA. March 14, 1997.

Johns, Cheryl. *Pentecostal Formation: A Pedagogy Among The Oppressed*. Journal of Pentecostal Theology Supplement. Winona Lake, IN: Eisenbrauns. 2010.

Kantzer, Kenneth S., and Stanley N. Gundry, eds. *Perspectives on Evangelical Theology*. Grand Rapids: Baker, 1979.

Kato, Byang H. *Biblical Christianity in Africa*. Achimota, Ghana: Africa Christian, 1985.

Kim, Hyun-Sook. "The Hermeneutical-Praxis Paradigm and Practical Theology." *Religious Education* 102/4 (2007) 419–36.

Kisau, Paul M. "Acts of The Apostles." In *Africa Bible Commentary*, edited by Tokunboh Adeyemo, 1323–74. Nairobi: Word Alive, 2006.

Klein, William, Craig Blomberg, and R. Hubbard Jr. *Introduction to Biblical Interpretation*. Dallas: Word, 1993.

Knight, Henry H., III. *A Future for Truth: Evangelical Theology in a Postmodern World*. Nashville: Abingdon, 1997.

Kraft, Charles H. "Interpreting in Cultural Context." In *Rightly Divided: Readings in Biblical Hermeneutics*, edited by Roy B. Zuck, 245–57. Grand Rapids: Kregel, 1996.

Kyomya, Michael. *A Guide to Interpreting Scripture: Context, Harmony and Application*. Nairobi: Hippo, 2010.

Bibliography

Ladd, G. E. *The New Testament and Criticism*. Grand Rapids: Eerdmans, 1967.

Land, Steven J. *Pentecostal Spirituality: A Passion for the Kingdom*. JPTSup 1. Sheffield, UK: Sheffield Academic Press, 1993.

Lawrence, B. F. *The Apostolic Faith Restored*. St. Louis: Gospel Publishing House, 1916.

Lehmann, Paul L. "'The Reformers' Use of the Bible." *Theology Today* 3 (1946–47) 12–26.

Levinson, John R. *Filled with the Spirit*. Grand Rapids: Eerdmans, 2009.

Lovett, Leonard. "Black Holiness Pentecostalism." In *Dictionary of Pentecostal and Charismatic Movements*, edited by Stanley M. Burgess et al., 76–77 Grand Rapids: Zondervan, 1988.

Lowenburg, Douglas P. "A Twenty-first Century Pentecostal Hermeneutic for Africa and Beyond." *Encounter: Journal for Pentecostal Ministry* 9 (2012) 1–41.

MacIntyre, Alisdair. *After Virtue: A Study in Moral Theory*. 2nd ed. Notre Dame: University of Notre Dame Press, 1984.

———. *Whose Justice? Which Rationality?* Notre Dame: University of Notre Dame Press, 1988.

Manus, Ukachukwu Chris. *Intercultural Hermeneutics in Africa: Methods and Approaches*. Nairobi: Acton, 2003.

Marsden, George. "Everyone One's Own Interpreter? The Bible, Science, and Authority in Mid-Nineteenth-Century America." In *The Bible In America: Essays in Cultural History*, edited by Nathan O. Hatch and Mark Noll, 82–95. New York: Oxford University Press, 1982.

McLean, Mark. "Toward a Pentecostal Hermeneutic." *Pneuma* 6/2 (1984) 35–56.

McQuillian, Jeff. *The Literary Crisis: False Claims, Real Solutions*. Portsmouth: Heinemann, 1998.

Mead, Walter Russell. "God's Country?" *Foreign Affairs* (September-October 2006) N.p. http://www.foreignaffairs.com/articles/61914/walter-russell-mead/gods-country.

Mesters, Carlos. "The Use of the Bible in Christian Communities of the Common People." In *The Bible And Liberation*, edited by Norman Gottwald and Richard Horsley, 12–31. Maryknoll, NY: Orbis, 1993.

Michaels, J. Ramsey. "Evidences of the Spirit, or the Spirit as Evidence? Some Non-Pentecostal Reflections." In *Initial Evidence*, edited by Gary B. McGee, 202–18. Peabody, MA: Hendrickson, 1991.

Middleton, J. Richard, and Brian Walsh. *The Transforming Vision: Shaping A Christian World View*. Downers Grove, IL: InterVarsity, 1984.

———. *Truth Is Stranger Than It Used To Be: Biblical Faith in a Postmodern Age*. Downers Grove, IL: InterVarsity, 1995.

Miller, Thomas W. *Canadian Pentecostals: A History of the Pentecostal Assemblies of Canada*. Mississauga, ON: Full Gospel, 1994.

Mugambi, J. N. K. "Foundations for an African Approach to Biblical Hermeneutics." In *Interpreting the New Testament in Africa*, edited by Mary N. Getui et al., 9–29. Nairobi: Acton, 2001.

Murphy, Nancey. *Beyond Liberalism and Fundamentalism: How Modern and Postmodern Philosophy Set The Theological Agenda*. Valley Forge, PA: Trinity, 1996.

Murphy, Nancey, Brad Kallenberg, and Mark Nation, eds. *Virtues and Practices in the Christian Tradition: Christian Ethics after MacIntyre*. Harrisburg, PA: Trinity, 1997.

Myland, D. Wesley. *The Latter Rain Covenant and Pentecostal Power*. Chicago: Evangel, 1910.

Bibliography

Nelson, Douglas J. "For Such A Time As This: The Story of William Seymour and the Azusa Street Revival." PhD diss., University of Birmingham, 1981.

Ngewa, Samuel, Mark Shaw, and Tite Tienou, eds. *Issues in African Christian Theology*. Nairobi: East African Educational, 1998.

Niebuhr, H. Richard. *The Meaning of Revelation*. New York: Macmillan, 1962.

Nienkrichen, Charles W. *A. B. Simpson and the Pentecostal Movement: A Study in Continuity, Crisis, and Change*. Peabody, MA: Hendrickson, 1992.

Noel, Bradley T. *Pentecostal and Postmodern Hermeneutics: Comparisons and Contemporary Impact*. Eugene, OR: Wipf & Stock, 2010.

Noll, Mark A. *A History of Christianity in the United States and Canada*. Grand Rapids: Eerdmans, 1992.

Norwoood, Frederick A. *The Story of American Methodism: A History of the United Methodists and Their Relations*. Nashville: Abingdon, 1974.

Oleka, Sam. "Interpreting and Applying the Bible in an African Context." In *Issues In African Christian Theology*, edited by Samuel Ngewa et al., 104–25. Nairobi: East African Educational, 1998.

Oss, Douglas. "Canon as Context: The Function of *Sensus Plenior* in Evangelical Hermeneutics." *Grace Theological Journal* 9/1 (1988) 103–14.

Outler, A. "Toward a Post-Critical Hermeneutics." *Theology Today* 42 (1985) 281–91.

Pannenberg, Wolfhart. "The Crisis of the Scripture Principle in Protestant Theology." *Dialog* 2 (1963) 13–27.

Pinnock, Clark H. *The Scripture Principle: Reclaiming the Full Authority of the Bible*. 2nd ed. Grand Rapids: Baker Academic, 2006.

Poloma, Margaret. *The Assemblies of God at the Crossroads*. Knoxville: University of Tennessee Press, 1989.

———. "The Spirit Bade Me Go: Pentacostalism and Global Religion." Paper prepared for presentation at the Association for the Sociology of Religion Annual Meetings, August 11–13, 2000. Washington, D.C. http://hirr.hartsem.edu/research/pentecostalism_polomaart1.html

Ramm, Bernard. *Protestant Biblical Interpretation*. 3rd rev. ed. Grand Rapids: Baker, 1993.

Ricoeur, Paul. *Essays on Biblical Interpretation*. Philadelphia: Fortress, 1980.

Robbins, Vernon K. *Exploring the Texture of Texts: A Guide to Socio-Rhetorical Interpretation*. Valley Forge, PA: Trinity, 1996.

Robinson, E. B. "Myland, David Wesley." In *Dictionary of Pentecostal and Charismatic Movements*, edited by Stanley Burgess et al., 632–33 Grand Rapids: Zondervan, 1988.

Roebeck, Cecil M., Jr. "Making Sense of Pentecostalism in a Global Context." Paper, 28th Annual Meeting of the Society of Pentecostal Studies, Springfield, MI, March 1999.

———. "Pentecostal Origins From A Global Perspective." In *All Together In One Place: Theological Papers from the Brighten Conference on World Evangelization*, edited by Harold D. Hunter and Peter Hocken, 23–37. Sheffield, UK: Sheffield Academic Press, 1993.

———. "Taking Stock of Pentecostalism: The Personal Reflections of a Retiring Editor." *Pneuma* 15/1 (1993) 57–65.

Rudd, Douglas. *When The Spirit Came Upon Them*. Mississauga, ON: PAOC, 2002.

Satterthwaite, P. E., and D. F. Wright, eds. *A Pathway into the Scriptures*. Grand Rapids: Eerdmans, 1994.

Bibliography

Spittler, Russell P. "Are Pentecostals and Charismatics Fundamentalists? A Review of American Use of These Categories." In *Charismatic Christianity as a Global Culture*, edited by Karla Poewe, 103–16. Columbia: University of South Carolina Press, 1994.

———. *Perspectives on the New Pentecostals*. Grand Rapids: Baker, 1976.

———. "Scripture and the Theological Enterprise: View from a Big Canoe." In *The Use of the Bible in Theology: Evangelical Options*, edited by Robert K. Johnston, 45–62. Atlanta: John Knox, 1985.

Stein, Robert H. *A Basic Guide to Interpreting the Bible: Playing by the Rules*. Grand Rapids: Baker, 1994.

Stendahl, Krister. "Biblical Theology, Contemporary." In *Interpreter's Dictionary of the Bible*, edited by G. A. Buttrich, 1:418–32. Nashville: Abingdon, 1976.

Stout, Harry. "Theological Commitment and American Religious History." *Theological Education* 25 (1989) 44–59.

Straus, Mark L. *How to Read the Bible in Changing Times: Understanding and Applying God's Word Today*. Grand Rapids: Baker, 2011.

Stronstad, Roger. "Pentecostal Experience and Hermeneutics." *Paraclete* 15 (1992) 16–28.

———. "Pentecostal Hermeneutics." *Pneuma* 15/2 (1993) 215–22.

———. "Trends in Pentecostal Hermeneutics." *Paraclete* 22/3 (1988) 1–11.

Summond, Jean-Jacques. *Word and Spirit at Play: Towards a Charismatic Theology*. London: SCM, 1994.

Synon, Vinson, ed. *Aspects of Pentecostal-Charismatic Origins*. Plainfield, NJ: Logos, 1975.

———. "The Origins of the Pentecostal Movement." http://www.oru.edu.library/special_collections/holy_spirit_research_center/pentecostal_history.php.

Tate, W. Randolph. *Biblical Interpretation: An Integrated Approach*. Peabody, MA: Hendrickson, 1991.

Taylor, G. F. *The Spirit and the Bride: A Scriptural Presentation of the Operations, Manifestation, Gifts and Fruit of the Holy Sprit in His Relation to the Bride, with special reference to the "Latter Rain" Revival*. Dunn, NC: George F. Taylor, 1907. www.pctii.org/arc/taylor_bk.html.

Thiselton, A. C. "The Hermeneutical Dynamics of 'Reading Luke' as Interpretation, Reflection and Formation." In *Reading Luke*, edited by Craig Bartholomew et al., 3–52. Grand Rapids: Zondervan, 2005.

———. *New Horizons in Hermeneutics: The Theory and Practice of Transforming Biblical Reading*. Grand Rapids: Zondervan, 1992.

———. "Why Hasn't Reader-Response Criticism Caught on in New Testament Studies? A Diagnosis Suggesting Five Reasons." In *The Promise of Hermeneutics*, by Roger Lundin et al., 154–63. Grand Rapids: Eerdmans, 1999.

Thomas, John Christopher. "Reading the Bible from within Our Traditions: A Pentecostal Hermeneutic as Test Case." In *Between Two Horizons: Spanning New Testament Studies and Systematic Theology*, edited by Joel B. Green and Max Turner, 108–22. Grand Rapids: Eerdmans, 2000.

———. "Women, Pentecostals and the Bible: An Experiment in Pentecostal Hermeneutics." *Journal of Pentecostal Theology* 5 (1994) 41–56.

Turner, George Allen. "The Baptism of the Holy Spirit in the Wesleyan Tradition." *Wesleyan Theological Journal*. http://www.lcoggt.org/Articles/bapt_of_the_holy_spirit_in_wes_trn.htm.

Bibliography

Turner, Max. "Luke and the Spirit: Renewing Theological Interpretation of Biblical Pneumatology." In *Reading Luke: Interpretation, Reflection, Formation*, edited by Craig Bartholomew et al., 267–93. Grand Rapids: Zondervan, 2005.

Ukachukwu, Chris Manus. *Intercultural Hermeneutics in Africa: Methods and Approaches*. Nairobi: Acton, 2003.

UNESCO Institute for Statistics. "Adult and Youth Literacy: Global Trends in Gender Parity." September, 2010. http://www.unesco.org/education/ild2010/FactSheet2010_Lit_EN.pdf.

Vanhoozer, Kevin J. "The Reader in New Testament Interpretation." In *Hearing the New Testament: Strategies for Interpretation*, edited by Joel B. Green, 301–28. Grand Rapids: Eerdmans, 1995.

Wacker, Grant. "The Demise of Biblical Civilization." In *The Bible In America: Essays in Cultural History*, edited by Nathan O. Hatch and Mark Noll, 121–38. New York: Oxford University Press, 1982.

———. *Early Pentecostals and American Culture*. Cambridge, MA: Harvard University Press, 2001.

———. "The Functions of Faith in Early Pentecostalism." *Harvard Theological Review* 77 (1984) 358–75.

Wall, R. W. *The Acts of the Apostles: Introduction, Commentary, and Reflections*. The New Interpreter's Bible 10. Nashville: Abingdon, 2002.

Weber, Timothy. *Living in the Shadow of the Second Coming: America Premillenialism,1873–1982*. Chicago: University of Chicago Press, 1987.

———. "The Two-Edged Sword: The Fundamentalist Use of the Bible." In *The Bible in America: Essays in Cultural History*, edited by Nathan O. Hatch and Mark Noll, 99–120 New York: Oxford University Press, 1982.

Webster, John. *Holy Scripture: A Dogmatic Sketch*. Cambridge: Cambridge University Press, 2003.

Willis, Lewis J., ed. *Assembly Addresses of the General Overseers: Sermons that Guided the Church*. Cleveland: Pathway, 1986.

Wooden, R. Glenn. "Guided by God: Divine Aid in Interpretation in the Dead Sea Scrolls and the New Testament." In *Christian Beginnings and the Dead Sea Scrolls*, edited by John J. Collins and Craig A. Evans, 101–20. Grand Rapids: Baker, 2006.

———. "The Role of 'The Septuagint' in the Formation of the Biblical Canons." In *Exploring the Origins of the Bible*, edited by Craig A. Evans and Emanuel Tov, 129–46. Grand Rapids: Baker Academics, 2008.

Yong, Amos. *Spirit—Word—Community: Theological Hermeneutics in Trinitarian Perspective*. Eugene, OR: Wipf & Stock, 2002.

www.ingramcontent.com/pod-product-compliance
Lightning Source LLC
Chambersburg PA
CBHW062042220426

43662CB00010B/1606